RotoVision

GRIDS

the structure of graphic design

Andre Jute

RotoVision

A RotoVision book
Published and distributed by RotoVision SA
Rue Du Bugnon 7
1299 Crans-Pres-Celigny
Switzerland
Tel: +44 (22) 776 0511
Fax: +44 (22) 776 0889

RotoVision SA, Sales & Production Office
Sheridan House, 112/116A Western Road
HOVE BN3 1DD
Tel: +44 (0) 1273 72 72 68
Fax: +44 (0) 1273 72 72 69

Distributed to the trade in the United States:
Watson-Guptill Publications
1515 Broadway
New York, NY 10036

ISBN 2-88046-277-0

Production and separation in Singapore by
ProVision Pte Ltd
Tel: +65 334 7720
Fax: +65 334 7721

Contents

4 Introduction

Historical perspective of the grid
How to use *Grids*

7 The purpose of the grid

Repeatability
Composition
Communication

13 Elements of the grid

Paper size
Measuring systems
Type distinctions
Building a collection of fonts
Recommended type combinations
Print area defined by margins
Allocating columns

39 Making a quick grid

The quick basic grid
Refinements

47 Constructing a proper grid

External factors
Translating thumbnails to full-size pages
Column and other guides
Type selection
The smallest line-space as the key
Column width in relation to typesize
Leading
Text and illustration on the baseline
Illustration depth
Drawing the complete grid
Viewing a grid
Running and service items
Type and picture areas

81 Grid, template and stylebook

Printed grid
Acetate overlay
Stylebook
Template
Style-sheets

103 Introducing the free grids

Using the grids on the disk

A4 three column
A4 four column
US letter three column
US letter four column
A4 three-fold leaflet
A4 four-fold leaflet
US letter three-fold leaflet
US letter four-fold leaflet
A3 poster
Tabloid poster
Packaging
Books
Acetate overlay and printed grid

123 Grids at work

Raising gardening aspirations
Gardens Illustrated/BBC *Gardeners' World*
Cataloging a limitless product
PhotoDisc
Grids for professionals in a hurry
Time/*Harvard Business Review*/*Wired*/
MacPower
Student travel
Globeplotter/Eurotrain
A uniformly square product: selling music
Opus 3/Harmonia
Mundi/Naxos/Collins/Chandos/Gimell

ON THE DISK
GALLERY OF GRIDS
SET UP AS TEMPLATES
FOR YOU TO COPY, ADAPT AND USE,
COMPLETE WITH MEASUREMENTS

158 Index

160 Acknowledgments

Grids on the bundled disk

Grids on the bundled disk
A4 three-column A43CMAC
A43CIBM
A4 four-column A44CMAC
A44CIBM
US letter three-column
USL3CMAC USL3CIBM
US letter four-column USL4CMAC
USL4CIBM
A3 leaflets A423FMAC A423FIBM
US letter leaflets L23FMAC L23FIBM
A3 poster A3PTRMAC A3PTRIBM
Tabloid poster TAPTRMAC TAPTRIBM
Packaging PACKMAC PACKIBM
Book BKMAC BKIBM
Acetate overlay and printable grid FILMMAC
FILMIBM

4 The historical perspective of the grid

From the time when civilized man first found the need to record information as a series of tabular or narrative symbols, written material has always required a basic grid of some sort; regularly shaped blocks of stone or clay tablets were simply easier to stack. Handwriting, when it evolved on rectangular sheets of papyrus or vellum, was on straight lines and demanded a minimum requirement of margins on all four sides.

The scribes of the Middle Ages, forerunners of today's graphic designers, set many of the parameters and constraints, in terms of columns, margins and spacing, which the literate Western world continues to hold sacrosanct. These same scribes were, until our own century, some of the last graphic communicators to retain direct control of the format of their output, although this was, of course, only on a one-off basis.

The invention and development of printing with movable type in the mid-15th century, enhanced the need for a regular system of control over the thousands of letters cast in metal or carved out of wood, which comprised each page of what was, arguably, the most momentous technical advance for mankind since the invention of the wheel. However, the rectangular 'formes' in which the printer locked up the individual letters in lines and columns of type, stifled any innovative use of the grid, at the same time as removing control from the scribes whose main concern had been aesthetically pleasing and creative communication.

The perceived typographic strait-jacket imposed by the invention of letterpress typesetting and printing, remained firmly in place for most of the following four centuries. Although the painstaking engraving of complete pages of words into wood, copper or steel, along with the discovery of lithography, went some way towards alleviating this constraint, it was at the expense of the phenomenal speed and economy of individually cast, moveable, re-usable type.

Innovative, asymmetric use of the grid, as practiced between the wars at the Bauhaus and advocated by Jan Tschichold, came as a breath of fresh air, but was, in practice, so difficult, time-consuming and expensive in terms of print production, that it was only practiced by an elite minority. The Bauhaus designers were, however, among the first to produce accurate layouts with detailed printing instructions. In so doing they took design decisions back into the studio, out of the hands of the printer.

Thoughtful designers, especially from the beginning of the 20th century, had always been aware of the possibilities of the grid. With the arrival of the first primitive photosetting systems following the Second World War, they also saw that the return of control from the printer carried potential disaster in the hands of many typographers unused to the freedom inherent in this latest technology. A group of Swiss designers set out to address the problem of formalizing the grid, both for their own use and as a teaching aid. Foremost among this group was Josef Müller-Brockmann, who in 1961 published an account of his principles in *The Graphic Artist and his Design Problems*. But the world had to wait another twenty years for the appearance of his *Grid Systems*, the first practical handbook to deal with the subject. Two years later, Postscript and the Macintosh arrived to fulfil the promise of photosetting, putting control of the format firmly back into the hands of every designer.

Meanwhile that most potent symbol of man's aspirations, NASA, had already formally adopted the use of the grid for all their communications, as had many governments, most multinational corporations – and graphic designers.

How to use *Grids*, the book and the disk

This is a technical handbook and sourcebook for professional graphic designers, and for students intending to practice as professionals. Except for occasional brief commentaries, *Grids* therefore concentrates on studio practice and examples of published work, and assumes that the reader already has a grounding in the more general arts, as well as the supporting technicalities of reprographics.

Grids is intended to be read straight through for familiarization, then used as a text to be followed in the creation of real designs. It is therefore organized in the order in which a designer considers, either consciously or subconsciously from experience, the elements necessary to create a grid for a coherent design which will communicate the intended message effectively.

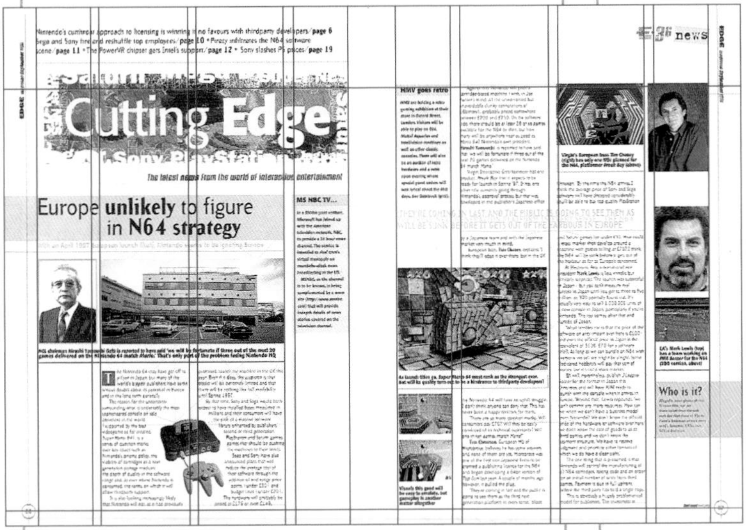
Cutting Edge

Europe unlikely to figure in N64 strategy

MS NBC TV...

HMV goes retro

Who is it?

The examples on the left show (above) a grid utilizing different column widths for Edge *magazine and (below) for* Drapers Record *a more uniform width column system has been applied.*

News

International News

C&A tracks shopping patterns

Clothes top sales league for July

Lingerie is uplifted by the padded bra

Surplus stock show is planned for Paris

Euro expansion for Sander

UK manufacturers sign up for Turkish trade mission

In Brief

6

The purpose of the grid

The primary purpose of the grid is to create order out of chaos. The grid helps the consumer to find material in the expected place every time, either when leisurely turning over the pages of a glossy magazine, or when rapidly scanning a professional journal for relevant information. This primary purpose holds true even with projects which tend by their very nature towards disintegration. Thus it forces the designer to think constructively, and in a structured manner.

The designer should regard grids as an aid to readability, recognition and understanding, never as a strait-jacket. If either text or art refuse to fit the grid, then the grid is not working. Do not force the material – redesign the grid.

The grid, together with its associated style-sheets, can be made to work so hard that when both are fully developed and agreed with the client, a significant proportion of the entire job is done. However, designing a grid and setting up style-sheets is expert work and demands all the designer's attention, skill and knowledge. Experienced designers therefore spend a significant amount of time fine-tuning their grids and style-sheets, because they know that the effort will be more than repaid in time saved later, and in the far better appearance of the finished project.

Besides being indispensable to the readability and appearance of a finished job, of all the tools available to help the designer to present a concept in a thoroughly professional manner, none is more powerful than the grid.

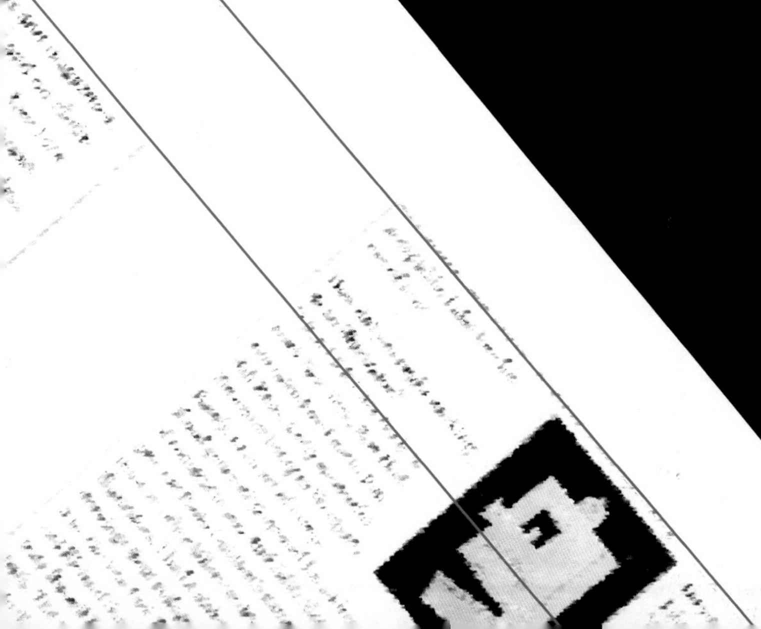

The purpose of the grid

The grid is a professional tool of objectivity in applied aesthetics, and its practical purposes fall into three classes:

- repeatability
- composition
- communication.

How the advantage and practices of the grid are divided into these classes, and what value is given to each, depends upon your point of view.

The designer never works in a vacuum. You have the background of 40 centuries of the arts behind you, the views of the communities in which you work and at which your work is aimed, the ideas of other designers, the budget for the project, and the input of the creator of the material you must work with – all of which have an influence, either subtle or explicit.

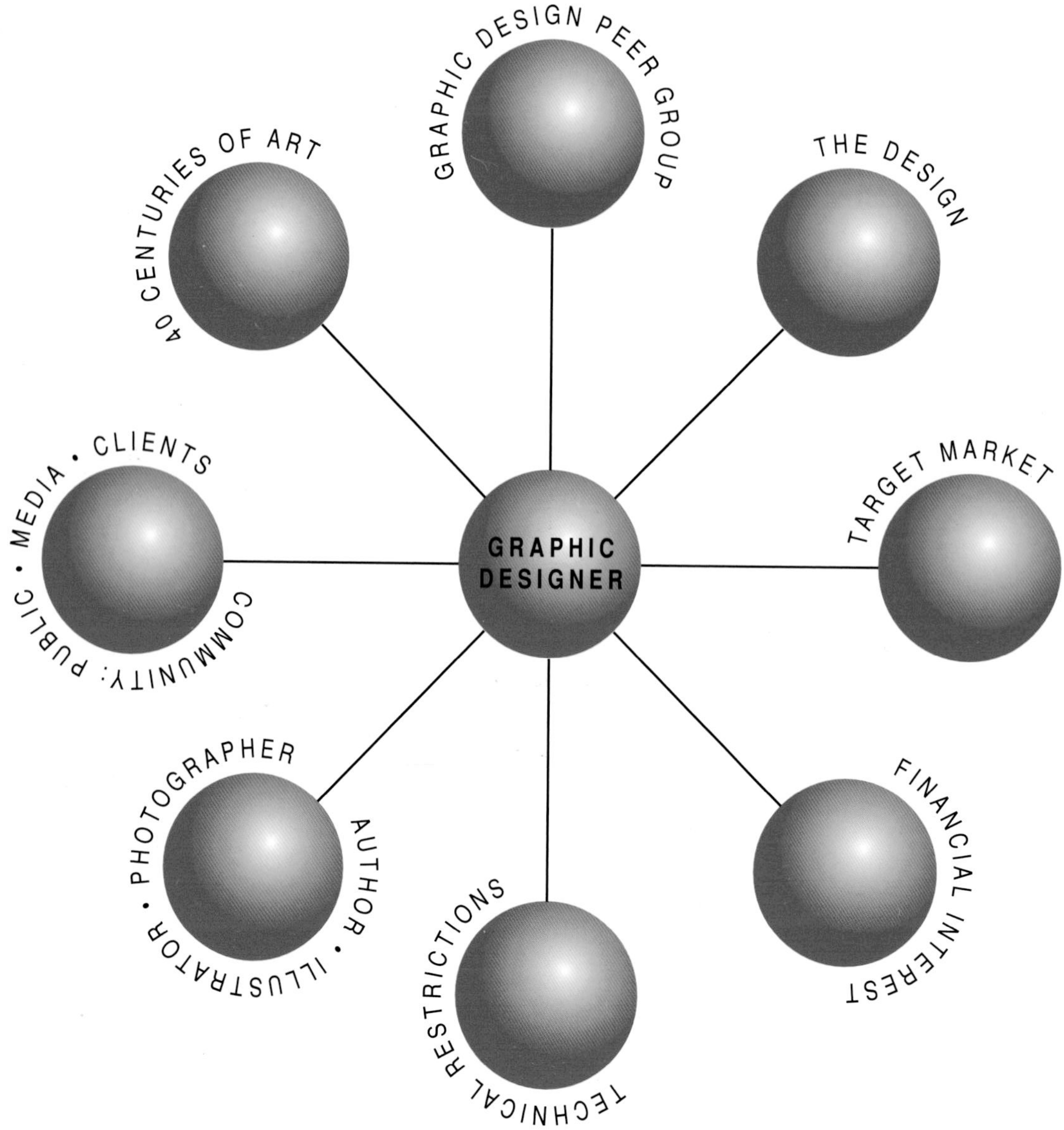

Repeatability

Imagine if on every new page you had first to draw out the margins, columns and baselines for each line of text before you could start placing the text and art. Yet that was essentially standard practice until a generation ago.

Repeatability is achieved by using one or more of the application tools of the grid – printed card, acetate overlay, computer template, text and illustration specification – to make similar pages in multi-page designs look the same, or to give multiple single designs a unity of appearance, or to give a multiplicity of designs for varying purposes a 'corporate identity' for a single organization. A substantial amount of time is invested in making the basic template perfect, because any errors on it will be endlessly repeated.

Repeatability is not only of benefit to graphic designers. Many people value the benefit to readers of finding material in the expected place every time so highly that they would consider repeatability the chief ornament of the communication function of the grid.

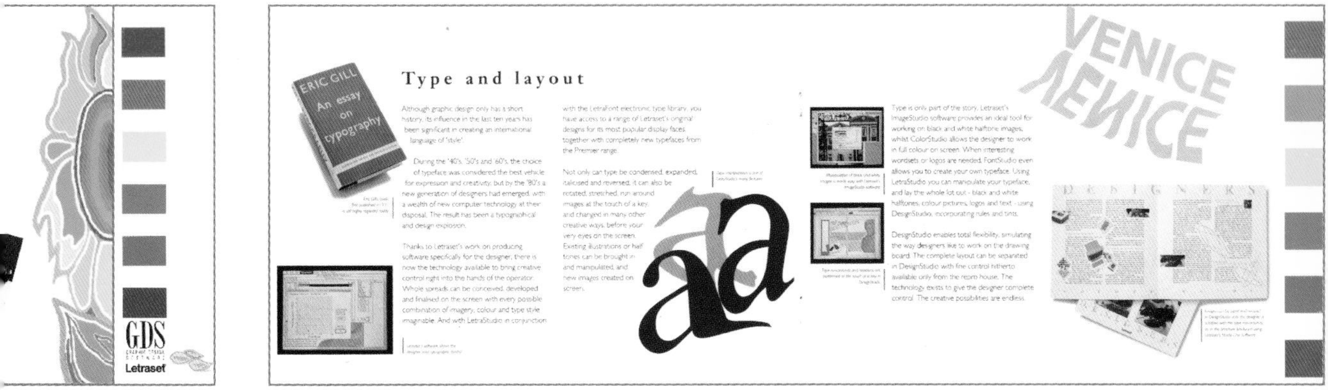

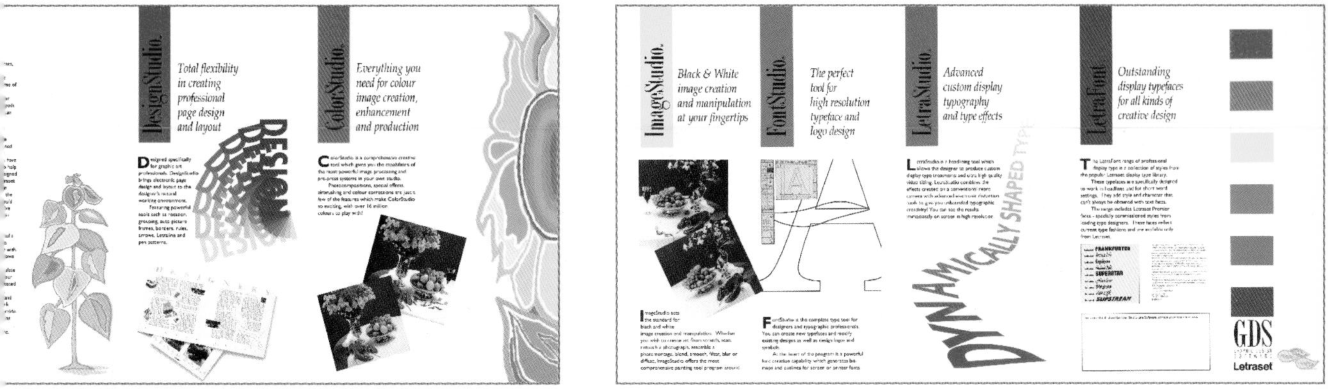

The two leaflets above the grid, and the disposition of the ornaments within it, communicate instantly to the target market (it is incidental that the clients of Letraset are themselves graphic designers).

Repeatability need not be a strait-jacket. The brochure immediately above has leaves of unequal width, so that when it is folded the flower motif remains visible.

10 Composition

Graphic designers are trained to appreciate compositional precepts inherited from aesthetic schools dating back to classical Rome; but in everyday practice such elevated principles are reduced to rules of thumb, modified by experience.

The grid incorporates the compositional wisdom of the ages into a format that is rigid in aspects where flexibility would be disastrous – as in varied leading for large-scale text – and flexible in varying degrees precisely as required for matters where you must apply initiative and taste. Two important instances in which you must use such initiative are:

- blending inflexible body text linearity with the flow of illustration, photography and display text made possible by the computer;
- arranging size, shape and balance of elements to provide the correct relative emphasis and aid comprehension without damaging repeatability.

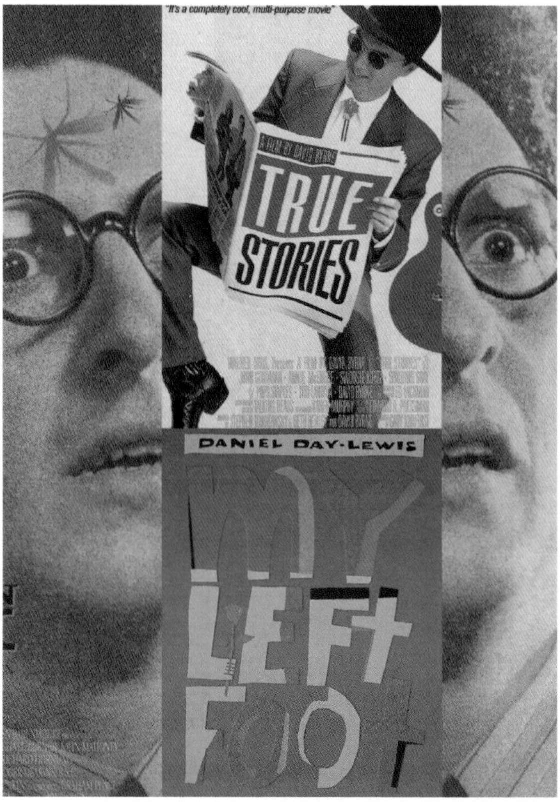

The grid above is very simple, consisting of two columns, each divided in half, with an additional column divider space in between the two halves.

With so much illustration and a riot of display faces in the illustrations, the designer has rigidly controlled the explanatory body copy and used it to determine the flow of the reader's eye. Text and illustration are placed in the grid to enhance rhythm and tension.

This is a 'reverse composition'. The white backgrounds to the type and some of the illustrations are essential to this design, standing in for the white space the full-bleed illustrations have totally consumed.

Communication

The purpose of graphic design is to communicate the message. Period. 'The message' is the message intended by whoever wrote the text, or the original creator of the illustrations in a mainly illustrated item. Thus the designer's personality should never be visible.

The grid is a modesty-screen between your personality and the reader, and helps avoid small lapses of concentration, or even straightforward incompetence, impinging on the ultimate consumer of the message. The grid eliminates the idle variations which you might consider clever but which merely interpose between the reader and the message.

Positive communicative aspects of the grid are that readers can:

- rely on finding given elements in the same place, for instance columns in a magazine;
- rely on the designer to guide them to important elements via compositional and type variation plus the disposition of space.

The grid is not merely a Eurocentric device, and is not tied to any language. Because it belongs to the very structure of communication, its application is universal.

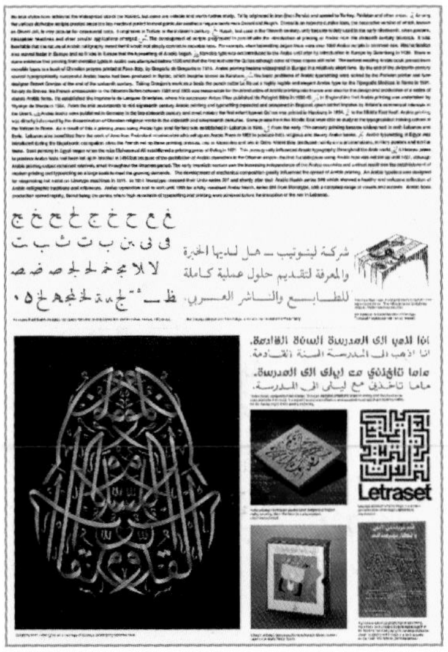

Above are examples of the way the same grid can be used as a base on which to create many layout variations.

eliveries top of
ndies' wish list

focus on kidswear at M&S

Elements of the grid

The grid is a mechanism, and like all mechanisms is most easily understood when broken into its component parts, each of which can then be concentrated on and mastered separately. Like every other mechanism, the grid is constructed from its smallest part upwards to its largest assembly, and the purpose of each part is best understood by reference to the purpose of the whole. As components are added, the earlier parts may have to be adjusted, sometimes repeatedly to mesh with the later additions.

The construction of the grid is, in theory, relatively simple. First the page size is specified, usually in ISO (International Standards Organisation) sizes, for example A4, A5, although American and British sizes are still quite commonly used in their respective parts of the world.

Margins at head, foot, binding and fore edge are next applied in order to determine the print area. This may, if necessary, then be divided into any combination of columns. Additional white space can then be distributed by means of placing body text, display text and illustrations within the print area.

The choice of typography is a skill which takes many years of practice to develop and perfect. A basic knowledge of the suitability of text and display, serif and sans serif type, together with the combination and manipulation of type faces, weights and sizes, is imperative before embarking on any graphic project, or building your own collection of fonts. It is also necessary to understand the point system, and to gain a knowledge of the various, initially confusing, type measuring systems in use throughout the Western world.

14 Paper: ISO sizes

Contrary to what one would think, paper size is rarely within the designers decision-making province. The job arrives as 'a three-fold A4 leaflet' or a magazine of so many pages of such a paper quality cut to a size (usually by the production chaser) such that together with its staples and envelope or wrapper it falls within a particular postage class by weight. The most common size range for European and Asian designers, and for Americans working on the world stage, to choose from is the ISO series, commonly called 'DIN' (Deutsche Industrie Normen) because it originated in Germany. The A series are trimmed sizes, the B series untrimmed sizes which allow for folding and intermediate sizes, the C series envelope papers, and the RA series oversizes of the A series which allow for trimming bleeds back to the A size. It is normal practice to design to the full size of A papers, bleed over their edges, and let the printer choose the oversize to print on.

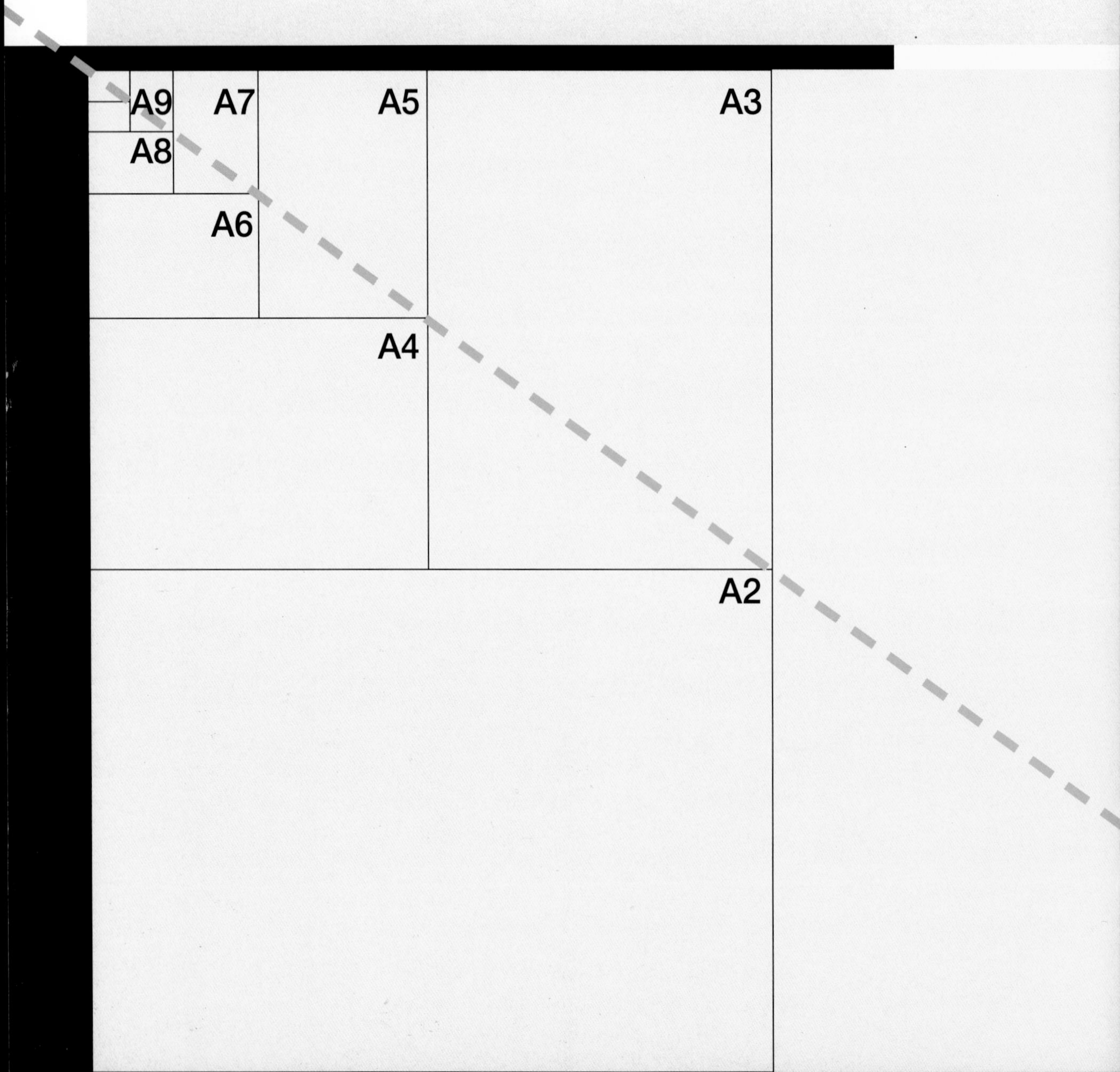

Paper: Imperial and American sizes

ISO sizes are each precisely half of the next larger size, which avoids waste. British and American sizes are arbitrary, though many of them fold to pleasingly-proportioned subdivisions.

British papers have names like Elephant, and range unfolded and untrimmed from 17in x 13.5in to 30in x 22in. Some of these sizes are still available and in use in small-scale specialist book publishing, but increasingly the British or 'imperial' sizes are being replaced by the metric ISO series. For the designer in practice, only three American trimmed sizes are of importance. They are American letter (8.5in x 11in), legal (8.5in x 14in), and 'American A3' (17in x 11in), plus the 'proofing oversize' of the last which is 18in x 12in.

The world is now such a village that almost every important American designer works with the ISO sizes. The importance of the American sizes is that much of the machinery a designer uses, for example laser printers and scanners, is primarily designed to use them.

A1

3

4

3

2

ISO	inches	mm
A0	33.11 x 46.81	841 x 1189
RA0	33.86 x 48.03	860 x 1220
SRA0	38.58 x 50.39	980 x 1280
A0	33.11 x 46.81	841 x 1189
B0	39.37 x 55.67	1000 x 1414
A0	33.11 x 46.81	841 x 1189
A1	23.39 x 33.11	594 x 841
A2	16.54 x 23.39	420 x 594
A3	11.69 x 16.54	297 x 420
A4	8.27 x 11.69	210 x 297
A5	5.83 x 8.27	148 x 210
A6	4.13 x 5.83	105 x 148
A7	2.91 x 4.13	74 x 105
A8	2.05 x 2.91	52 x 74
A9	1.46 x 2.05	37 x 52
A10	1.02 x 1.46	26 x 37

The difference between a metric A4 sheet and an American letter sheet is that the American measure is wider and shorter than the metric one. The white block is the actual size of the difference. It is good practice to work on sizes that fit standard file covers and filing cabinets, and other paper holders and storage devices.

If material is to be printed on both metric and American sizes, the only way to ensure that page numbers will correspond is to design different margins for the different formats and thus ensure that the print area remains the same.

Paper: paper finish and typeface choice

Typefaces change their character according to the kind of paper on which they are printed. You are strongly advised to have the fonts you own or intend using printed on a variety of papers.

Opposite and below is a small sample of common faces which you can add to and have printed on various papers. All are shown in 14pt with 20 per cent leading, but the test should be conducted with a variety of sizes, especially in text faces, where 1pt can on some papers make the difference between legibility and disaster. (Selection and notes after John R Biggs.)

Though in mass-market magazines and catalogs it is often impossible, on thin paper particular attention should be paid to the showthrough of illustrations and type. Mirrored or handed design may be essential if thin or otherwise less than totally opaque paper is to be used.

Illustrations only to the full extent of each band, and only to be backed by either illustration to the full extent of the band or a full text block. Bleed permitted only when backed by bleed in the same position.

Baskerville is a transitional face of unaffected simplicity suitable for a wide range of uses. It can become very light on gloss paper, but that may in some circumstances be an advantage.

Have a block of Gill Sans printed on different papers and compare its behavior. *Here is a line of italic for comparison.*

This is Plantin, which looks best on art paper or any smooth paper. *This is the italic for comparison.*

Rockwell has a heavy color on both smooth and rough papers. *This is the italic for comparison.*

Bembo is a very beautiful old face intended for use on antique papers. *This line of italic is for comparison.*

Bodoni is a typical modern face. Its color is fairly constant on all kinds of paper, though the fine serif tends to become rather faint on very glossy paper.
A line of italic of this excellent all-round typeface for comparison with the roman.

Caslon was designed at a time when printing was done on a hand-press on damp handmade paper. It gains character on rough papers. There are many modern versions to choose from.

Caslon 540, from ATF in 1902, is the first modern version of this popular font. **Caslon 3, also from ATF, is a bolder version of 1905. Both were designed and modified specifically for 20th century setting technologies, papers and press speeds.** Caslon 224 from ITC is an adaptation by Ed Benquiat in 1983 which offers several weights suitable for different papers. Book. Medium. **Bold. Black.**

Typography: naming type parts

Two main purposes of the grid are to organize various typefaces and sizes into a pleasing and practical relationship with each other; and to integrate type and illustrations of varying format, origin and execution into a pleasing and practical relationship with each other. It follows as a precondition to the making of a good grid that you must have enough knowledge of type to choose the best combination of faces and sizes for the particular document.

Type is a very large subject in its own right, and can be a veritable lifetime study. We therefore give only a skeleton outline of type – concentrating instead on the interaction of type with the grid in the success of the completed design.

Before we can classify type, we must agree a language of description.

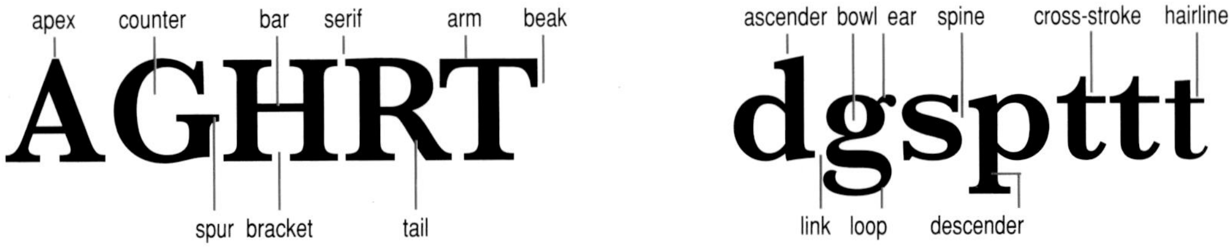

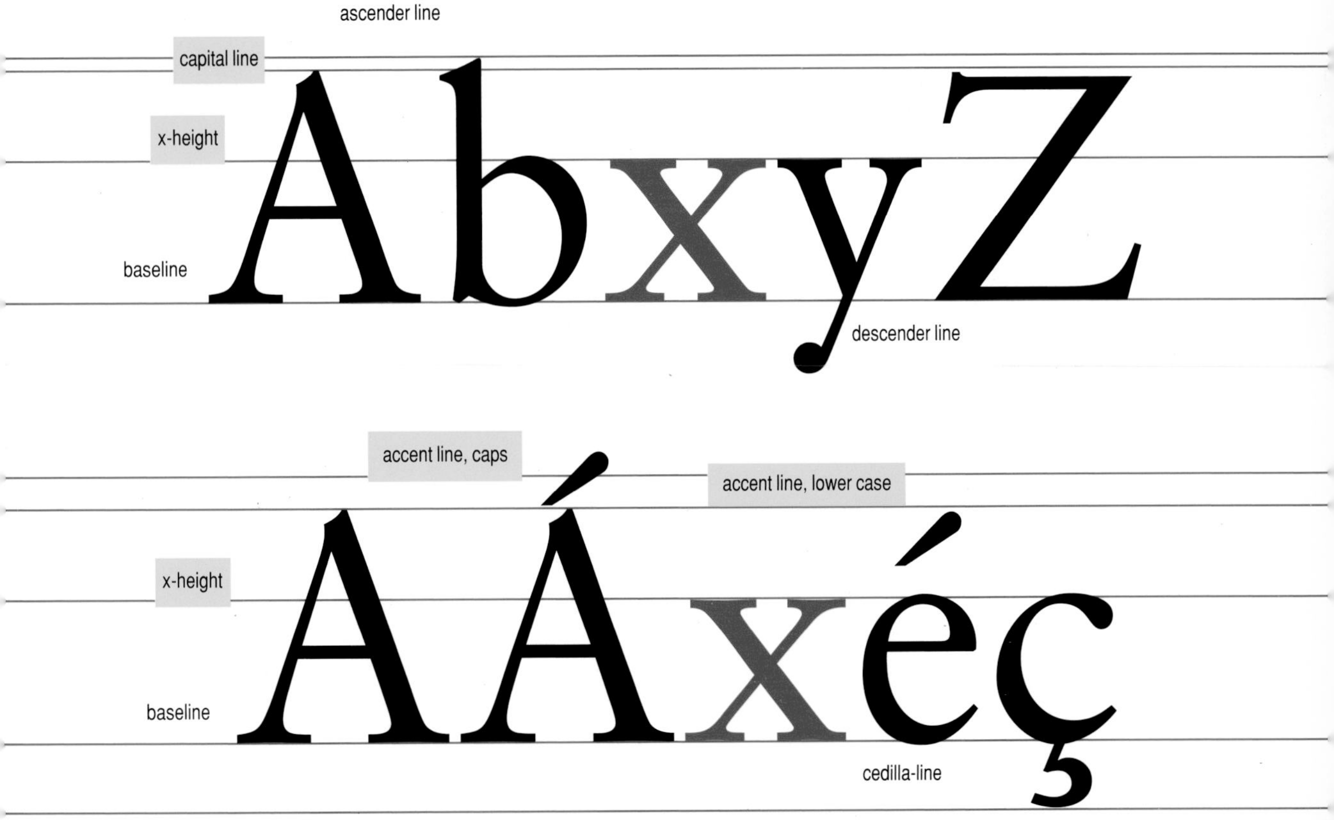

The top of a line of type can be measured either as the capital height, the ascender height or the accented capital height.

Serif

Old Face

Bembo *Aldus Manutius 1495*

Plantin *Christophe Plantin c1560*

Garamond *Jean Jannon c1621*

Sabon *Jan Tschichold 1965*

Transitional

Baskerville *John Baskerville 1772*

Times *Stanley Morison 1932*

Modern

Bodoni *Giambattista Bodoni 1798*

Walbaum *J. F. Walbaum c1804*

Slab

Rockwell *Inland Typefoundry 1910*

Incised

Perpetua *Eric Gill 1925–32*

PERPETUA TITLING

TRAJAN CAROL TWOMBLY 1989

Sans serif

Gill Sans *Eric Gill 1928–1930*
Helvetica *Max Miedinger 1957*
Univers *Adrian Frutiger 1957*
Akzidenz Grotesk *Berthold 1896*

Other types

Script
Zapf Chancery
Blackletter
Old English Text
DECORATED
SLIPSTREAM
Mechanical
OCR-A

The angle of stress is an important indicator of the period of a serif font. At first it mimics that in handwriting, but the modern face would be very uncomfortable to create by hand because the pen would have to be at a right-angle to the writing to make perfectly upright stresses.

Typography: measuring systems

The grid is a logical and consistent tool to relate type and images on the page. It was devised by typographers, as graphic designers were known until midway through the 20th century. It is therefore merely a matter of evolution that the inventors of the grid should choose as their smallest unit the line-space, which is equal to the typesize plus the leading. Typesize, leading and line-space are specified in points.

Unfortunately, type is one of the oldest artifacts of man's cultural history. As in everything with so much history, there is a confusion of standards.
The first successful type measuring system was invented by Pierre Fournier in 1675. The system still in use in Europe is an improvement of the Fournier system introduced by Firmin Didot (1712–1768). It is based on the 'French foot' of 30cm (called the 'line gauge'), which contains 798 points. 12 points make a cicero, so the line gauge of 798 points contains 66.5 ciceros – hardly a convenient calculation base. But designers and printers did become accustomed to it.

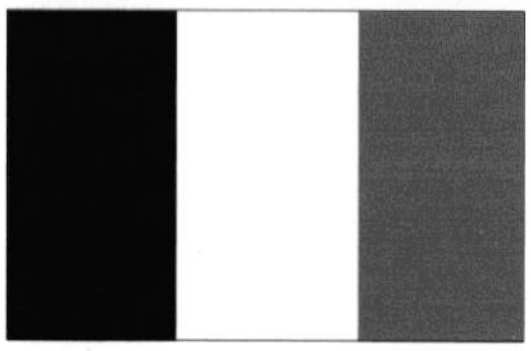

Didot

1m = 2,660 points
12 points = 1 cicero = 4.51mm
1 French foot = 30cm = 1 line gauge = 798 points = 66.5 ciceros
1mm = 2.66 points
1pt = 0.376mm

Anglo-American

1 imperial foot = 12 inches
1 inch = 72 points
1 point = 0.013833in
12 points = 1 pica = 0.166in
6 picas = 1 inch

<>Didot<>Anglo-American<>

1 Didot point = 0.0148in = 1.07 Anglo-American points
12 Didot points = 1 cicero = 0.1776in
1 Anglo-American point = 0.3514mm = 0.9345 Didot points
12 Anglo-American points = 1 pica = 4.216mm

Cicero = Augustin = 'aug' in Dutch

Cicero = Riga tipographica = 'riga' in Italian

You have to be very sharp-eyed to see that 12 Didot points are deeper than 12 Anglo-American points, but over a few inches the difference soon becomes evident. Both red bars are 432 points long.

The smaller Braggadocio S is 96 Anglo-American points, the bigger one is 96 Didot points.

Typography: Anglo-American and computer points

The Anglo-American system, used in the USA, UK, and around much of the Pacific Rim, also uses points, but its points are 72 to the inch. 12 points make one pica (sometimes still called a 'pica em') and six picas make an inch.

Neither the French system nor the Anglo-American system relates to the metric system, in which everything is measured in millimeters, which is slowly conquering the world.
In any event, computer setting is now so prevalent, and computerized final page make-up so nearly universal, that the practising designer selects a points base after considering where the fonts chosen for the design were digitized. If the fonts are from a British or American 'foundry' (a courtesy title extended to the better software houses), points and picas may be chosen, if the fonts are from a German, Dutch or Swiss supplier, points and ciceros may be chosen. Or you can mix systems and let the computer do the arithmetic.

The computer allows seamless mixing and matching of different measuring systems. Books can be specified in a mixture of millimeters, picas and points.

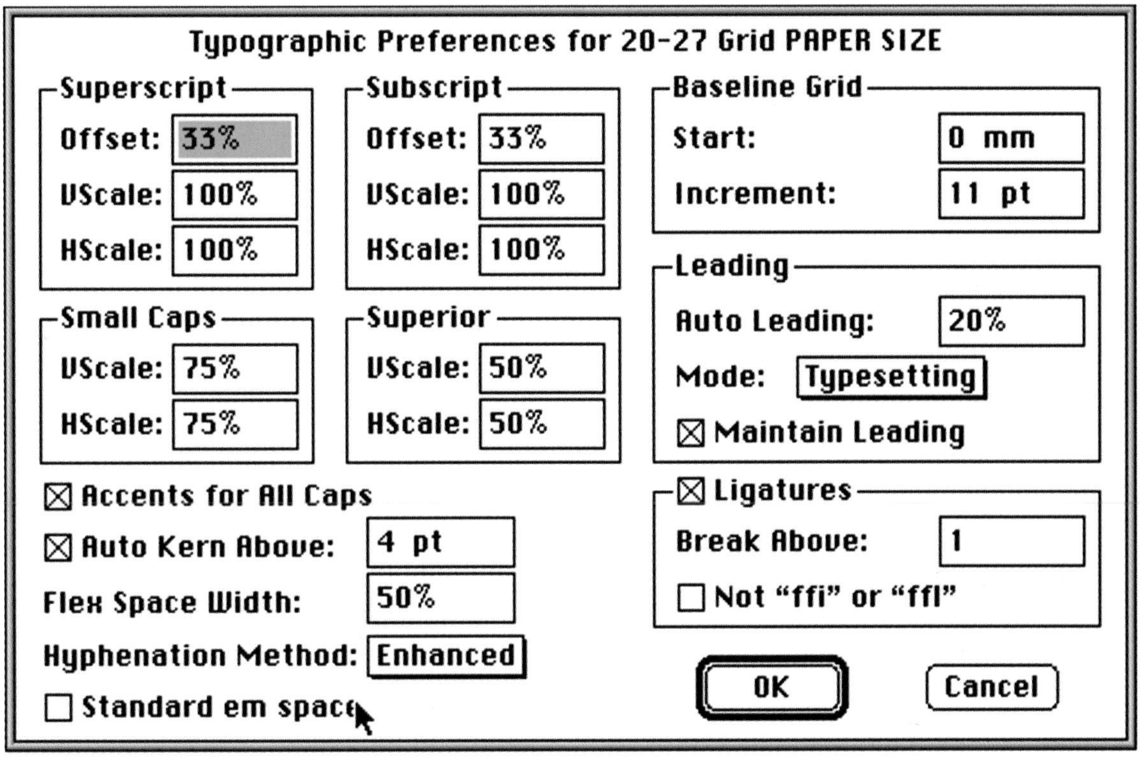

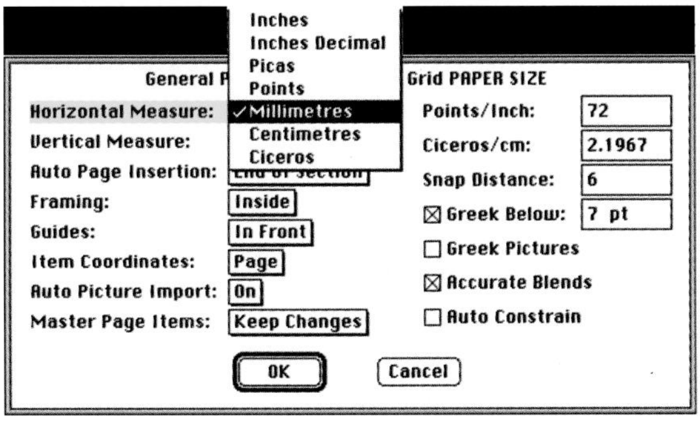

Typography: measuring type

When fonts were cast in hot metal, the designer was forced to use the available sizes: for text fonts usually 8 or 9, 10, 12, 14, 18 and 24pt, and for display fonts up to 48 or often 60pt, and sometimes 72pt. Only specialized newspaper 'small classified' fonts were 7pt and smaller, but Times went down as far as 4pt. The larger fonts, sometimes from 48pt upwards and always from 72pt upwards, were cut in wood, and the available choice depended on what the typesetter held or would buy in for the job.

PostScript allows you to set in any fraction of a point. The 'appearing size' of a font, from the top of the ascender to the bottom of the descender, is not its actual point size. The point size is that measured from baseline to baseline when the type is set solid, without leading. This takes into account the natural space above and below the type. The measurement from baseline to baseline, including leading, is known as the line-space.

9pt
10pt
12pt
14pt
18pt
24pt
36pt
48pt
72pt
96pt

4pt 6pt 7pt 8pt 10.375pt 19.625pt

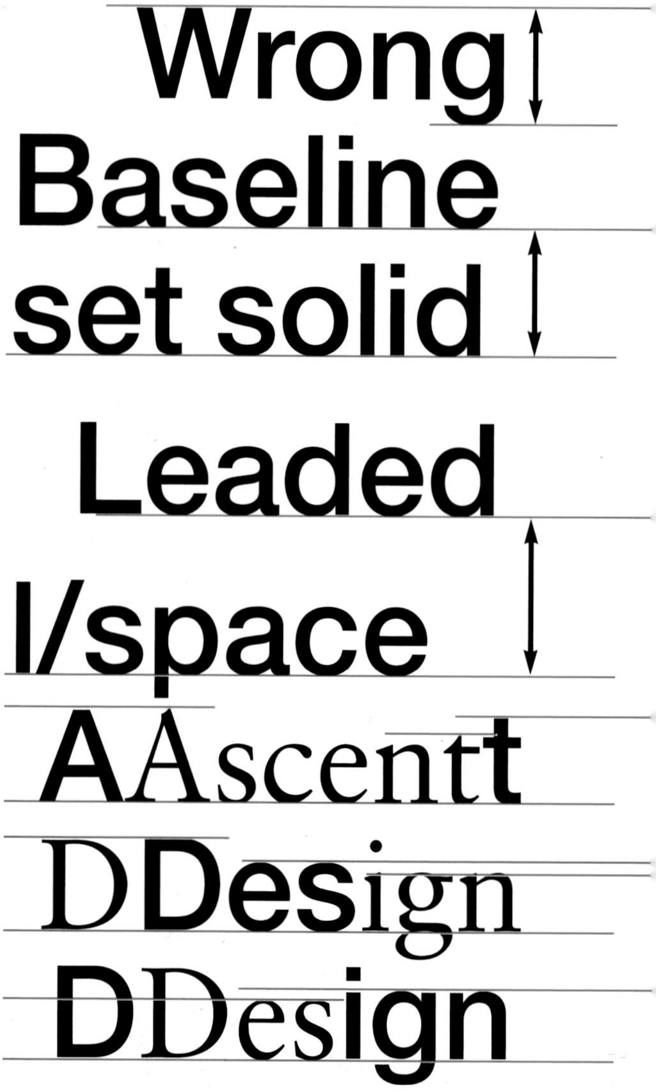

All type featured in this column is 48pt, set in a mixture of Helvetica (sans) and Sabon (serif), but Sabon is a 'smaller appearing' face than Helvetica.

Typography: swash and drop caps

Many decorative fonts and capitals are available ready-made from the same sources as the more orthodox fonts.

Or designers with illustrative and/or photomanipulative skills or contacts can create their own; often these later come on to the general market as well. There are specialized font creation programs to design text fonts, a very complicated business, but most of the programs a graphic designer owns can be used innovatively to make display fonts.

These are called swash capitals or, if advertised to the DTP market, drop caps. You should specify in the style-sheet accompanying the grid that drop capitals or swash initials may be applied only to paragraphs at least one line deeper than the 'drop'.

An alternative is to have the text start on the baseline of the swash letter.

Special titling fonts, made up entirely of capitals, are also available. Examples are Perpetua Titling and Trajan. Their distinctive feature is that they are optimized for the larger point-sizes, with kerning that looks awful if used at text sizes.

Display fonts need not be as special – or as much trouble and expense – as those on this spread. They can be different widths, weights, sizes or formats of standard text fonts. Or they can be manipulations of standard PostScript fonts, found on the menu bars of many graphics computers and programs as 'font styles'.

Display fonts can be standard text fonts in the larger sizes; or they may be special designs with absolutely no application for setting running text in bulk-reading sizes. The general rule of thumb is that the designer should use such fonts once only per page or per job, and only one of them at a time.

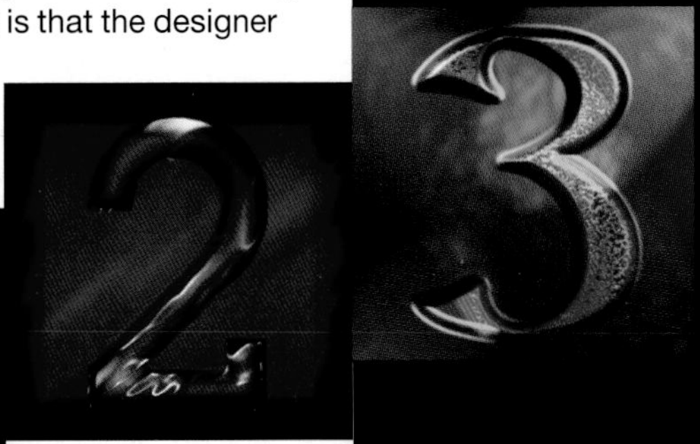

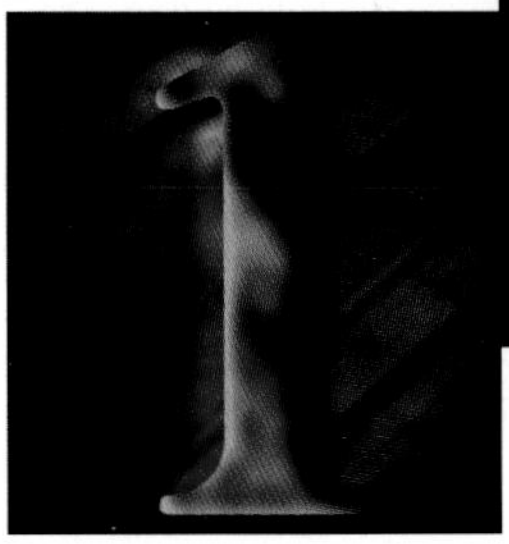

Some designers create their own display and decorative fonts for special purposes. On the left is Countdown by Michael O'Dwyer, above Ekol-V by André Jute.

Typography: type manipulation and styling

Though it is frowned upon in purist circles, it is possible to manipulate a single typeface either expertly through graphics programs or in many cases more easily straight from the menu bar, as in the examples on yellow below. There may be occasions and jobs which warrant these makeshifts.

But just above that level, fonts are available in sets of four, containing plain, bold, italic and bold-italic versions, and even specialized fonts are not outrageously expensive in the overall perspective of a design and print job.

Designers making templates for others to follow even on modest jobs should specify in their style-sheets that all styles must be applied via the font menu (which uses PostScript outlines), and not by keyboard short-cuts which create inferior computer-generated styling emulations.

Plain **Bold** *Italic* ***BoldItalic***

Cont. Underline Word Underline

Outline Shadow ~~Strikethrough~~

SMALL CAPS ALL CAPS

Super^{script} Sub$_{script}$ Superior^2

Bold+Outline+Shadow

Bold+Italic+O/L+Shadow

Plain FAUX **Bold** *Italic* ***BoldItalic***

Plain TRUE **Bold** *Italic* ***BoldItalic***

FAUX SMALL CAPS TRUE SMALL CAPS

Typography: expert fonts

When hot-metal setting was prevalent, the typesetter would automatically create the refinements on this page. Today, with computer setting, they are under the control of the graphic designer: you should include them, or specify them in the style-sheets for others to follow.

True small caps, non-lining figures, true fractions, ligatures, alternative (swash) characters, accents and diacritical marks may be specified or implied in the house styles of magazine and book publishers and the better newspapers, and are almost always required for corporate work. You may in any event decide that the job requires such refinement: you will find that it is not the cost of the additional fonts which is critical, but the labor involved in setting the refinements.

Regular Garamond

The quick brown fox jumps over the lazy dog

1234567890&

Small Caps & OSF

The quick brown fox jumps over the lazy dog

1234567890&

J. F. Smith, M.D.

Expert

ﬁﬀﬁﬄﬂﬀ ¾⅔¼½⅛⅜⅝⅓⅞

1234567890$,.

Alternative

ertazctnQt

THE QUICK BROWN FOX JUMPS OVER THE LAZY DOG

Titling

THE QUICK BROWN FOX JUMPS VER THE LAZY DOG

01234567890&

Standard:

ff fi fl ffi ffl

Ligatures: ﬀ ﬁ ﬂ ﬃ ﬄ

•ITC Garamond Light The quick brown fox jumps over the lazy dog. THE QUICK BROWN FOX JUMPS OVER THE LAZY DOG. 123456790 *The quick brown fox jumps over the lazy dog. THE QUICK BROWN FOX JUMPS OVER THE LAZY DOG. 123456790*
•ITC Garamond Book The quick brown fox jumps over the lazy dog. THE QUICK BROWN FOX JUMPS OVER THE LAZY DOG. 123456790 *The quick brown fox jumps over the lazy dog. THE QUICK BROWN FOX JUMPS OVER THE LAZY DOG. 123456790*
•ITC Garamond Bold The quick brown fox jumps over the lazy dog. THE QUICK BROWN FOX JUMPS OVER THE LAZY DOG. 123456790 ***The quick brown fox jumps over the lazy dog. THE QUICK BROWN FOX JUMPS OVER THE LAZY DOG. 123456790***
•ITC Garamond Ultra The quick brown fox jumps over the lazy dog. THE QUICK BROWN FOX JUMPS OVER THE LAZY DOG. 123456790 ***The quick brown fox jumps over the lazy dog. THE QUICK BROWN FOX JUMPS OVER THE LAZY DOG. 123456790***
•ITC Garamond Light Condensed The quick brown fox jumps over the lazy dog. THE QUICK BROWN FOX JUMPS OVER THE LAZY DOG. 123456790 *The quick brown fox jumps over the lazy dog. THE QUICK BROWN FOX JUMPS OVER THE LAZY DOG. 123456790*
•ITC Garamond Book Condensed The quick brown fox jumps over the lazy dog. THE QUICK BROWN FOX JUMPS OVER THE LAZY DOG. 123456790 *The quick brown fox jumps over the lazy dog. THE QUICK BROWN FOX JUMPS OVER THE LAZY DOG. 123456790*
•ITC Garamond Bold Condensed The quick brown fox jumps over the lazy dog. THE QUICK BROWN FOX JUMPS OVER THE LAZY DOG. 123456790 ***The quick brown fox jumps over the lazy dog. THE QUICK BROWN FOX JUMPS OVER THE LAZY DOG. 123456790***
•ITC Garamond Ultra Condensed The quick brown fox jumps over the lazy dog. THE QUICK BROWN FOX JUMPS OVER THE LAZY DOG. 123456790 ***The quick brown fox jumps over the lazy dog. THE QUICK BROWN FOX JUMPS OVER THE LAZY DOG. 123456790***
•ITC Garamond Light Narrow The quick brown fox jumps over the lazy dog. THE QUICK BROWN FOX JUMPS OVER THE LAZY DOG. 123456790 *The quick brown fox jumps over the lazy dog. THE QUICK BROWN FOX JUMPS OVER THE LAZY DOG. 123456790*
•ITC Garamond Book Narrow The quick brown fox jumps over the lazy dog. THE QUICK BROWN FOX JUMPS OVER THE LAZY DOG. 123456790 *The quick brown fox jumps over the lazy dog. THE QUICK BROWN FOX JUMPS OVER THE LAZY DOG. 123456790*
•ITC Garamond Bold Narrow The quick brown fox jumps over the lazy dog. THE QUICK BROWN FOX JUMPS OVER THE LAZY DOG. 123456790 ***The quick brown fox jumps over the lazy dog. THE QUICK BROWN FOX JUMPS OVER THE LAZY DOG. 123456790***

ITC's Garamond is available in four weights – light, medium or 'book', bold and ultra-bold – and three widths – standard, condensed and narrow. With the corresponding italics, 22 combinations of type width, weight and emphasis give you generous control over column widths, style-sheets and the resulting gray appearance of the page.

Typography: width and weight

Rather than being seduced by the multitude of fonts which has accompanied the growth of desktop publishing, it is far more useful for the vast majority of design assignments to concentrate on a few type families.

As few as two – one serif, one sans – will do if they are available in a wide range of weights and widths plus special faces such as true small capitals and fractions, alternatives and titling characters. Many great designers consistently use no more than a handful or two of font families.

The computer allows digital compression and expansion of standard fonts, but this facility must be used with great restraint unless bizarrely contorted, improbably proportioned type is actually desired.

In addition, Adobe and Apple are both developing technologies in which selected specially-prepared vector-described fonts may be smoothly and sometimes extensively altered on combinations of several 'axes' of width, weight, oblique angle, serif, stroke stress and width, and other key distinguishing features.

95 Black ***96 Black***
85 Heavy ***86 Heavy***
75 Bold ***76 Bold***
65 Medium *66 Medium*
55 Roman *56 Italic*
45 Light *46 Light*
35 Thin *36 Thin*
25 Ultralight *26 Ultralight*

Typography: building a collection of fonts

Virtually every design needs fonts.

Electronic fonts are unimaginably cheap compared to traditional or even photoset fonts. And whereas traditional typesetters intended by 'a font' only a single weight in a single style in a single size, in the vector-font age we intend by 'a font' usually at least two styles each in two weights in any and all arbitrary sizes the designer wants to specify.

The low cost of individual fonts has led to an upsurge in font design, so that it can, paradoxically, be expensive to collect a broad range of fonts. As we have seen, you are best advised to start with a few fonts and come to know them intimately, adding gradually to the collection.

The high-quality fonts on this spread are given away with many applications and with PostScript laser printers, or sold at low cost in promotions by the great electronic 'foundries'.

24pt Avant Garde Book & *Oblique* **Avant Garde Demi & *Oblique*** Bookman & *Italic* **Bookman Demi & *Italic*** Helvetica & *Oblique* **Helvetica Bold & *Oblique*** Narrow Helvetica & *Oblique* **Narrow Helvetica Bold & *Oblique*** New Century Schoolbook & *Italic* **New Century Schoolbook Bold & *Italic*** Palatino & *Italic* **Palatino Bold & *Italic*** Times & *Italic* **Times Bold & *Italic*** Courier *Zapf Chancery* (Symbol) Σψμβολαβχδεφγηιφκλμνοπθρ (Zapf Dingbats)✺❁❐❆ ✤❉■❇❂❁▼▲

11pt Avant Garde Book & *Oblique* **Avant Garde Demi & *Oblique*** Bookman & *Italic* **Bookman Demi & *Italic*** Helvetica & *Oblique* **Helvetica Bold & *Oblique*** Narrow Helvetica & *Oblique* **Narrow Helvetica Bold & *Oblique*** New Century Schoolbook & *Italic* **New Century Schoolbook Bold & *Italic*** Palatino & *Italic* **Palatino Bold & *Italic*** Times & *Italic* **Times Bold & *Italic*** Courier *Zapf Chancery* (Symbol) Σψμβολ (Dingbats)✺❁❐❆ ✤❉■❇❂❁▼▲

The designs cast into the grids for demonstration in the following spreads use the common fonts most designers already have (on this spread), or are likely to acquire soon (overleaf).

Sophisticated fonts are also sometimes bundled with high-level programs. On this page is Tekton, a very sophisticated multiple master font which Adobe gave away with one version of their Type on Call CD-ROM, which itself comes free of charge with several applications or can be bought separately for less than the cost of one of the fonts bundled with it.

Multiple masters are fonts in which the user may exercise control over one or more of the font's design parameters, called axes, such as weight, width, angle of stress, oblique angle, and in some master fonts much more esoteric aspects of font design.

This is Tekton, a multiple master font
in which the designer has control over weight and width. This is
Tekton, a multiple master font in which the
designer has control over weight and width.
This is Tekton, a multiple master font in
which the designer has control over
weight and width. This is Tekton, a multiple master
font in which the designer has control over weight and width.
This is Tekton, a multiple master font in which
the designer has control over weight and
width. This is Tekton, a multiple master
font in which the designer has
control over weight and width. **This is**
Tekton, a multiple master font in which the
designer has control over weight and width.
This is Tekton, a multiple
master font in
which the

These are the text and display faces used in the sample documents. When you are using the grids from the disk you can replace them with any similar or otherwise suitable fonts. In fact, it is good practice to substitute fonts in workable grids in order to discover how grids work.

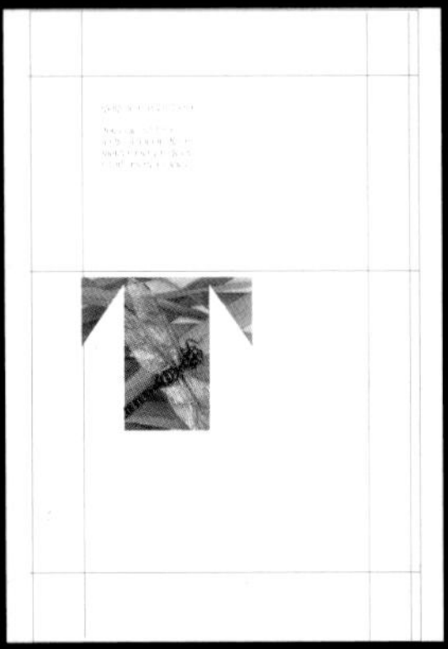

10.5/12.5pt Sabon and italic and small caps for the running titles. The swash capitals used to open chapters are from André Jute's Ekol-V series.

italic

*SCAPS*Sabon

GOOD
DEEDS
IN THE
GHETTO

Bodoni Book is an elegant font, which in *Book Italic looked just right on the recycled paper of this school newsletter.* There is also a Plain Bodoni **and an accompanying BoldCondensed, not used in this design but shown here for comparison with the** Bodoni Book *and Italic.*

BoldIta***licEx***

traRockwel

Akzidenz Grotesk is a lively alternative to the overused Helvetica and the similarly too common Univers. It has a good range of weights.

AkzidenzGr

oteskBESu

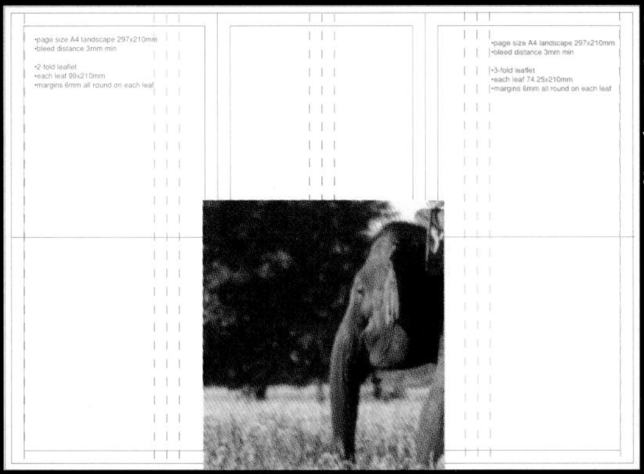

Gill Sans, bought by many designers as a display font, is also a good reading font, with a great deal of dignity and character.

GillSansBoldExtra

Walbaum, even in the Bold, is unexpected on a poster. That is already a good reason to use it. In addition it is a good strong face, very contained and impactful. Try also the Roman *and Italic versions for reading texts.*

BoldItalicBoldWalbaum

There is no reason why you should not create custom lettering for many jobs. Adobe's Illustrator and Photoshop, standard programs on most designers' desktops, are both convenient tools for this purpose. This quick'n'dirty placement sketch was made in Illustrator.

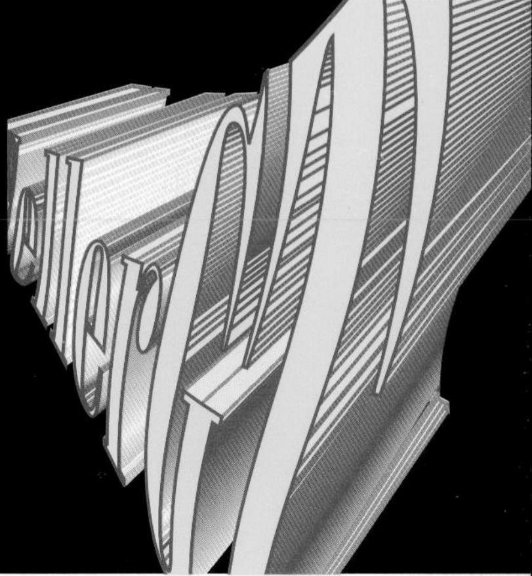

The reason the Helvetica/Times combination is so popular is that it works – most of the time. But every designer must guard against making it a thoughtless, automatic choice.

Helvetica

Times

Margins: defining elements of page, spread and 'color'

Though you will often have a quite precise advance idea of which type family or families will suit a particular job, no particular typesize, weight or width can be chosen until the column width is established. But the column width is never chosen as an independent, self-standing entity. It is always arrived at indirectly, as a function of the type area, which in turn depends on the margins chosen.

First, you must determine the margins which will give the type and illustrations on the page the desired proportions and overall appearance according to your understanding of the message to be conveyed and the expected readership. Thus margins are specified with a particular purpose in mind, rather than arbitrarily.

It is generally accepted that margins and the resulting type area look best when they stand in a mathematical relationship to the page size. There is no 'right' page or grid proportion, but the most famous of these relationships is the 'golden section', in which the page is proportioned 34:21 and the print area is as deep as the full page is wide, with the margins in the proportions 2:3:4:6.

There are only a few books and magazines which can afford such elegantly neutral layout. When the opportunity arises, many designers prefer to use the space to create other impressions (see bottom of facing page).

What remains after allocating the margins is the print area. Although it may later be divided into columns, initially the designer will view it as a block of gray on the page in order to judge proportions and overall impact.

In practice, most designers make their grids on spreads rather than pages. The gutter represents the space on a spread comprising two inside or back-edge margins.

The relationship of margins to each other and to the print area is a crucial design decision and is as important as that of the typeface.

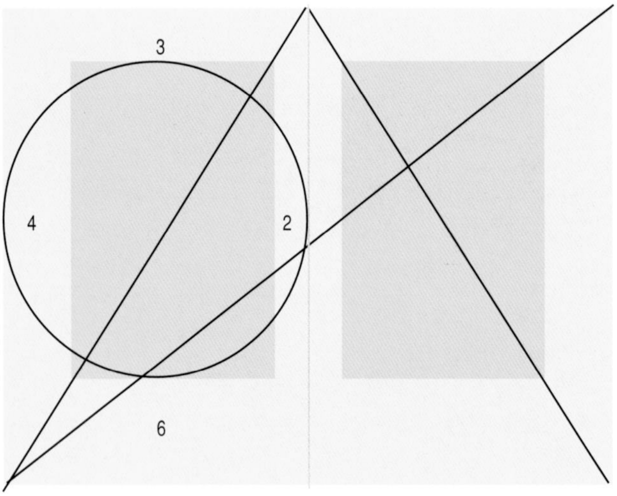

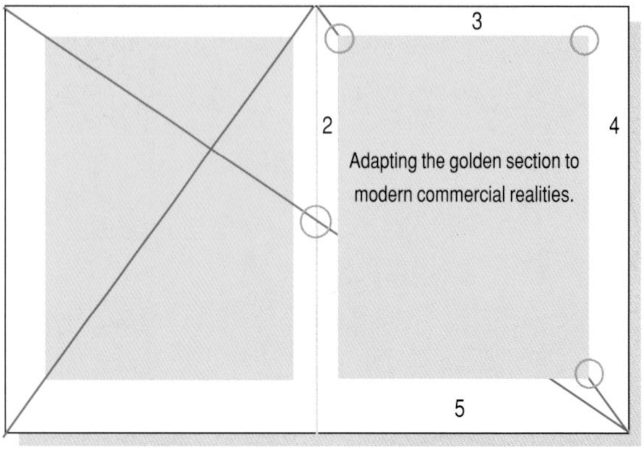

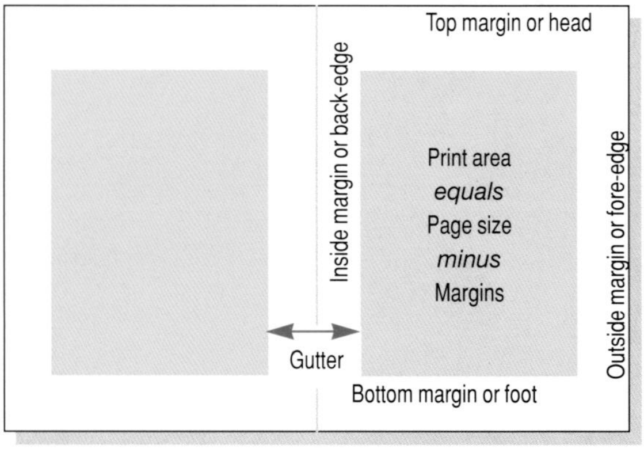

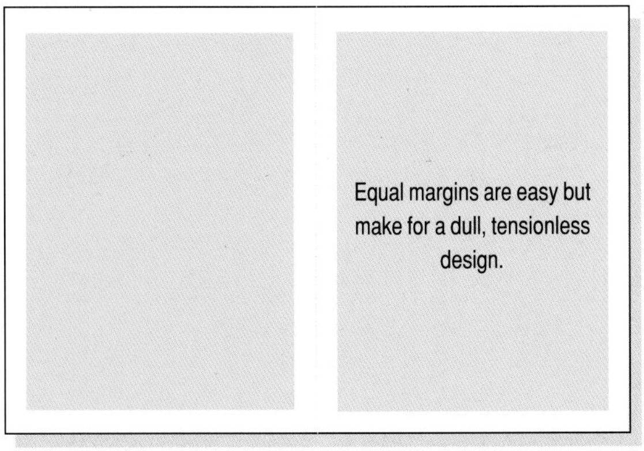
Equal margins are easy but make for a dull, tensionless design.

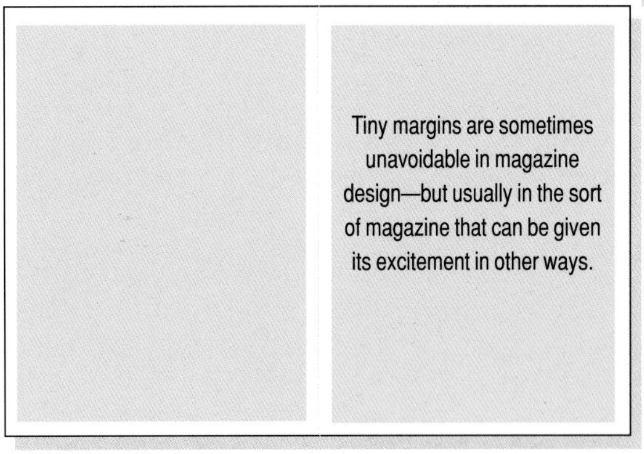
Tiny margins are sometimes unavoidable in magazine design—but usually in the sort of magazine that can be given its excitement in other ways.

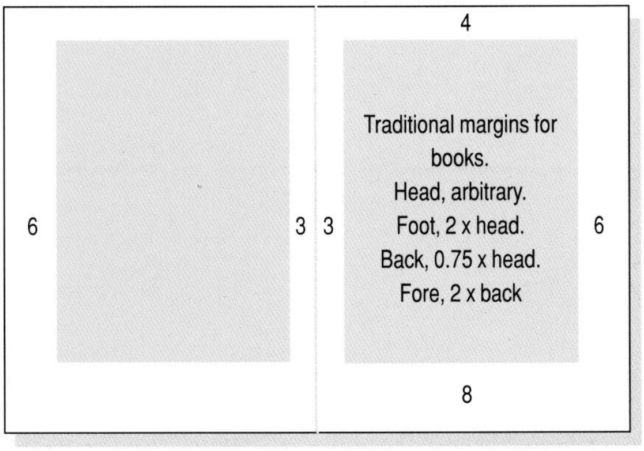
4
6
3
3
6
Traditional margins for books.
Head, arbitrary.
Foot, 2 x head.
Back, 0.75 x head.
Fore, 2 x back
8

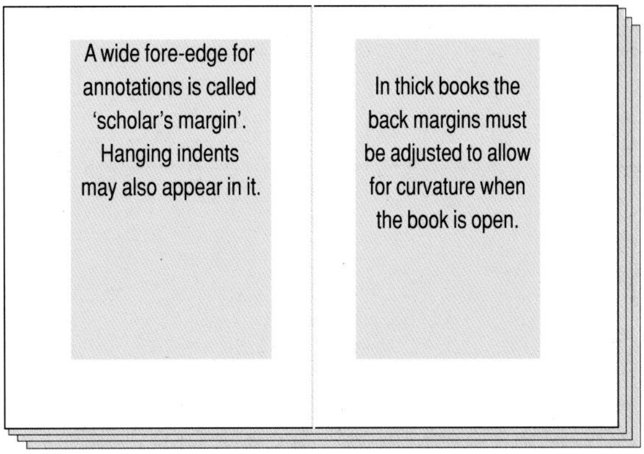
A wide fore-edge for annotations is called 'scholar's margin'. Hanging indents may also appear in it.
In thick books the back margins must be adjusted to allow for curvature when the book is open.

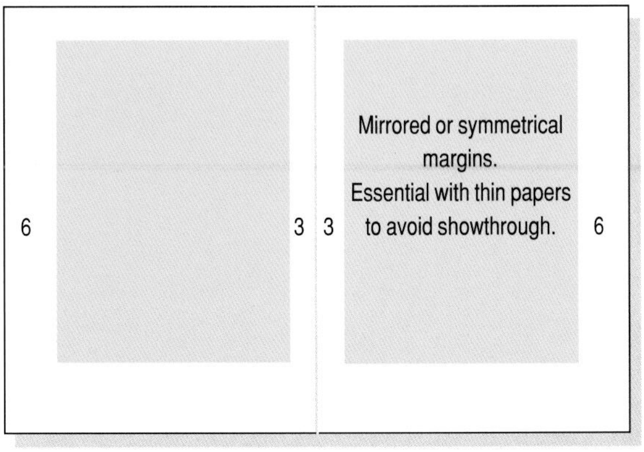
6
3
3
6
Mirrored or symmetrical margins.
Essential with thin papers to avoid showthrough.

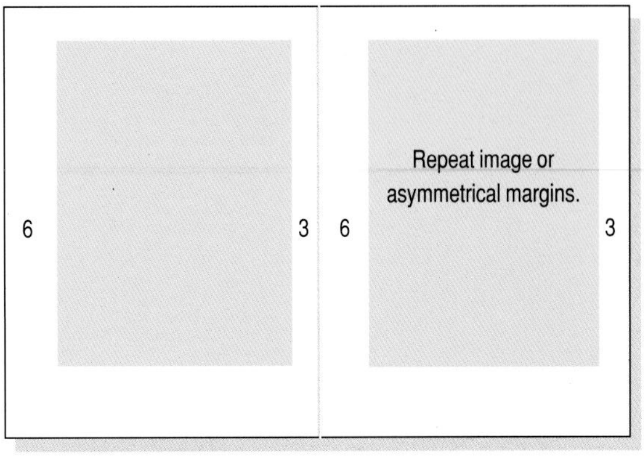
6
3
6
3
Repeat image or asymmetrical margins.

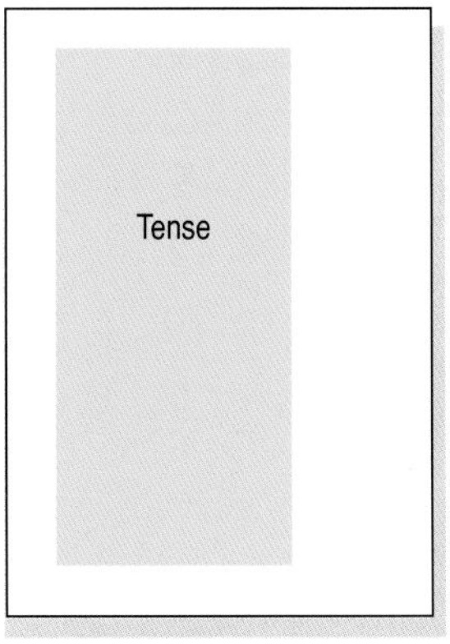
Tense

Informal

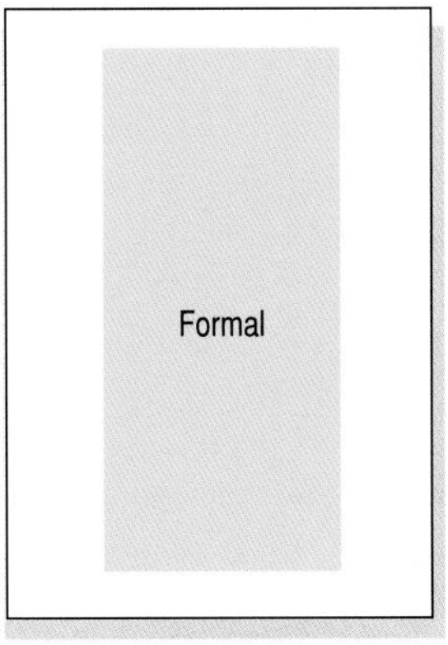
Formal

Elegant and luxurious

After the margins are decided upon, the print area thus established may, as a preliminary estimate, be broken up into columns. Sketches must be made to precise scale, which with pencil and grayliner can take a lot of practice and time. However, the computer can make scaled 'sketches' very quickly, permitting many more variations to be considered.

You should keep in mind that any column widths indicated at this 'doodling' stage will almost certainly have to be adjusted once the typeface and typesizes come to be selected. However, making thumbnails is a worthwhile exercise which allows comparisons to be made which cannot conveniently be done with full-size working models, where the details tend to obscure the larger issues.

In each row on this spread the left-hand column shows the print area. The other columns show only three of the multitude of possible layouts. These designs would be for text-heavy pages; more spacious pages are on the next spread.

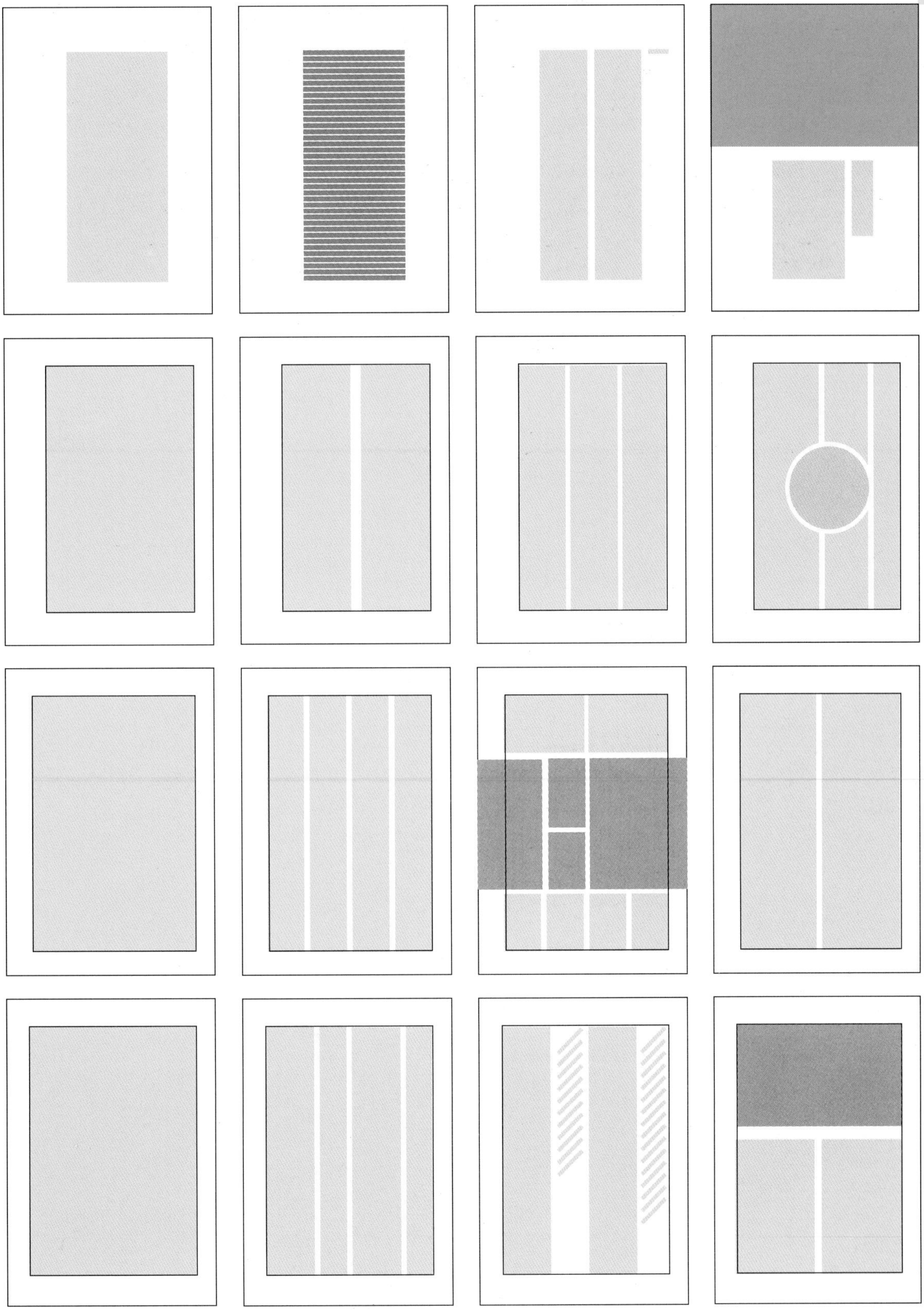

You should always grasp the concept of the most difficult pages first; those are inevitably the pages most loaded with text and hence allowing the least flexibility in allocating white space. Most of the pages on the previous spread fall into that category.

After deciding how the most densely-populated pages will look, you then have a good grasp of what can be done with those pages where more flexibility is possible. More flexibility almost always means that more white space can be allocated.

As before, the caveat is that the column widths and text/display weights as well as illustrative placements will have to be adjusted when the grid is drawn.

But, once more, the advantage of thumbnails over full-size work is that the principles may be abstracted from the details and very quickly multiplied, varied, altered, considered, and accepted or altered again.

The left-hand column once again shows the print area, which need not all be used.

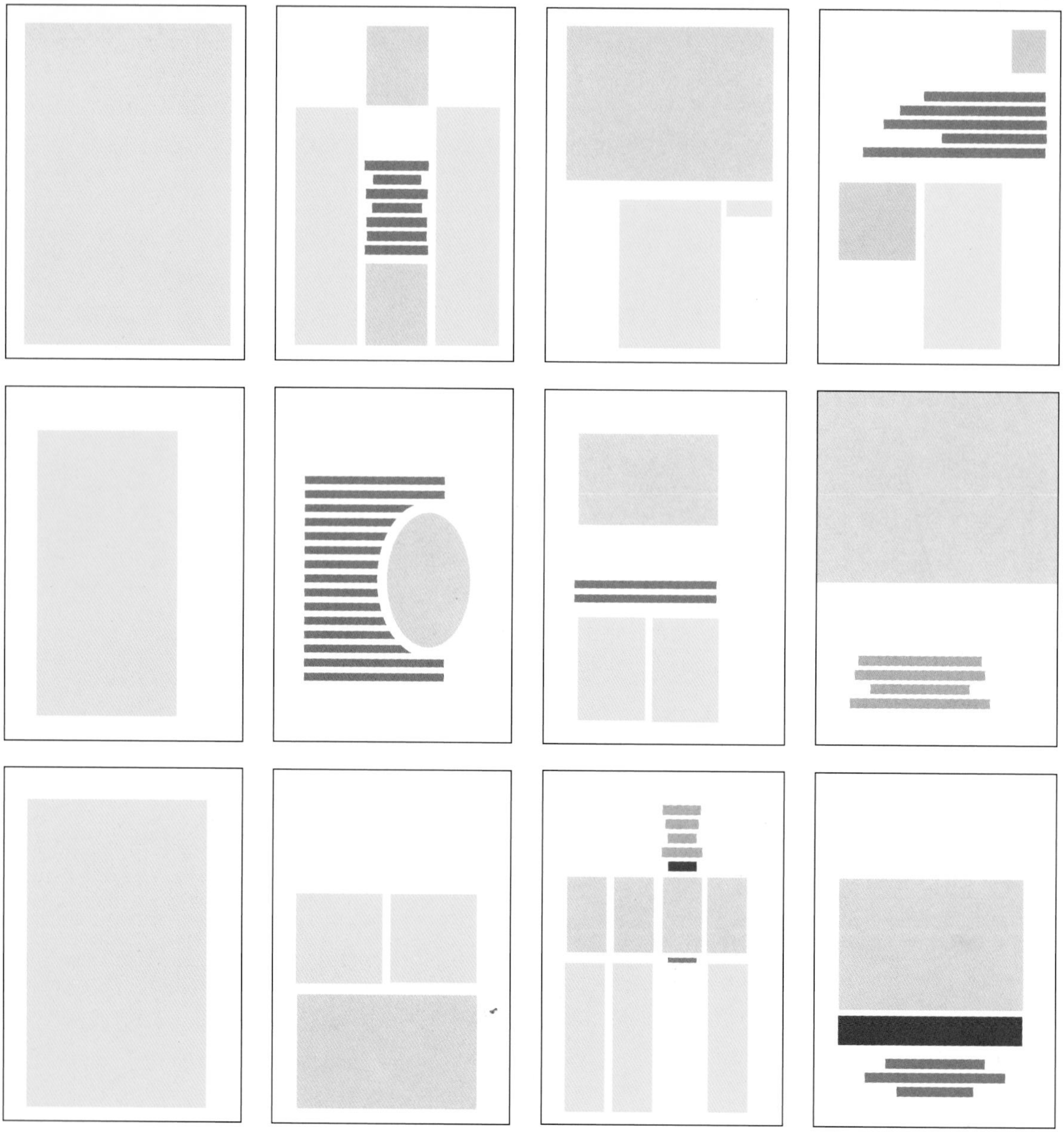

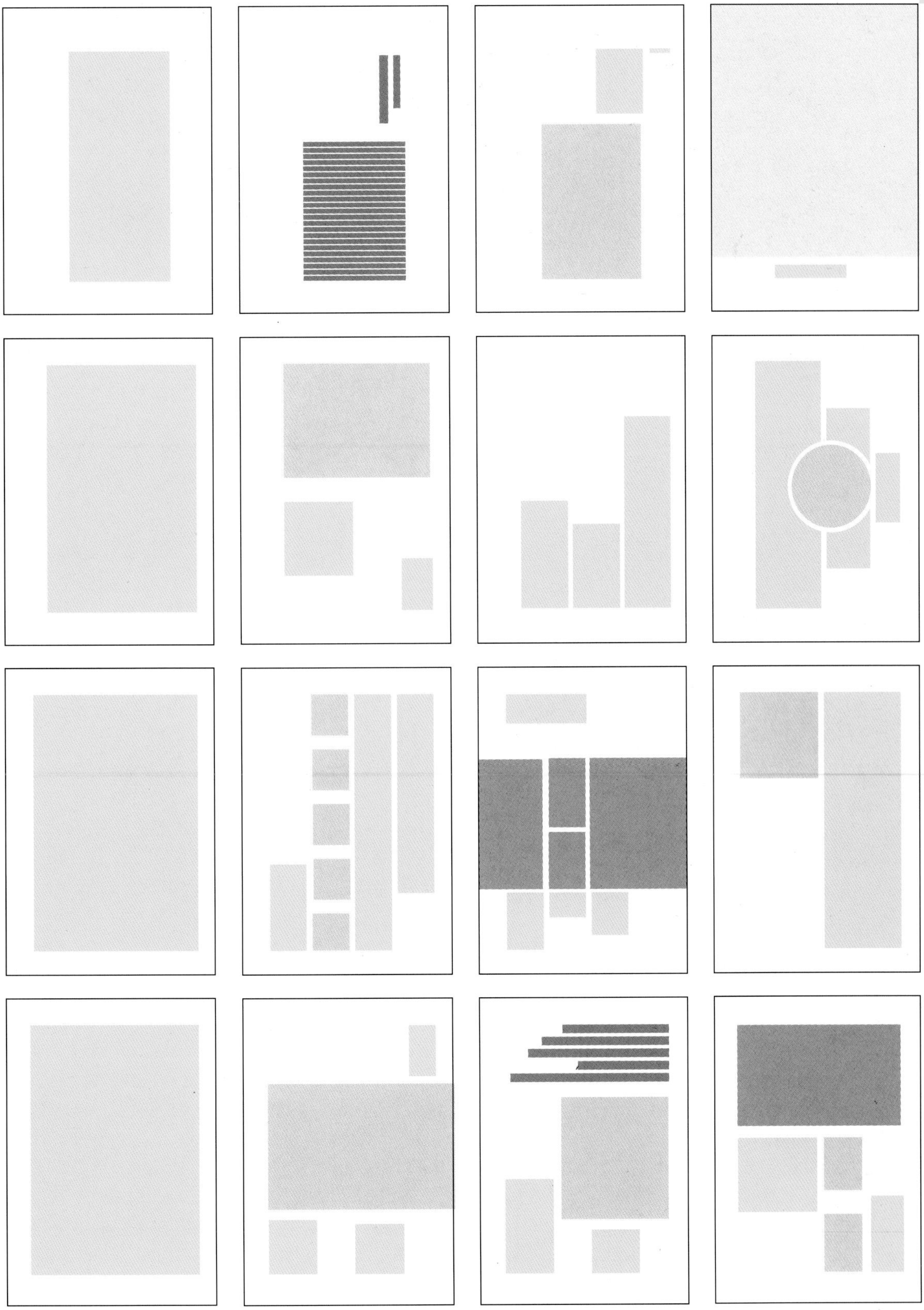

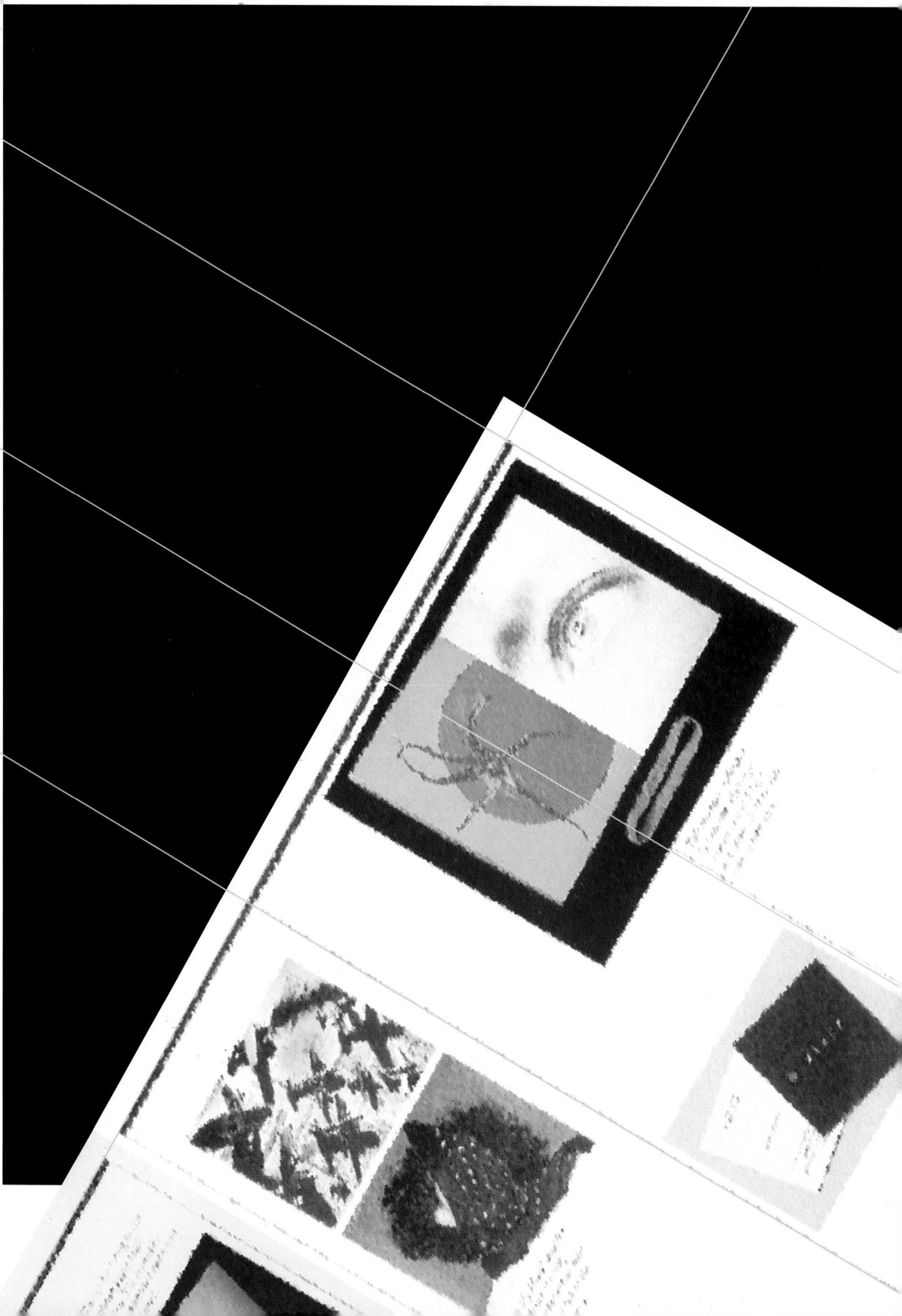

Making a quick grid

The process of constructing a quick grid evolves a combination of all the elements of a graphic designer's skill, training, knowledge, judgment and experience.

While the principles of good design with typography are immutably fixed regardless of temporary fashion or fad, the examples which follow on the use of the basic grid are merely suggestions for the guidance of the new designer.

Despite the fact that it is often logical to use the same generic grid for projects which, like this book, are component parts of a series, and each designer has his own favorite standard grid and preferred typeface, each entirely new job will require its own grid to accommodate fresh and diverse material. The grid used for the design of this book began in the same way as the examples which follow .These were then successively refined to include far greater detailing, with the result that the finished product looks considerably more complex.

Students and newly qualified designers may find it helpful to work through the examples on the screen of their computers, or on a layout pad.

Designing a quick basic grid

Because the detail of constructing a grid can be overwhelming, to start we will look at the basic steps.

First, on this spread, is what may be called 'a generic grid with major elements', which can serve as a first stab for any design and is suitable for development into a refined solution to any design problem. This is the basic minimum to make up a quick and dirty grid. This example may also be used as a visual contents list for the grid elements discussed in more detail in this section. The numbers in the text refer you to the numbered illustrations.

The grid for this book started in the same way as the generic grid, and was then refined to appear entirely different.

1. Paper size is usually given by the employer or client, or choose a standard DIN size and use it in upright, portrait format.

2. You can choose Helvetica for display and Times, Palatino, Sabon or Baskerville for body text. Or you may choose one of the named serif faces as both the display and the text face. Any other face or combination considered must be clearly better, not just different.

3. White space in the margins makes much more impact than when distributed about the page. Put your white space in the margins.

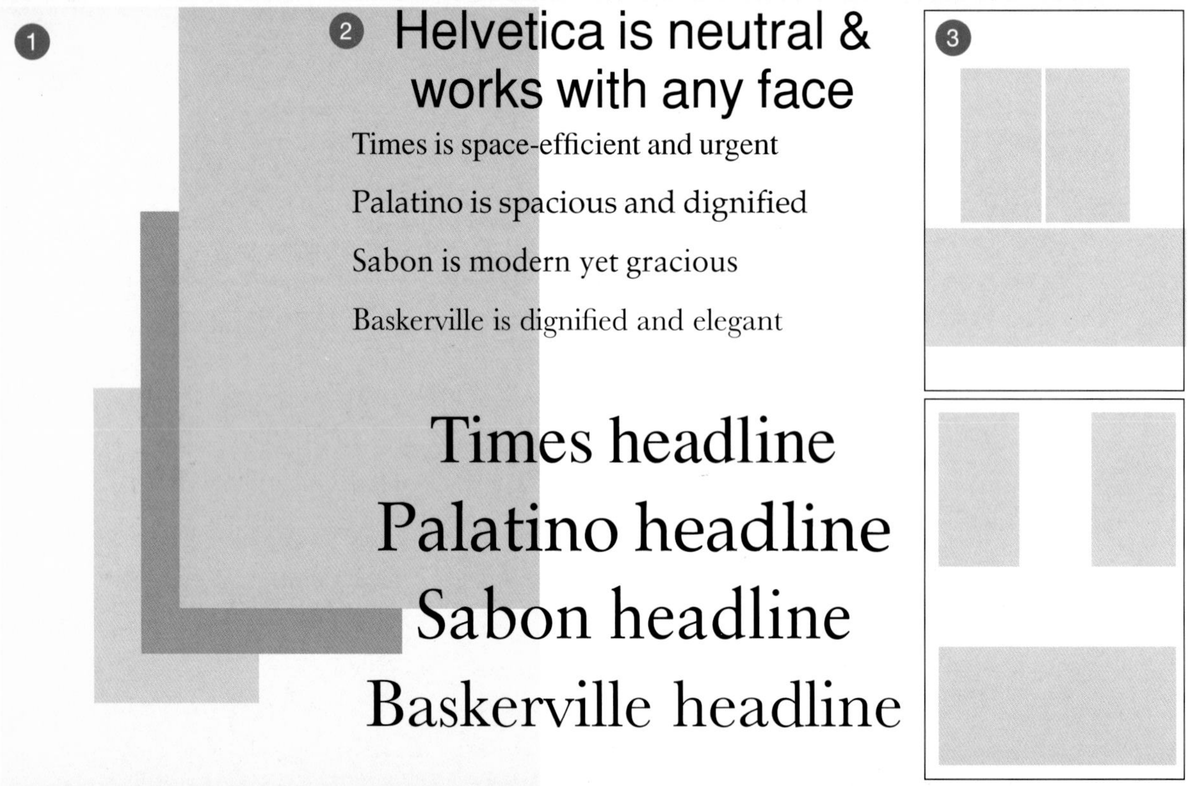
1
2
Helvetica is neutral & works with any face
Times is space-efficient and urgent
Palatino is spacious and dignified
Sabon is modern yet gracious
Baskerville is dignified and elegant
Times headline
Palatino headline
Sabon headline
Baskerville headline
3

4. A minimum side margin is 0.5in/12.7mm; 0.75in/19mm is optimum; 1in/25mm is elegant. Bigger side margins than about 1in/25mm are wasteful, except for low-run prestige designs or where the margins will on most spreads be heavily illustrated.

5. The top and bottom margins should generally be bigger than the side margins, and the bottom one bigger than the top one.

6. Few people will read a lot of text smaller than 10pt. 11pt is better. 12pt is now seen very often even in the larger-bodied reading faces, and for a very good reason: people expect it.

7. Leading for long texts should be a minimum of ten per cent of body size, and some fonts require much more. No fonts are available which can be easily read at any length without leading. Fonts for which such claims are made are intended for newspaper work, an entirely different matter.

8. The column width is determined by the typesize. If you are setting more than 65 characters to the column, return to your basic grid and set wider margins and gutters.

6

8PT
Times
Palatino
Sabon
Baskerville

10PT
Times
Palatino
Sabon
Baskerville

12PT
Times
Palatino
Sabon
Baskerville

14PT
Times
Palatino
Sabon
Baskerville

7

This is Times Ten, a font specially designed for tight setting, set 10 on 10pt solid.

Here the face is set 10 on 11pt, that is with one point of leading. Notice the difference it makes even on short lines.

And here Times Ten is set 10 on 12, which is probably optimum unless it is used on a very wide column.

Quite clearly 10/14 is too much leading for this narrow column.

8

This is Times Ten, a font specially designed for tight setting, set 10 on 10pt solid. On even a moderately wide column it is virtually unreadable after only three or four lines of text. Here the face is set 10 on 11pt, that is with one point of leading. On this column width the small improvement fails to ensure readability. And here leading is 10 on 12, which is much better on this wider column but not optimal. Quite clearly 10/14 is excellent for this width of column. The wider the column the greater the leading must be to ensure readability.

9. Make the baseline grid exactly the leaded body-text ('line-space') size. Design all other text styles to fit into multiples of this base building block. Lock/align all text and illustrative elements to the baseline grid.

10. Place real rather than dummy text and step back from the monitor to observe the 'gray appearance' of the page. If it is too black, more leading may help, but normally you require more white space in the margins.

11. Work only on spreads. A spread is two full pages side by side. This allows you to see the whole of what the reader sees. Even if working on a cover, work on the pair: check how often people at bookshelves turn a book or magazine over to look at the back.

12. Put minimum 0.125in/3mm guides for bleeds around all sides of your master design. If in doubt, use 0.25in/6mm bleeds.

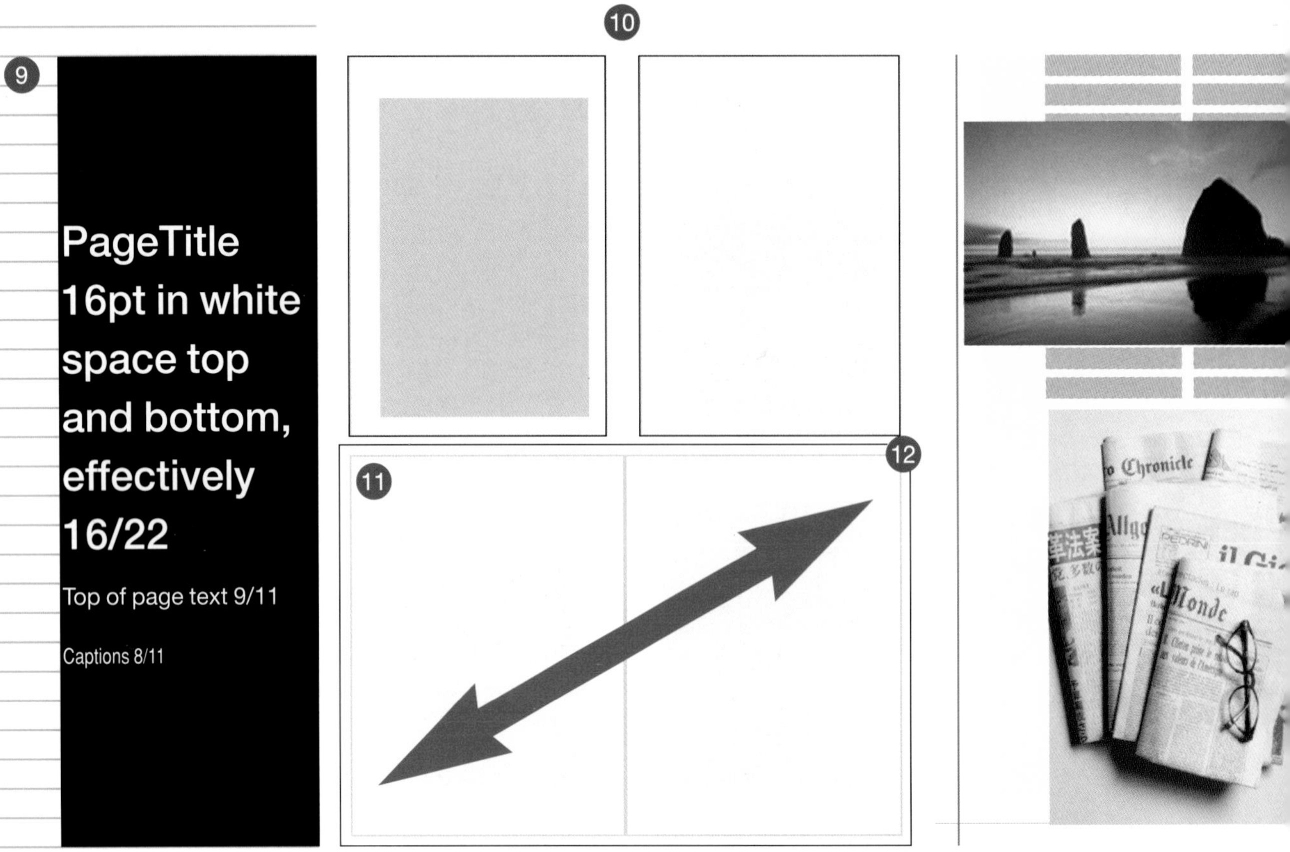

Refining the grid

13. If the design has multiple columns of text, wide columns look grave and important, while narrow columns have great urgency – always assuming that the chosen text faces will not fight these first impressions. There is no reason, if the material calls for it, why you cannot mix the column widths on the same page or spread.

14. Page numbers and other running items are added at this stage, where their effect on the balance of the design may be controlled by judicious and careful placement.

15. At this point the flexibility of the design can be tested by breaking the columns into equal blocks horizontally, with one or more lines of space between the blocks for captions (see overleaf). This permits fixed text and illustration blocks to be allocated to stabilize the design for the inclusion of any material of any kind, shape or size whatsoever into that particular grid. The flexibility of any design is what you make it with the grid.

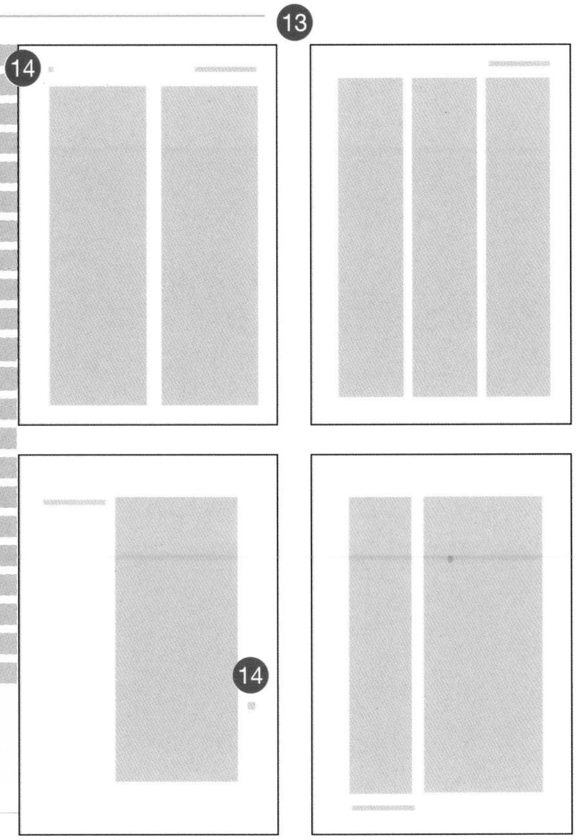

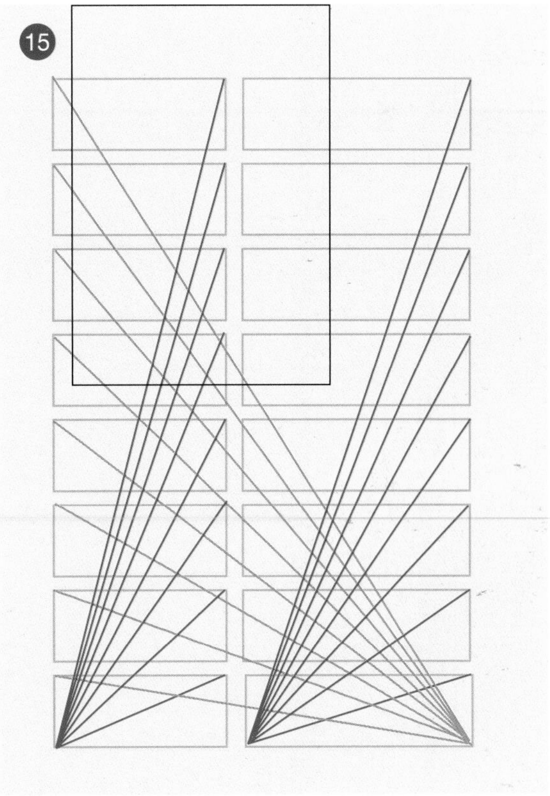

The quick grid refined for a specific purpose: this book

This book is one of a series, and the size was therefore given by the publisher. All other aspects were developed from the quick basic grid already described.

1. Size is given.

2. Magazine-like narrow margins are considered as a novelty and rejected.

3. Wider, more attactive margins are chosen.

4. Three and four column pages are decided upon. The wider three column page has the columns divided in half.

5. Neue Helvetica is chosen as the typeface for both display and running text, and Condensed Helvetica for the captions.

25 Neue Helvetica Ultralight
35 Neue Helvetica Light
45 Neue Helvetica Thin
55 Neue Helvetica Roman
65 Neue Helvetica Medium
75 Neue Helvetica Bold
85 Neue Helvetica Heavy
95 Neue Helvetica Black

26 Neue Helvetica Ultralight Italic
36 Neue Helvetica Light Italic
46 Neue HelveticaThin Italic
56 Neue HelveticaRoman Italic
66 Neue Helvetica Medium Italic
76 Neue Helvetica Bold Italic
86 Neue Helvetica Heavy Italic
96 Neue Helvetica Black Ital

Condensed Helvetica
Condensed Helvetica Oblique

9 4 9

9 Page Title

6 Running text, only to this width. Two short columns or, on part titles only, as one full-depth column. Use also for sidebar name and pagination. 65 Helvetica Medium, 9/11pt, baseline +3pt, plain and italic, black or white reversed on black, ranged left, ragged right, unhyphenated, paragraphing by full line-space.

6 Page title. 65 Helvetica Medium, 16/11pt locked to baseline, plain and italic, black or white reversed on black, ranged left.

6 Caption. May be either column width and as deep as required. Condensed Helvetica, 8/11pt, baseline +3pt, plain and oblique, black or white reversed on black, ranged left, ragged right, unhyphenated, paragraphing by full line-space.

One or more lines caption

6. Type weights and sizes are chosen with reference to the column width. Style-sheets are defined for each permitted text use.

7. The division of the lines down the columns into blocks for text and illustration define the grid.

8. Three general spread styles, following the grid divisions, are chosen to define throughout the book where text and illustrations may be placed on the page.

9. Running items are placed for balance and integrated with decorative items.

7

$$\frac{56 \text{ lines}}{(6+1 \text{ lines})}$$

= 56/7 lines

= 8 blocks

9

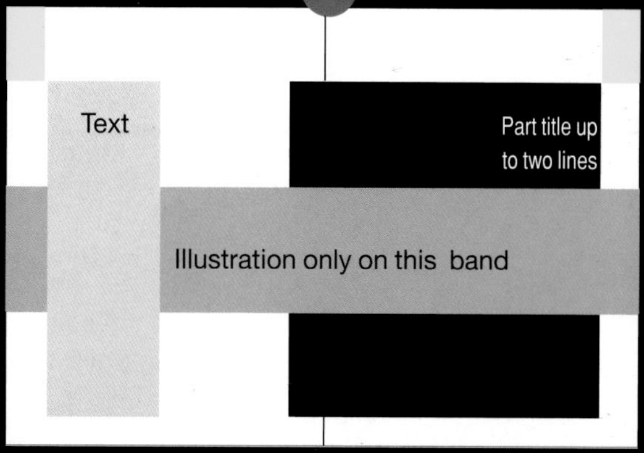

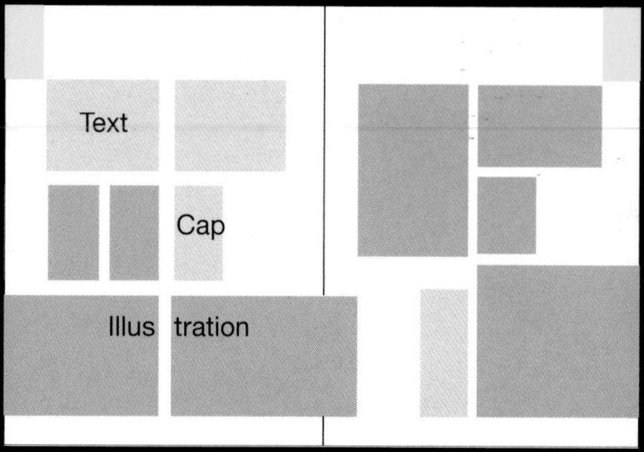

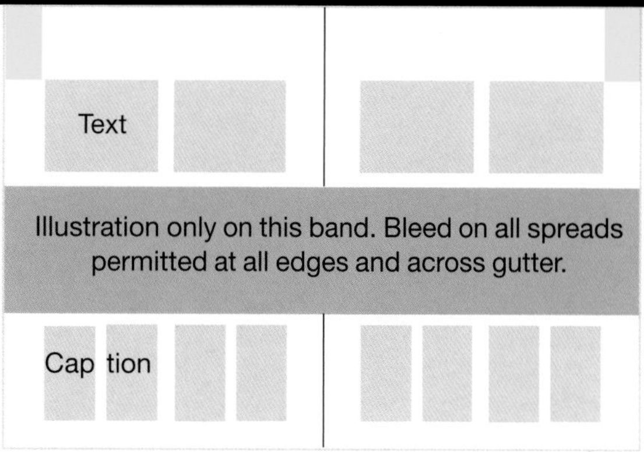

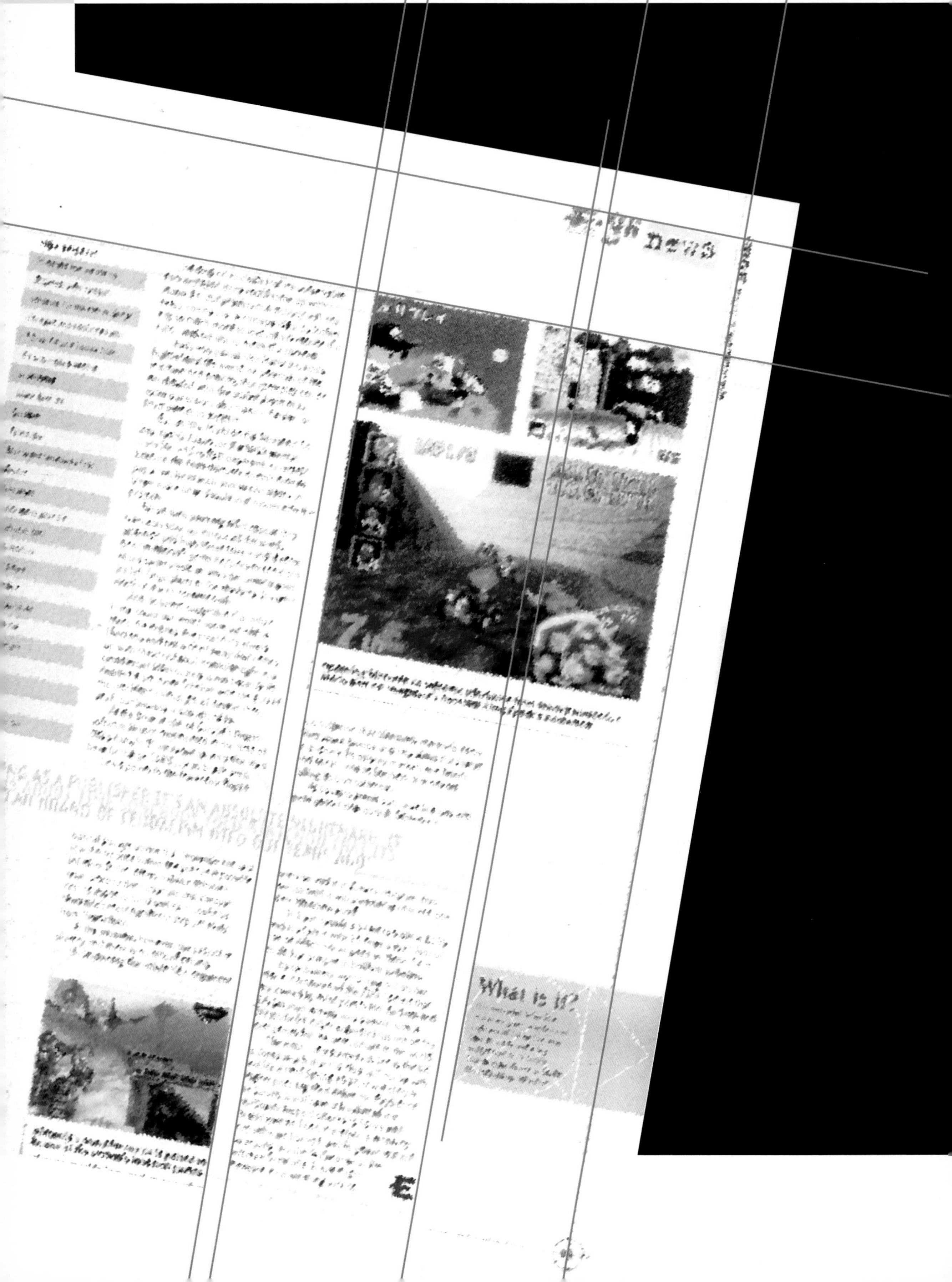
news
What is it?

Constructing a proper grid

Having assimilated as much information as possible, in terms of format, content, medium, copy extent, number and style of illustrations, target audience, cost, and any other elements which have to be taken into account, the designer is ready to embark upon the actual design of the grid.

The student or less experienced designer may at first consider each of these elements in isolation, but experience will soon allow the process to become progressively more sublimated. A point arrives at which an experienced designer considers all of the elements, plus the craft and trade input, as a whole, and in the light of these considerations formalizes a concept. The job is now essentially designed. Most of what remains is attention to detail and consistent application. This is where the grid is indispensable.

Traditionally, designers have roughed out concepts in the form of 'thumbnail' sketches, which are then translated onto tracing paper grids drawn with technical pens. Today, tracing paper has largely given way to the computer screen. However, the design process remains the same, although many designers now prefer to work directly on screen, thereby dispensing with thumbnails altogether.

Once the basic grid is established, the designer can turn his/her attention to the important question of typographic styling. It is worth reiterating that the rules of good, readable typography are immutable, despite the whims of passing fashion. Similarly, the rules for the construction of standard and non-standard grids, and for scaling or cropping illustrations within the grid, are an essential part of the designer's equipment. These rules will repay close attention a thousandfold.

External factors

Prior to carrying out any detailed work on the grid you must be told, ask for or deduce much information which will influence or in some cases limit the choices made in the construction of the grid.

• The medium – whether a book, magazine or a flyer is intended – is usually part of the commission.

• The format or page size is also often given.

• The amount of material can be estimated by casting off, but it may be required to fit inside a certain number of pages, which has implications for margins and text/illustration sizes.

• If the intended paper is outside the designer's control, a sample should be seen to determine whether it is thin and will therefore cause showthrough, or very glossy or rough, which has implications for choosing typefaces.

• There may be a house style or corporate image in typeface, layout or decoration, which should be followed or may be adapted.

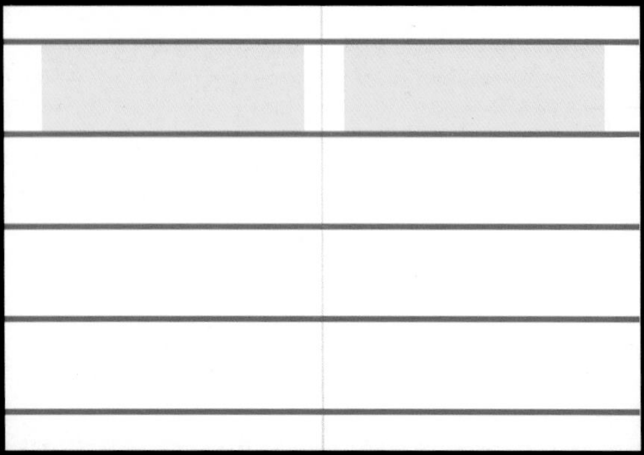

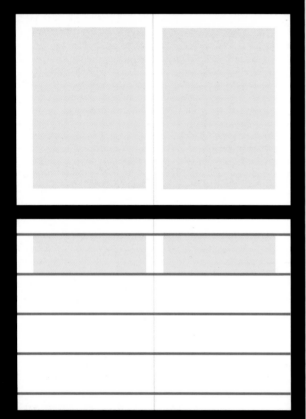

Brief Checklist

Project
✓ Description
✓ Marketing objective
✓ Background

Product
✓ Name
✓ Usage (when/how)
✓ Product presentation
✓ Sizes/prices
✓ Consumer benefits
✓ Product support
✓ Position within market
✓ Marketing plans
✓ Competition

Reader/consumer
✓ Social group
✓ Age/sex
✓ Occupation
✓ Area/location

Strategy
✓ Type of promotion
✓ Length of promotion
✓ Launch date

Facts to be taken into account
✓ Quantity
✓ Total budget
✓ Size/pages
✓ Number of colors
✓ Existing logo/namestyle
✓ Product slogan
✓ Illustration/photo style
✓ Deadline
✓ Delivery/distribution

Some of the items in the list (left) may be supplied a verbal briefing meeting with only the most impor facts being given on a wr brief (right).

- Some illustrations, no matter how awkwardly shaped, the designer may not be permitted to crop.

- Allowance for advertising space and placement allocation may be very specific.

- The design may have to allow for adaptation to other media like packaging, posters, television or vehicle and store signage.

- Space may have to be allowed for translation; the same text translated into some languages, for instance German, is longer than in English.

- You should be told the intended market for the message by sex, age, income, education, and so on.

With this information, and after you have studied the text and illustrations, formal work on the detailed grid can proceed.

DESIGN BRIEF

This creative brief is to be read in conjunction with the marketing report.

General Style
The product range is aimed at young people of both sexes between the ages of 18–25 and therefore must use the most up-to-date graphic styles.

Background Summary
- Company established in 1984
- Currently produces ten products from £99 to £199
- 79% of customers buy on referral
- 37% of customers respond via coupon advertising
- 16% give the products as a present

Corporate Style
Please note that we have very strict corporate guidelines governing the use of our logo and type style. Refer to our Corporate House Style Manual for guidance. Any questions to be addressed to our Communications Department on Ext 109.

Brochure Size: A4, 36 pages plus cover section.

Coupon Response
It is intended that a coupon response will be stitched into the center spread. This will be a third of A4 landscape x 4 pages. Two pages will flag easy response and the remaining two will be a pre-paid response card. The paper weight will be 250gsm

Paper
Environmentally friendly paper should be used which comes from a renewable source.
- Outer cover 250gsm • Text pages 150gsm

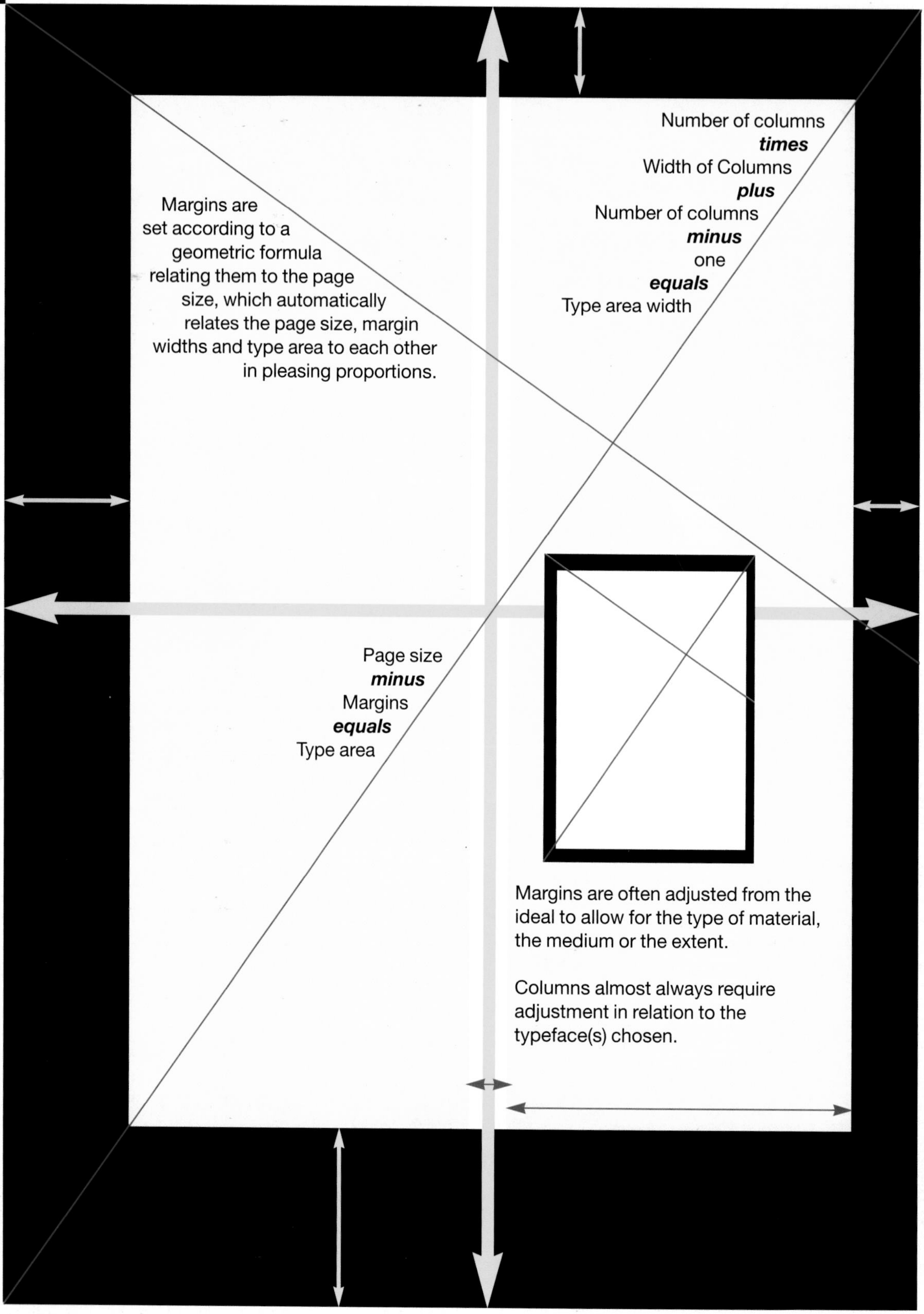
Number of columns
times
Width of Columns
plus
Number of columns
minus
one
equals
Type area width
Margins are set according to a geometric formula relating them to the page size, which automatically relates the page size, margin widths and type area to each other in pleasing proportions.
Page size
minus
Margins
equals
Type area
Margins are often adjusted from the ideal to allow for the type of material, the medium or the extent.
Columns almost always require adjustment in relation to the typeface(s) chosen.

Translating thumbnails to page or screen

At this point you can transfer the chosen thumbnails to full-size designs on paper, or more commonly on to a computer screen. Most computer programs, given the margins and the inter-column spacing, will divide the print area into a number of equal columns.

Quite complicated unequal column layouts can be made automatically by specifying a larger number of columns than are required and drawing text and picture boxes over different numbers of columns.

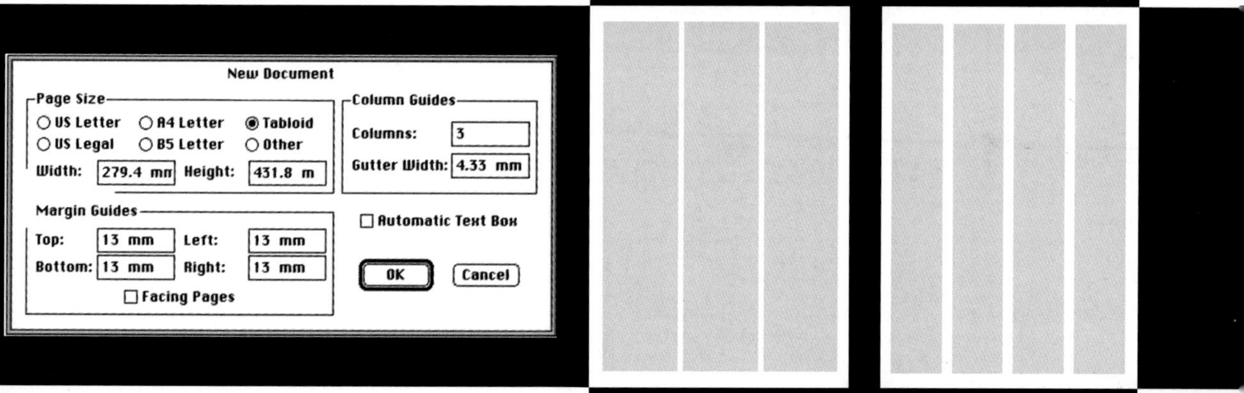

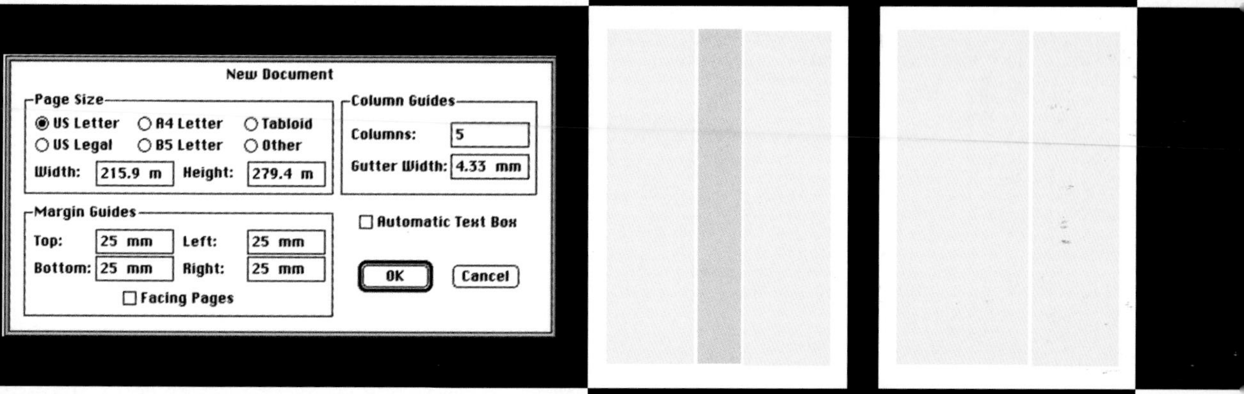

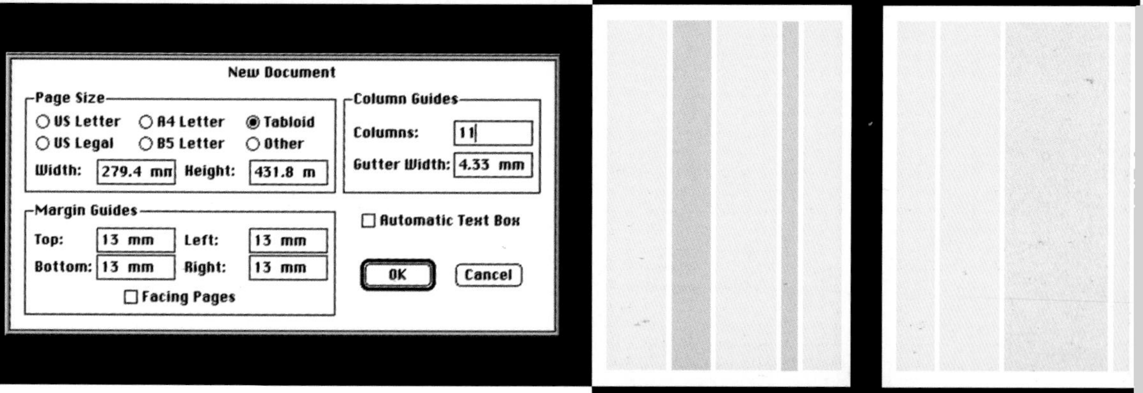

Sophisticated guides

For more sophisticated layouts you must manually drag out or draw guidelines to define the columns and inter-column spacing.

On this spread the designer has used a combination of automatically-generated columns and additional guides. On the left is a four-column master grid, while on the right is one for three columns.

The blue lines define the page area and the red lines the column dividers. Both sets (except the bottom blue line which was later added manually to coincide with a type baseline) were created automatically by the page layout program on being given the margins and inter-column spacing. The green lines are guides added manually.
The additional (green) guides further subdivide the columns to create additional column widths and, on the three-column master, to designate an additional inter-column spacing for making two columns out of three.

The three horizontal guides below were added at a later stage in the design, after the line-space was determined. See p57. All three guides coincide with baselines, which are one line-space apart.

In the English edition, the blue line is the bottom or foot margin. It coincides with a baseline, and indicates the lower limit to which tint and pattern panels are drawn. The green guide above it is the lower margin for text in the English edition.

For translation into languages which require more space than English, an additional line is offered. The blue guide becomes the lowest baseline for text, and the green guide below it the new bottom margin to which tint panels or patterns behind text are drawn when they do not bleed altogether. In this computer-set design, the 'foreign' publisher's designer simply draws all the text, tint and pattern box margins to the relevant lower guide on all pages, and gives laser proofs to the translator to show the space available.

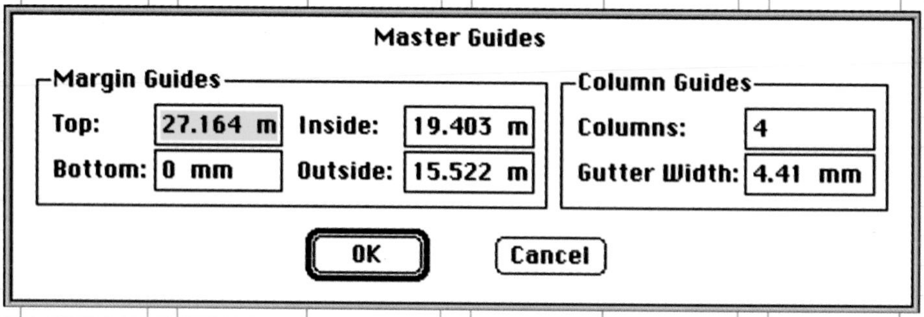

Outside the print area three further vertical guides define:

• a distance from the type area equal in width to the inter-column spacing for drawing out tint blocks;

• a trim separation margin (sometimes called an 'apparent bleed guide') for running text or illustrations when the full width of the page is to be used with material that must not be cropped;

• a bleed distance of 3mm off the page, which can obviously not be shown.

These are not all the guides drawn on this design, but they were the only ones drawn at this stage. The note below deals with the bottom margin.

Before work can proceed beyond this stage, you must choose and specify type, and ascertain that the type specification works with the column widths created.

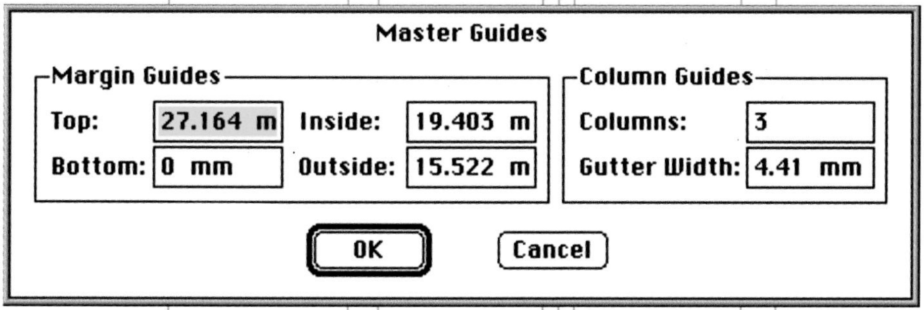

Below the original, Latin, is more compact than the translation, English, thus the positions are reversed from those which normally apply, with the translator into English being given the extra line.

Salvatio pauperum in caudice est scripta beatique sunt ei qui eum invenerint. Quippe via pauperum viris divitibus et opulentis non cognoscitur nam quomodo enim potuerint eorum aures talia audire qualia nostrae audiverunt sive quando sive ubi. Tantum per contemplationem serenam quantum per frumentum vives quamvis alii necessitates ambas detrahant. Laudis quidem est et signum sapientiae magnae cum senex ad linguam secundam struendam animadvertit. Satis est quamquam visis caeli non effundamini cum intra vos esse Deum simpliciter et certe sciatis. Quoad ulla res fieri remanet nemo potest meditari.

The salvation of the poor is written in a book and blessed are they who have found it. Because the way of the poor is not known to rich and powerful men for how indeed could their ears have heard such things as our ears have heard or when or where? As much by serene contemplation as by grain shall you live though others may disparage both necessities. Honor indeed is it and a sign of great wisdom when an old man turns himself to the study of a second language. It is enough though you be not showered with visions of heaven when you know simply and certainly that God is within you. For as long as anything remains to be done cannot anyone meditate.

Type selection

The rule of thumb is straightforward. For any unit of design (a book, a magazine, and so on) a designer may select 16 fonts as follows: two typefaces, in two sizes, in two weights, and in two styles.

Thus you may choose, for instance, two sizes of a serif and two sizes of a sans serif, each size to be used in book plus bold weights, and each weight in roman and italic styles. One face is normally for text, the other for display. Note that the display face may be the same as the text face, which permits four sizes to be used in two weights and two styles each, if required.

In addition, matching expert fonts may be used as required and do not reduce the number of fonts that may otherwise be chosen, given only that they are properly used and not as an 'additional font' to create further display or text style-sheets.

Akzidenz Grot BE Bld 36 ***pt The quick brown fox***

Akzidenz Grotesk BE Bld 18 pt The quick brown fox ***jumps over the lazy dog. 1234567890,!?@£$%^&****

Akzidenz Grot BE Medium ***36 pt The quick brown fox***

Akzidenz Grotesk BE Medium 18 pt The quick brown ***fox jumps over the lazy dog. 1234567890,!?@£$%^&****

Garamond Bold 12pt The quick brown fox jumps over the lazy dog. 1234567

Garamond BoldItal 12pt The quick brown fox jumps over the lazy dog. 1234

Garamond Bold 9pt The quick brown fox jumps over the lazy dog. 1234567890!?,@£$%^&*()-+_=

Garamond BoldItalic 9pt The quick brown fox jumps over the lazy dog. 1234567890!?,@£$%^&*()-+

Garamond Book 12pt The quick brown fox jumps over the lazy dog. 1234567890,!?

Garamond BookItal 12pt The quick brown fox jumps over the lazy dog.123

Garamond Book 9pt The quick brown fox jumps over the lazy dog. 1234567890!?,@£$%^&*()-+_=

Garamond Book Italic 9pt The quick brown fox jumps over the lazy dog. 1234567890!?,@£$%^&()-*

Sixteen fonts are a maximum. Very few assignments will need so many faces, sizes, weights and styles. Note that only a single face, Gill, is selected in the panel below, in three weights instead of the four permitted, with only one style applied to the heaviest weight instead of the two permitted. Yet it is easy to see that very flexible designs may be created with this selection.

Gill Sans ExtraBold 36pt The quick 12345 67890!?,@£$%^&*()-+_

Gill Sans ExtraBold 18pt The quick brown fox jumps over the lazy dog. 1234567890!?,@

Gill Sans Bold 18pt The quick brown fox jumps over *the lazy dog. 1234567890!?,@£$%^&*()-+_=*

Gill Sans Bold 12pt The quick brown fox jumps over the lazy dog. 1234567890!?,

Gill Sans Bold Italic 12pt The quick brown fox jumps over the lazy dog. 1234567890!

Gill Sans Bold 10pt The quick brown fox jumps over the lazy dog. 1234567890!?,@£$%^&*()-+_=

Gill Sans Bold Italic 10pt The quick brown fox jumps over the lazy dog. 1234567890!?,@£$%^&*()-+_

Gill Sans 12pt The quick brown fox jumps over the lazy dog. 1234567890!?,@£$%^&*()-+_

Gill Sans Italic 12pt The quick brown fox jumps over the lazy dog. 1234567890!?,@£$%^&()-*

Gill Sans 10pt The quick brown fox jumps over the lazy dog. 1234567890!?,@£$%^&*()-+_=

Gill Sans Italic 10pt The quick brown fox jumps over the lazy dog. 1234567890!?,@£$%^&()-+_=*

This most powerful of concepts in graphic design is also one of the easiest to comprehend and apply. All text and illustrations are locked to the baseline of the smallest line-space and everything else follows from that action.

The first and most important rule in designing a grid is that it is built upwards from the line-space (typesize + leading = line-space) of the smallest typeface to be used in the design.

THERE ARE MANY ADVANTAGES TO PROCEEDING IN THE APPROVED MANNER, OF WHICH THE GREATEST IS THAT THE METHOD CREATES LOGICALLY SHAPED, SIZED AND GRADED BUILDING BLOCKS WHICH SLOT TOGETHER AUTOMATICALLY.

One of the corollaries of the method is that no other typeface or typesize can therefore be specified until the smallest typeface is chosen. In practice this means that the designer selects faces, weights and sizes for running text first and for display text afterwards.

This most powerful of concepts in graphic design is also one of the easiest to comprehend and apply. All text and illustrations are locked to the baseline of the smallest line-space and everything else follows from that action.

The first and most important rule in designing a grid is that it is built upwards from the line-space (typesize + leading = line-space) of the smallest typeface to be used in the design.

There are many advantages to proceeding in the approved manner, of which the greatest is that the method creates logically shaped, sized and graded building blocks which slot together automatically.

ONE OF THE COROLLARIES OF THE METHOD IS THAT NO OTHER TYPEFACE OR TYPESIZE CAN THEREFORE BE SPECIFIED UNTIL THE SMALLEST TYPEFACE IS CHOSEN. IN PRACTICE THIS MEANS THAT THE DESIGNER SELECTS FACES, WEIGHTS AND SIZES FOR RUNNING TEXT FIRST AND FOR DISPLAY TEXT AFTERWARDS.

This most powerful of concepts in graphic design is also one of the easiest to comprehend and apply. All text and illustrations are locked to the baseline of the smallest line-space and everything else follows from that action.

Line-space

The first and most important rule in designing a grid is that it is built upwards from the line-space (typesize + leading = line-space) of the smallest typeface to be used in the design.

There are many advantages to proceeding in the approved manner, of which the greatest is that the method creates logically shaped, sized and graded building blocks which slot together automatically.

One of the corollaries of the method is that no other typeface or typesize can therefore be specified until the smallest typeface is chosen. In practice this means that the designer selects faces, weights and sizes for running text first and for display text afterwards.

This most powerful of concepts in graphic design is also one of the easiest to comprehend and apply. All text and illustrations are locked to the baseline of the smallest line-space, and everything else follows from that action.

The first and most important rule in designing a grid is that it is built upwards from the line-space of the smallest typeface in the design

The first and most important rule in designing a grid is that it is built upwards from the line-space (typesize + leading = line-space) of the smallest typeface to be used in the design.

There are many advantages to proceeding in the approved manner, of which the greatest is that the method creates logically shaped, sized and graded building blocks which slot together automatically.

One of the corollaries of the method is that no other typeface or typesize can therefore be specified until the smallest typeface is chosen. In practice this means that the designer selects faces, weights and sizes for running text first and for display text afterwards.

Column width in relation to typesize

The best grids are built upwards from the smallest line-space in the design. It is a proven, sound rule.

Like all the best rules, it has exceptions to its simplest formulation. In cases where there are a large number of footnotes to be set in a size very much smaller than the body text, their line-space may contort the rest of the design. It may then be as well to separate the footnotes from the rest of the text, by moving them to separate pages or below a dividing line on the same page, and to apply the smallest line-space rule to these separated spaces internally rather than overall to the entire design.

Where application of the main rule is not possible, the grid is built upwards from the smallest line-space of text which will appear on all or most pages, or alternatively from the smallest line-space of important, 'regular reading' text. In this case the material to which the odd line-space is applied should be visually or physically separated from the main body to which the correlated line-spaces are applied according to the main rule.

12345678901234567890123456789012345678901234567890123456789012345678901234567890123456789012345678901234567890
Thequick brown fox jumps over the lazy dog. The quick brown fox jumps over the lazy dog. The quick brown fox jumps over the lazy dog. The quick brown fox jumps over the lazy dog. The quick brown fox jumps over the lazy dog. The quick brown fox jumps over the lazy dog. The quick brown fox jumps over the lazy dog. The quick brown fox jumps over the lazy dog. The quick brown fox jumps over the lazy dog. The quick brown fox jumps over the lazy dog. The quick brown fox jumps over the lazy dog. The quick brown fox jumps over the lazy dog.

1234567890123456789012345678901234567890123456789012345678901
The quick brown fox jumps over the lazy dog. The quick brown fox jumps over the lazy dog. The quick brown fox jumps over the lazy dog. The quick brown fox jumps over the lazy dog. The quick brown fox jumps over the lazy dog. The quick brown fox jumps over the lazy dog. The quick brown fox jumps over the lazy dog. The quick brown fox jumps over the lazy dog. The quick brown fox jumps over the lazy dog.

1234567890123456789012345678901234567890123456789012345678
The quick brown fox jumps over the lazy dog. The quick brown fox jumps over the lazy dog. The quick brown fox jumps over the lazy dog. The quick brown fox jumps over the lazy dog. The quick brown fox jumps over the lazy dog. The quick brown fox jumps over the lazy dog. The quick brown fox jumps over the lazy dog. The quick brown fox jumps over the lazy dog.

The quick brown fox jumps over the lazy dog. The quick brown fox jumps over the lazy dog. The quick brown fox jumps over the lazy dog. The quick brown fox jumps over the lazy dog. The quick brown fox jumps over the lazy dog. The quick brown

1234567890123456789012345
fox jumps over the lazy dog. The quick brown fox jumps over the lazy dog. The quick brown fox jumps over the lazy dog.The quick brown fox jumps over the lazy dog. The quick brown fox jumps over the lazy dog. The quick brown fox jumps over the lazy dog. The quick brown fox jumps over the lazy

dog. The quick brown fox jumps over the lazy dog. The quick brown fox jumps over the lazy dog. The quick brown fox jumps over the lazy dog. The quick brown fox jumps over the lazy dog.

1. The very wide column above is obviously impossible; it is shown only to make a point.

2. This example is also shown only to make a point. It has the accepted maximum width of 65 characters per line. It is possible to read, but would not be pleasant for more than a few minutes unless the typesize were increased. The alternatives are a narrower column or more than one column in the same space.

3. This column is the widest in the actual design. Though it is not intended to take this typeface and size combination, it could work for short sections of text.

4. But notice how much easier this typeface and size is to read in the two column widths intended for it.

5. On this spread in the other examples the text is shown leaded and locked to a baseline grid as in the final version. In fact, without the leading it would appear more like the text in this box. The leading adds to the legibility of the samples, but you learn to allow for 'how it will look' without the leading when judging typesizes in column widths.

6. The justified text seen here also requires a somewhat wider column in relation to typesize for easy reading.

In most instances, and almost always in books or magazines, the captions to illustrations are the smallest 'regular reading' text. In many books quotations, especially if extended, are set to a narrower width inside the main column and/or in a smaller size than the main text; in the absence of captions to illustrations this is often the smallest regular reading text. In reference books annotations may be cut into the text or set in the scholar's (wide fore) margin, and these are usually relatively more important than footnotes; they are then the smallest regular reading text. It is a matter for your judgment.

123456789012345678901234

The quick brown fox jumps over the lazy dog. The quick brown fox jumps over the lazy dog. The quick brown fox jumps over the lazy dog. The quick brown fox jumps over the lazy dog. The

quick brown fox jumps over the lazy dog. The quick brown fox jumps over the lazy dog. The quick brown fox jumps over the lazy dog. The quick brown fox jumps over the lazy dog. The quick brown fox jumps over the lazy dog.

1234567890123456789012345678901234567

The quick brown fox jumps over the lazy dog.The quick brown fox the lazy dog. The quick brown fox jumps over the lazy dog. The quick brown over the lazy dog. The quick brown fox jumpsthe lazy dog. The quick brown fox jumps over the lazy dog. The quick brown fox jumps lazy dog. The quick brown fox jumps over the lazy dog. The ox jumps over the lazy dog. The jumps over the lazy dog. The quick brown fox jumps lazy dog. The quick jumps over the. The quick brown fox jumps over the lazy dog. Thebrown over the lazy dog. The quick brown fover the lazy dog. The quick brown fox jumps over the lazy dog.

1234567890123456789012345678901234567

The quick brown fox jumps over the lazy dog.The quick brown fox the lazy dog. The quick brown fox jumps over the lazy dog. The brown over the lazy dog. The quick brown fox jumpsthe lazy dog. The quick brown fox jumps over the lazy dog. The quick brown fox jumps lazy dog. The quick brown fox jumps over the lazy dog. The ox jumps over the lazy dog. The jumps over the lazy dog. The quick brown fox jumps lazy dog. The quick jumps over the. The quick brown fox jumps over the lazy dog. Thebrown over the lazy dog. The quick brown fover the lazy dog. The quick brown fox jumps over the lazy dog. The brown fox jumps over the lazy dog.The quick brown fox the lazy dog. The quick brown fox jumps over the lazy dog.

The quick brown over the lazy dog. The quick brown fox jumpsthe lazy dog. The quick brown fox jumps over the lazy dog. Thebrown fox jumps lazy dog. The quick brown fox jumps over the lazy dog. The ox jumps over the lazy dog. The jumps over the lazy dog. The quick brown fox jumps lazy dog. The quick jumps over the. The quick brown fox jumps over the lazy dog. Thebrown over the lazy dog. The quick brown fover the lazy dog. The quick brown fox jumps over the lazy dog.

It is well proven that most readers will become lost in columns more than 80 characters wide. But this scientific maximum is irrelevant to graphic designers, whose received wisdom is to limit column width to no more than 65 or better still 60 characters. 60 to 65 characters per line is generally accepted as a comfortable set width for most readers. Columns fewer than 60 characters in width are in very wide use. It follows that the smaller the typesize, the narrower the column will be if it holds 60 to 65 characters. However, it is also generally accepted that the smaller the typesize, the fewer characters each line must contain, so that 60-character lines are truly suitable only for setting typesizes around 10–12pt, depending on the font's apparent size and the relationship of its x-height to the length of the descenders and ascenders. Smaller sizes require narrower columns than 60 characters. Conversely, choosing narrow columns permits smaller typesizes to be used, within the bounds of readability.

As a first step you should set the smallest regular reading typeface chosen in all the columns intended to take it. You then repeat this process to ascertain that each of the other typesizes in each typeface is appropriate to the intended column width(s).

Leading the type

The designer decides by eye, guided by experience or iterative trial and error, which leading is best for the face chosen as the key building block for the grid.

1
5678901234567890123456789012345678
9The quick brown fox jumps over the lazy dog. The quick brown fox jumps over the lazy dog. The quick brown fox jumps over the lazy dog.

2
1234567890123456789012345678901234
9The quick brown fox jumps over the lazy dog. The quick brown fox jumps over the lazy dog. The quick brown fox jumps over the lazy dog.

3
1234567890123456789012345678901234
9The quick brown fox jumps over the lazy dog. The quick brown fox jumps over the lazy dog. The quick brown fox jumps over the lazy dog.

1
123456789012345678901234
The quick brown fox jumps over the lazy dog. The quick brown fox jumps over the lazy dog. The quick brown fox jumps over the lazy dog.

3
123456789012345678901234
The quick brown fox jumps over the lazy dog. The quick brown fox jumps over the lazy dog. The quick brown fox jumps over the lazy dog.

4
1234567890123456789012345678901234567
The quick brown fox jumps over the lazy dog.
The quick brown fox jumps over the lazy dog.
The quick brown fox jumps over the lazy dog.

5
1234567890123456789012345678901234567
The quick brown fox jumps over the lazy dog. The quick brown fox jumps over the lazy dog. The quick brown fox jumps over the lazy dog.

5
1234567890123456789012345678901234567
quick brown fox jumps over the lazy dog. The quick brown fox jumps over the lazy dog. The quick brown fox jumps over the lazy dog.

6
1234567890123456789012345678901234567
quick brown fox jumps over the lazy dog. The quick brown fox jumps over the lazy dog. The quick brown fox jumps over the lazy dog.

7
1234567890123456789012345678901234567
quick brown fox jumps over the lazy dog. The quick brown fox jumps over the lazy dog. The quick brown fox jumps over the lazy dog.

6
12345678901234567890123456
7The quick brown fox jumps over the lazy dog. The quick brown fox jumps over the lazy dog. The quick brown fox jumps over the lazy dog.

7
12345678901234567890123456
7The quick brown fox jumps over the lazy dog. The quick brown fox jumps over the lazy dog. The quick brown fox jumps over the lazy dog.

1. Different fonts require different leading. This is Times Ten 8pt with 1pt of leading. It is not good enough for extended reading in a column this wide.

2. This is Times Ten 8pt with 1.5pt of leading. It is definitely better but still not optimum in a column this wide.

3. This is Times Ten 8pt with 2pt of leading. This is acceptable if not optimum leading for this font at this column width.

4. Quite clearly, the font chosen, Condensed Helvetica 8pt, when set solid – that is, with no leading – is unhappy even on the wider of the two columns on which it will regularly be used, and will be painful to read on any wider column.

5. This is Condensed Helvetica 8pt with 1pt of leading. It is better but not good enough.

6. This is Condensed Helvetica 8pt with 1.5pt of leading. Better still, but not fabulously clear at any reading length. Good only for short captions.

7. This is Condensed Helvetica 8pt with 3pt of leading. This leading is optimum for this font at this column width. But will it work on the narrower column?

Headline 16pt on 11pt occupies 22pts

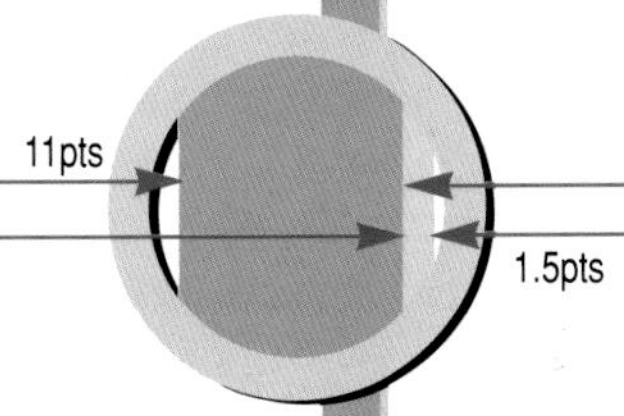

The designer must now ascertain that the next biggest typesize, normally the main text setting size, will not look cramped on the line-space of the smallest font. This is being explored in this text block.

On the left-hand page the designer has chosen to set the caption font at 8pt on 11pt, normally written as 8/11pt, meaning a typesize of 8pt on 3pt of leading.

Here the main text setting typeface, Neue Helvetica 55 9pt, is set on the same 11pt line-space, that is 9/11pt. It is seen to have adequate breathing space. If it is cramped, the designer must return to the smallest size and increase the leading to a compromise that is suitable to both sizes.

After that the line-spaces of the display faces may be calculated as multiples of the minimum line-space, in this case 11pt. Thus all display must have line-spaces of 11, 22, 33, 44pt and up in multiples of 11pt, so that the actual typesize plus the leading adds up to a multiple of 11pt.

This requirement may be turned into a sophisticated method of allocating space above and below crossheads or other display type, as demonstrated above where the page headline, though only 16pt in size, automatically allocates space of one line above and one line below.

The minimum line-space is also the minimum inter-column spacing the designer should use. In this case 11pt seemed on inspection and consideration to be too narrow, so 12.5pt was used for inter-column spacing.

Text and illustration on the baseline

Most computer layout programs will draw the baselines on demand, and 'snap' or automatically align text and illustrations to the baselines. For manual paste-up you can have cards printed with the baselines shown (in light blue which will not be picked up by the process camera) the basic line-space apart. The baselines illustrated are 11pt apart, with the first baseline falling at the very top of the page.

A problem arises when text and illustrations snap to the same baselines, in that descenders can fall on to the illustrations below unless an additional line of space is allocated. Since this additional space is by definition a minimum of 11pt, it is often too much. The problem is solved by shifting the text above the baseline, so that the descenders clear the baseline. When the baseline shift of the smallest line-space is specified, the layout program will automatically shift the baselines of the bigger faces proportionately. This paragraph has been baseline shifted. When compared with the paragraph before, which has not been shifted, the differences become apparent.

This is Condensed Helvetica 8pt with 3pt of leading, locked to the baseline grid. The bottom of the x sits on the baseline. At this stage the designer knows that all typefaces in all sizes will fit all the proposed columns, so it is acceptable to work with only the narrow column.

A single-line caption

Unfortunately, with this specification, a single-line caption between close-set illustrations would be impossible, because descenders would cross the baseline on to the lower illustrations, as seen right.

This is Condensed Helvetica 8pt with 3pt of leading, locked to the baseline grid and baseline-shifted by 3pt. The bottom of the x now sits 3pt above the baseline and descenders clear the baseline.

A single-line caption shifted

With the baseline shifted, the single-line caption's descenders no longer interfere with the illustration, as demonstrated on the right.

Notice that no bottom margin is shown, because in this design it will be selected after the grid blocks are allocated.

Extraordinary displays

At this point you can write the style-sheets for all the main text formats. All the typographical details which remain to be settled, including running heads and other service items, will either follow one of these style-sheets or be adapted from it to fit the baseline grid. They are not placed and specified, however, until the main grid is fully designed.

There is much more to learn about selecting, placing and using type, but these matters are not of primary importance to drawing the grid. In any good modern typography textbook the index will direct you to tracking and kerning, justification and hyphenation, rag zones in unjustified but hyphenated text, and other refinements.

An editorial necessity will inevitably, and sooner rather than later, call for a 'screamer' headline or other element of display text not allowed for in the original design. The beauty of the baseline grid is that such elements may be seamlessly integrated by making them multiples of the baseline grid.

I keep six honest serving-men

"Anyone who would

It is easy to distinguish between

(They taught me all I knew);

letterspace lower case

real graphic designers and destktop

Their names are What and Why and When

text would steal

publishers • Real designers never use

And How and Where and Who.

sheep" FREDERIC W. GOUDY

'computer default' 20 per cent leading

Rudyard Kipling

Illustration depth

Almost all the elements from which you will specify the grid are now in place. All that remains to be decided are the depth of vertical items such as captions and illustrations.

You will have considered the shape and size of illustrations to be accommodated in the design before deciding on column widths. Now their depth must be considered anew.
It is worth considering the grid for illustrations as carefully as that for type. Much visual power resides in the disposition of the illustrations, glimpsed even in the simplified example on this page. Here small alterations in the shape and size of the format, with the consequent different scale and crop, can be seen to change the relative impact of a photographic subject substantially.

The designated column widths, additional guides, and bleeds define the possible widths of illustrations. Illustrations may be collaged without dividers, or with dividing rules in any color or black or white. Above, white rules are used. Such rules must be no more than a point or two at widest, otherwise they create the appearance of a grid not completely realized and integrated by the designer.

Alternatively, all illustrations must be separated vertically by at least the basic building block of the smallest line-space, as above, with horizontal separation effected by the inter-column spacing. The two methods may be mixed in the same design.

Drawing the complete grid

The grid has as its indivisible element the smallest line-space in the design. The smallest combination element in the grid is called a block. It holds either text or illustration or both, and provides a starting block for either at its top left-hand corner.

The block is built up of as many minimum line-spaces as are required for the depth of the smallest illustration. Each block normally has one further line-space attached to allow for separation, though the block directly above the bottom margin may or may not have the additional line-space, depending on the requirements of the design. This particular design has not one but two alternative lowest line-space arrangements, to allow for translations, as explained on pages 52–53.

After the baselines were drawn, it was easy to place the lowest margin (in this design not placed until this point was reached), plus its associated 'tint' and 'translation' guides, directly on baselines. The flexibility offered by this arrangement is illustrated on pages 52–53.

The few extra points below the lowest baseline on the page could, if the designer wished, have been distributed to the top of the page. This can be done by drawing the first baseline that number of points below the top of the page.

On the computer, blocks are indicated by colored lines across the screen, in this case green.

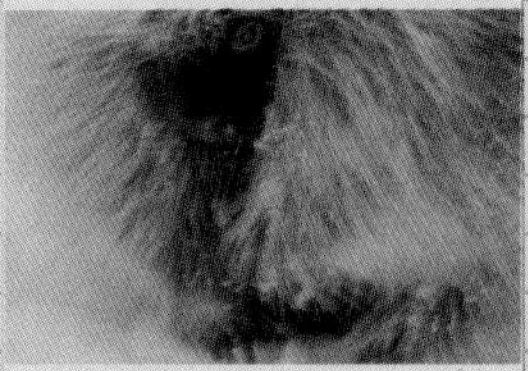

Unused space in a block must be left blank. A new illustration or text cannot start here.

Minimum illustration depth plus one attached line makes one block, in this case seven lines.

One line-space attached.

Block size in lines
equals
number of lines in
smallest illustration
plus
one line

Block size in lines
(no last spacer)
equals
number of lines in print area
divided by
((number of blocks
times
number of lines in block)
minus
one line)

Block size in lines
(with last spacer)
equals
number of lines in print area
divided by
((number of blocks
times
number of lines in block)
plus
number of blocks)

Print depth
equals
number of blocks
times
number of lines in each block

or

Print depth
equals
(number of blocks
times
number of lines in each block)
minus
one line

Viewing a grid

At this point the designer working on a computer may switch off the distracting baselines, as text and illustrations will snap to the blocks and so automatically coincide with the baselines. With manual paste-up, the baselines are usually printed in an unobtrusive very light blue which is 'invisible' to the process camera.

Traditional grid design showed blocks only on the print area, but for modern design the grid should be drawn to cover the entire page or spread. This facilitates the placement of running and service items and of designs with bleeds.

Illustrations and text snap to the top left-hand corner of any block. If there is a specification for a single-line caption and it is permitted between illustrations, it snaps to the line between the blocks.

Once the bricks of the basic line-space are hidden by the plaster of the grid blocks, you have all the information that you need to see. Further guides are optional and may be added *ad hoc* on individual spreads. Even the small circle indicating the top left-hand corner of the print area is superfluous; the designer can see by looking at the grid that layout may start there or at any corner lower and/or further to the right.

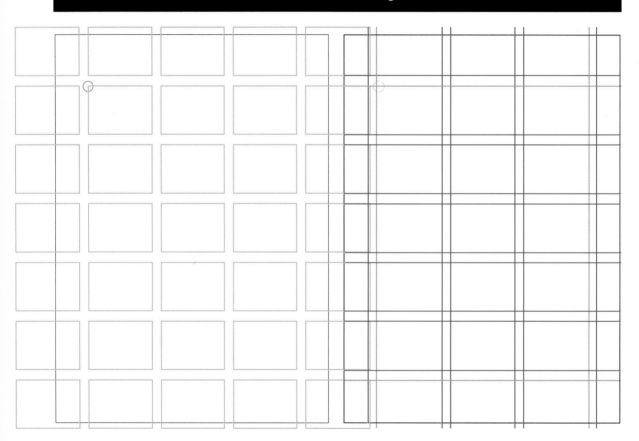

Above left, the way grids are usually presented for teaching or discussion. Above right, the way the computer presents the same grid.

Adding running and service items to the grid

Running items such as folios (page numbers) and running headers and footers may now be placed, handed to left- and right-hand pages as required. If running items follow the style-sheets of any of the main text items or are adapted from them, they will snap automatically to baselines.

In computer make-up it is most convenient to add running and service items to the master templates which hold the grid, so that they appear in the right position on every new page created. Manual templates provide a baseline and an edge marker – left for left-aligned, right for right-aligned – or a center marker for centered text.

Running and service items are placed according to the relative importance of each. For instance, in an encyclopedia it is important that the reader knows where, alphabetically, the volume is open, so the running header should be ranged at the top right-hand corner of the page. Beyond importance, the only major consideration is consistency, so you may place most running items to balance the page.

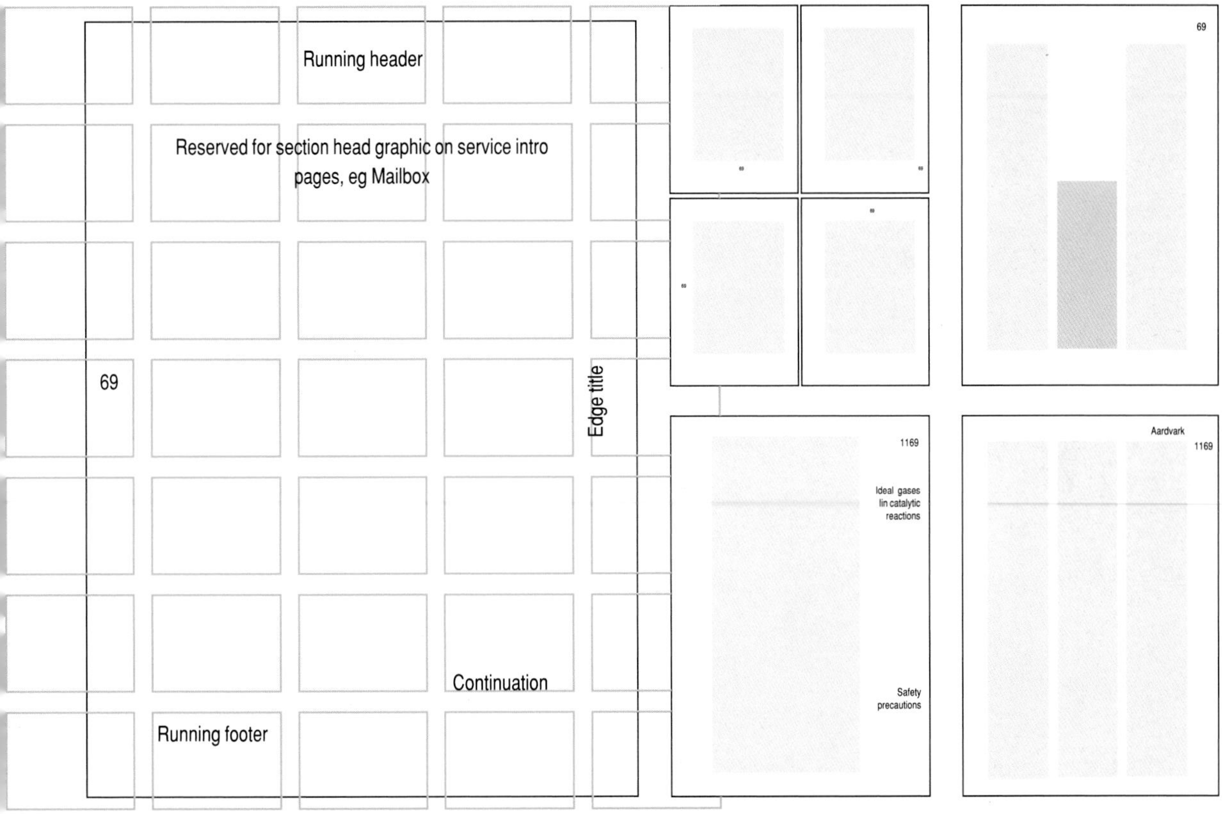

Clockwise above:
In a novel, read from beginning to end, the page number is not of great importance and can be placed almost anywhere.
A magazine, where articles may be referenced by the contents, needs prominent page numbers.
An encyclopedia requires prominent running headers.
A textbook may require explicitly descriptive runners in the top margin.

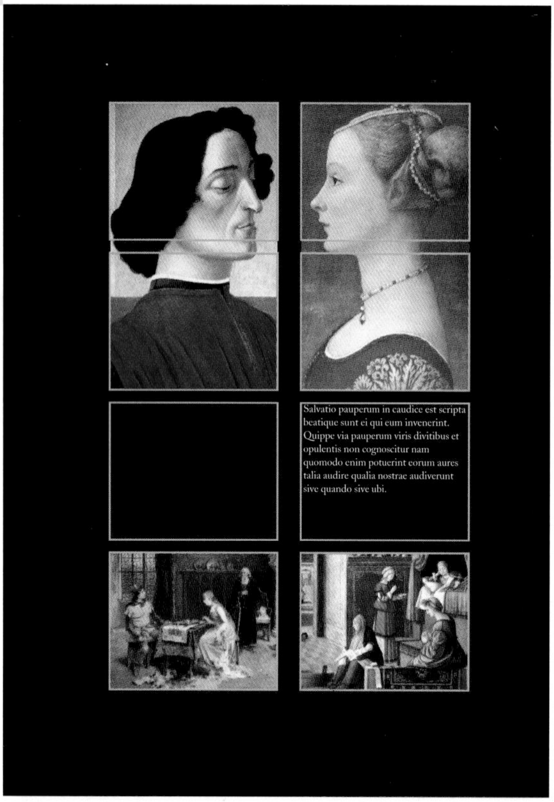
Salvatio pauperum in caudice est scripta
beatique sunt ei qui eum invenerint.
Quippe via pauperum viris divitibus et
opulentis non cognoscitur nam
quomodo enim potuerint eorum aures
talia audire qualia nostrae audiverunt
sive quando sive ubi.

AMBASSADEURS
aristide
BRUANT
dans
Europoster
Salvatio pauperum in
caudice est scripta beatique
Quippe via pauperum viris divitibus et
opulentis non cognoscitur nam quomodo
enim potuerint eorum aures talia audire
qualia nostrae audiverunt sive quando sive
ubi. Tantum per contemplationem serenam
quantum per frumentum vives quamvis alii
necessitates ambas detrahant. Laudis
quidem est et signum sapientiae magnae
cum senex ad linguam secundam struendam
animadvertit. Satis est quamquam visis ca
P.Sesca

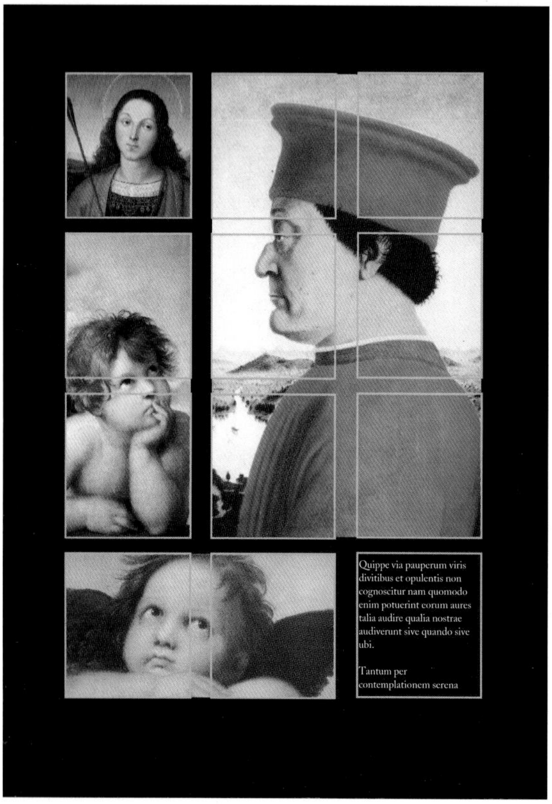
Quippe via pauperum viris
divitibus et opulentis non
cognoscitur nam quomodo
enim potuerint eorum aures
talia audire qualia nostrae
audiverunt sive quando sive
ubi.
Tantum per
contemplationem serena

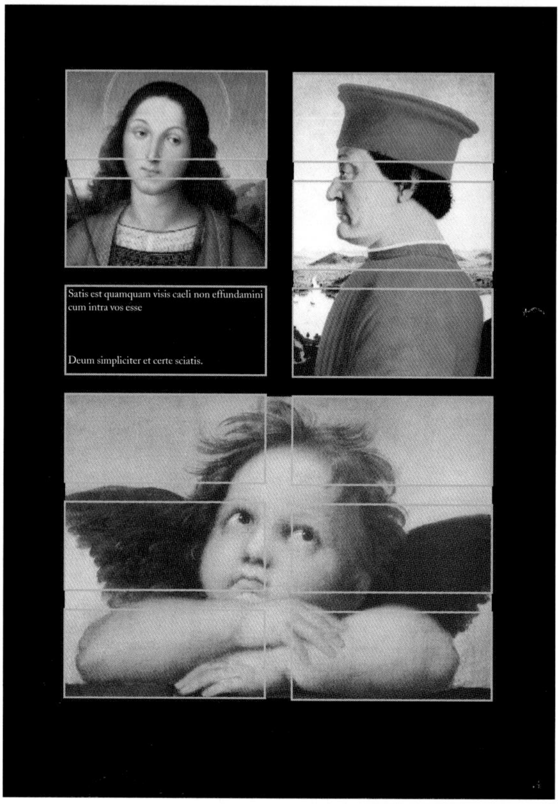
Satis est quamquam visis caeli non effundamini
cum intra vos esse
Deum simpliciter et certe sciatis.

Standard grids

Some grids are so convenient to so many design requirements that they have been given names of their own as a mark that they have received the imprimatur of experience. Thus graphic designers on the international circuit speak of a '20-block grid' or a '40-element' grid and everyone else knows what they mean. When one recognizes the work of a designer on sight, it is usually because of the grid he has made his own for that class of work and refined in many unique ways.

This spread illustrates eight-, 12-, 32- and 40-block portrait-format grids, plus two landscape 12-block grids, each in only one of the many possible arrangements of illustration and text.

Tantum per contemplationem
serenam quantum per frumentum
vives quamvis alii necessitates ambas
detrahant. Laudis quidem est et
signum sapientiae magnae cum sen

Tres Matti aeres
trond mon ami
super!
Salvatio pauperum in caudice est scripta beatique sunt ei qui eum invenerint. Quippe via pauperum viris divitibus et opulentis non cognoscitur nam quomodo enim potuerint eorum aures talia audire qualia nostrae audiverunt sive quando sive ubi. Tantum per
Tji riente delinnear
Per ad astra, omnia\.
Tres Matti
1221697

Mixed column grids on the same page

It is possible, and often done in sophisticated designs, to combine different column grids on the same page. This is normally done for grids on the same size pages, with matching margins and therefore print areas, and only in designs printed on paper where showthrough is not a consideration or where other arrangements can be made to avoid showthrough.

In this book there are three- and four-column page designs in which blocks (and half-blocks in some cases) may on each page be combined to make additional permutations. By placing the column arrangements of two page designs together, further permutations become possible.

There is an alternative way to achieve the flexibility of mixed grids without their complexity. This is to use multiple very narrow columns. The possible combinations offer much of the flexibility of mixed grids without their possible confusion, for instance in the hands of hard-pressed editorial staff on periodicals or daily journals. The larger the page size, the more useful this alternative method becomes, which is why it is popular with those privileged enough to design a broadsheet newspaper from scratch.

In computerized design, guides may be drawn to indicate the additional divisions. For manual paste-up all the possible column widths are often indicated on the printed template, and combined only when there are so many that they become confusing.

If the column width chosen for flexibility is too narrow even for the smallest typeface, it is necessary to specify that it will never be used singly except as white space.

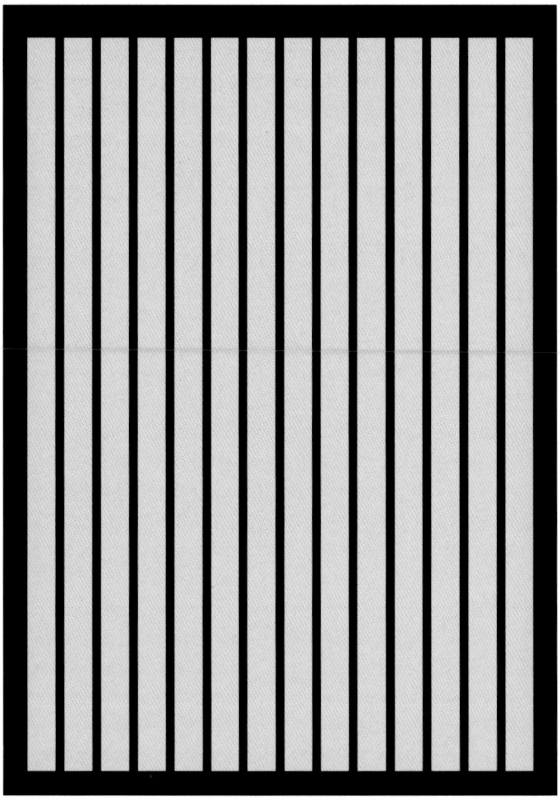

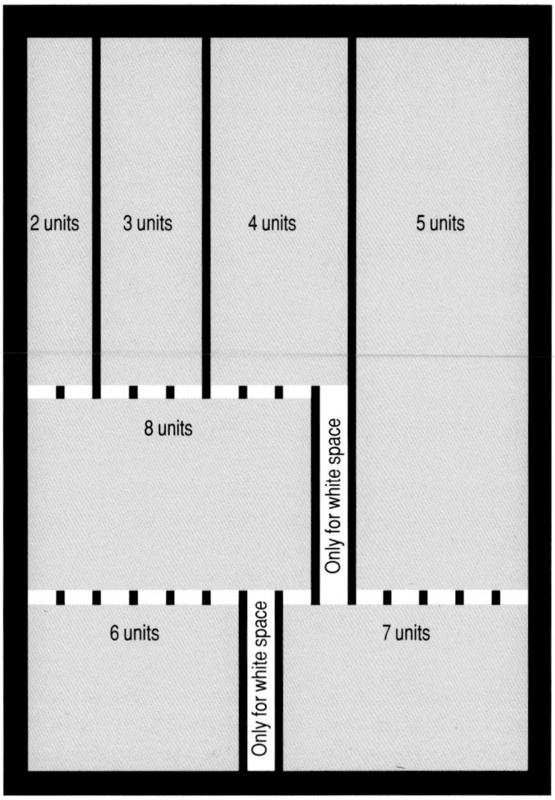

In the example above 14 columns are used to make widths from two units to eight units. A single unit is permitted only for white space.

Text inset

Text may and often does stand in a different relationship to illustrations, mechanical elements and decorations when separated from them by a full line or the full width of a column-divider. Text is today often run on to illustrations or photographs, either overprinted or reversed out. It is also used on tint panels or next to them, and next to rules.

The rule is simple. If the other panel is placed hard on the edge of text, whether beside or under it, the text must be inset from that edge by an absolute minimum of 4pt. It is also useful to have a rule of thumb for separating text from inter-column or horizontal divider rules. The author's personal rule is 4pt but many newspapers use 3pt. In a quality design 3pt or even 4pt can look mean. Six points for either inset or distancing usually guarantees that no reader will be irritated.

The quick brown fox jumped over the lazy dog. The quickjumped over the lazy dog. The quick brown fox jumped the lazy dog. The quick brown fox jumped the lazy. The quick brown fox jumped over the lazy. The quick fox jumped over the lazy dog. The brown fox jumped r the lazy dog. The quick brown jumped the lazy dog. The quick brown fox jumped the lazy dog. The quick brown fox jover the dog. The brown fox jumped over the lazy dog. The quick brown jumpedhe lazy dog. The quick brown fox jumped over lazy . The quick brown fox jumped over the lazy dog. The brown fox jumped over the dog. The quick brown

fox over the lazy dog. The fox jumped over the lazy dog. The fox jumped over the lazy dog. The fox jumped over the lazy dog. The fox jumped over the lazy dog. The fox jumped over the lazy dog. The fox jumped over the lazy dog. The fox jumped over the lazy . The fox jumped over the lazy dog. The fox jumped over the lazy dog. The fox jumped over the lazy dog. The fox jumped over the lazy dog. The fox jumped over the lazy dog. The fox over the lazy dog. The fox jumped over the lazy dog. The fox jumped over the lazy dog. The fox jumped over the lazy dog. The fox jumped over the lazy dog. The fox jumped over

the lazy dog. The fox jumped over the lazy dog. The fox jumped over the lazy dog. The fox jumped the lazy dog. The fox jumped over the lazy dog. The fox jumped over the lazy dog. The fox jumped over the lazy dog. The fox jumped over the lazy dog. The fox jumped over the lazy . The fox jumped over the lazy dog. The fox jumped over the lazy dog. The fox jumped over the lazy dog. The fox jumped over the lazy dog. The jumped over the lazy dog. The fox jumped over the lazy dog. The fox jumped over the lazy dog. fox jumped over the lazy dog. The fox

jumped over the lazy dog. The fox jumped over the lazy dog. jumped over the lazy dog. The fox jumped over the lazy dog. The fox jumped over the lazy dog. The foxover the lazy dog. The fox jumped over the lazy dog. The fox jumped over the lazy dog. The fox jumped over the lazy . The fox jumped over the lazy dog. The fox jumped over the lazy dog. The fox jumped over the lazy dog. The fox jumped over the lazy dog. The fox jumped over the lazy dog. The fox jumped over the lazy dog. The fox jumped over the lazy dog.

1. Text widely separated from an illustration uses the full width of the column. Text hard up against an illustration or tint panel must have an inset, and so must text printed on an illustration or on the panel if the edges would otherwise coincide. Here an 8pt inset is used for an obvious demonstration but in the rest of the book 4pt is used.

2. If the inset makes the narrowest column too narrow, you must reconsider the placement of the illustrations or tint panels, the typeface used or the column width.

3. The vertical rule is 3pt from the right-hand blocks of text. If the inter-column spacing is not wide enough to leave enough space between rule and text, it must be made wider. The horizontal rules are 3pt, 4pt and 6pt below the text. See the page opposite for proper use of horizontal rules. Throughout this book, in which rules and frames are used for demonstration (rather than decoration or separation), rules and frames are 0.75pt wide to ensure instant visibility.

Text runaround to illustrations

In traditional hot-metal setting and photosetting the amount of labor involved in running text around even a rectangular illustration was enormous. As a result, the technique was used only infrequently.

In computer setting, making a text runaround for an irregularly shaped illustration is as easy as dragging it on to the page and into position. Once you have learned to fill in the dialog boxes and layer the text and illustration boxes for trouble-free runarounds (which takes at most half a day with the page make-up software's manuals), it becomes a trivial exercise.

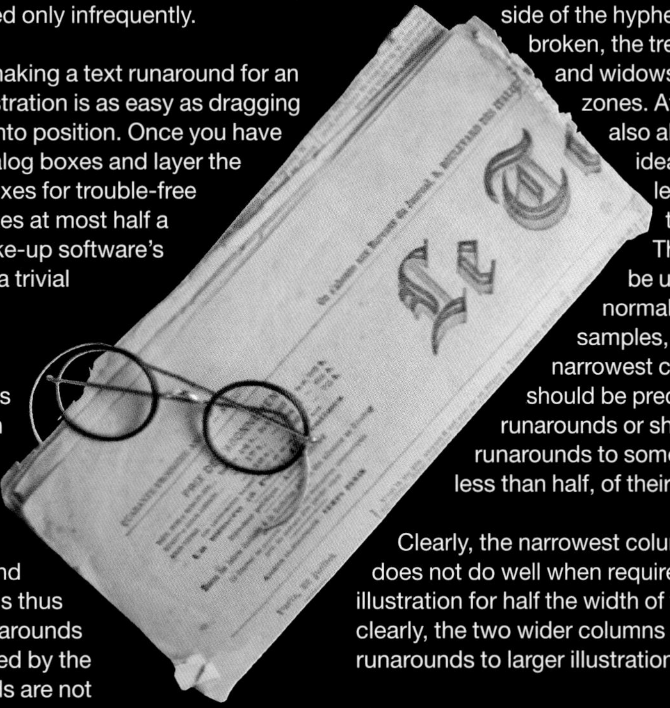

Sooner or later the question of runarounds arises for every design using an adapted standard grid, which describes all kinds of periodicals and many catalogs, brochures and other print designs. It is thus wise to check that runarounds can be accommodated by the grid, even if runarounds are not initially intended.

This is especially important in grids which will be used by others. A common example is the leading designer who delivers templates of the design to be executed by, for instance, magazine staff; or the head of a design team whose design will be used by make-up artists under conditions of such time pressure that supervision is, with the best intention in the world, often cursory.
As always, you should start with the narrowest column and determine what size of illustration may be offered to it for a runaround. A rule of thumb would be useful, but there seems to be no received wisdom on this point. One guide is to permit runarounds in columns wide enough to accommodate illustrations up to half the column width without adverse effects. After that it is a matter of judgment. In many designs such a rule in turn creates a rule in the stylebook that text in the narrowest column or columns should never be required to make runarounds.

It is useful to consider this requirement at the same time as making decisions about hyphenation and the consequent minimum number of characters either side of the hyphen in words to be broken, the treatment of orphans and widows, and also of rag zones. At this stage you will also already have a good idea of the minimum line-length the smallest typeface will bear. This information can be used to determine, normally by printing samples, whether the narrowest column or columns should be precluded from runarounds or should permit runarounds to some part, obviously less than half, of their width.

Clearly, the narrowest column on this page does not do well when required to run around an illustration for half the width of the column. Equally clearly, the two wider columns are comfortable with runarounds to larger illustrations.

This runaround text would be improved by justified setting and/or hyphenation (as shown in the example below). Where manual hyphenation is not possible or desirable, you must limit runarounds to justified, hyphenated columns, or to ragged-right columns wide enough not to require manual adjustment.

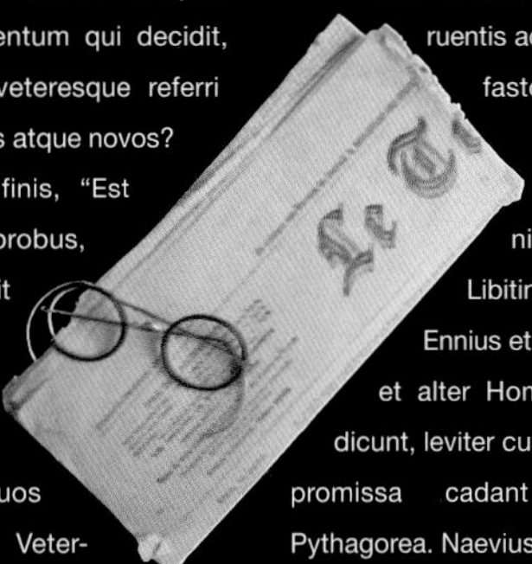

Si meliora dies, ut vina, poemata reddit, scire velim, chartis pretium quotus arroget annus. scriptor abhinc annos centum qui decidit, inter perfectos veteresque referri debet an inter vilis atque novos? Excludat iurgia finis, "Est vetus atque probus, centum qui perficit annos." Quid, qui deperiit minor uno mense vel anno, inter quos referendus erit? Veter-esne poetas, an quos et pra-esens et postera respuat aetas? "Iste quidem veteres inter ponetur honeste, qui vel mense brevi vel toto est iunior anno." Utor permisso, caudaeque pilos ut equinae paulatim vello unum, demo etiam unum, dum cadat elusus ratione ruentis acervi, qui redit in fastos et virtutem aestimat annis miraturque nihil nisi quod Libitina sacravit. Ennius et sapines et fortis et alter Homerus, ut critici dicunt, leviter curare videtur, quo promissa cadant et somnia Pythagorea. Naevius in manibus non est et mentibus haeret paene recens? Adeo sanctum est vetus finis omne poema. ambigitur quo-tiens, uter utro sit prior, aufert Pacuvius docti famam senis Accius alti, dicitur

74 Different depth blocks on one grid

Even if by the nature of the profession grids are required to be multi-functional devices, instances do arise where the format of the finished design, the proportions of the illustrations, or even an especially suitable typeface, require a unique design.

Furthermore, the rare, intrinsically once-off design almost always requires a new grid to accommodate the special needs of its illustrations and text. In these cases the grid needs to be flexible only internally, rather than externally over a number of related jobs.

It can therefore be specified and fine-tuned very precisely, with blocks of different depths to suit the material – as distinct from combinations of blocks of the 'standard' depth on, for instance, the 'corporate' grid, as in all the examples before this. Note, though, that all blocks of whatever depth must still be integer-multiples of the minimum line-space.

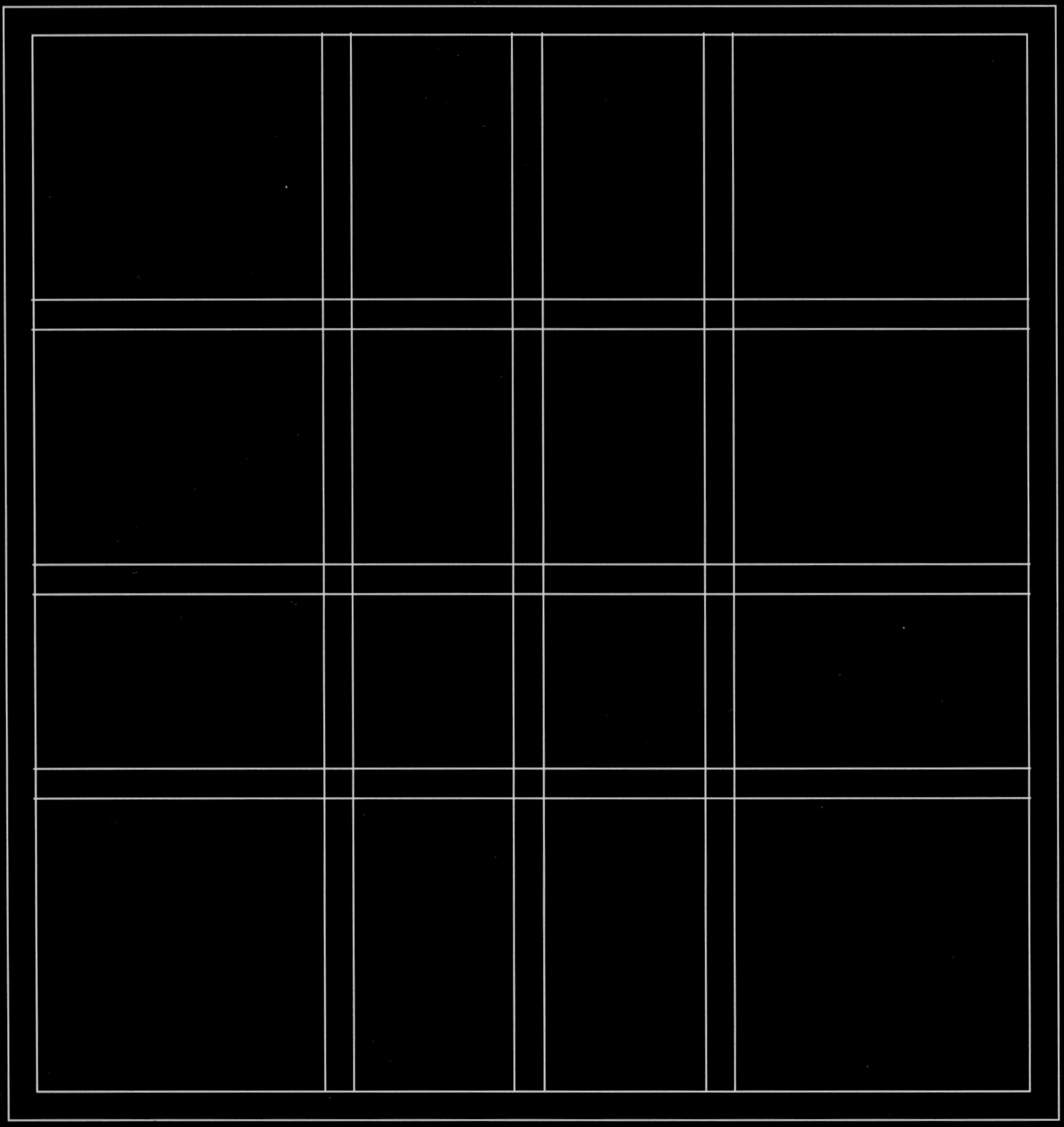

Design bands

In general practice a grid must in most instances serve many times for multiple purposes inside one publication or across publications. It is therefore often convenient for maximum flexibility to specify the grid with many rectangular blocks of small but equal depth which can be combined as required for larger illustrations and text blocks.

The blocks may also be combined into horizontal and vertical design bands, in which you reserve a group of blocks for text and another group of blocks for illustration. There may be one such specification for the entire publication or several designs allocated to specific pages. If the latter, a band of grouped blocks may on some pages, say article introductions in a magazine layout or part titles in a book, be allocated solely to white space, and another band to headlines and straplines (explanatory display under a headline). A pull-quote (text from the body copy repeated in display type) may also have a fixed position on each page.

When cropping is forbidden

Occasions arise when illustrations may not be cropped. This is not an uncommon requirement in some kinds of catalog work, but it is desirable to discover the restriction before design commences. Usually the illustrations are not the same format, some being landscape, some portrait. Even if they are of the same format, they may not be similarly proportioned, thus defeating attempts at scaling them to fit.

For the sake of demonstration, let us say a magazine page is returned by the client with the instruction that the grid, design and the layout must not be changed but all illustrations must be shown uncropped because the magazine page layout is now to be used in a catalog.

Above, the photographs were cropped for effect in the magazine.

On the right is the same page when the designer may not crop the photographs. The tint panels relate those photographs which do not fit to the grid. This is a standard method, often seen in catalogs where for legal and administrative reasons the client connections between illustrative items by aligning a group of them to the grid with a single tint block, as on the next spread.

The photographs have been left in the same position as before but obviously the illustrations could benefit from regrouping without disturbing the original framework.

The ideal, however, would be to redesign the page in order at least to group like formats with like, above and top right, while retaining the spirit of the original.

Another solution, if design change is not restricted, is shown on the right.

Perception and scale

In most cases, graphic designers automatically allocate illustrations to positions on the grid and scale them, usually very roughly, according to their relative sizes in human perspective, counting on the perspective and psycho-visual conditioning of the viewer's culture to connect (the jargon is 'make the closure') widely different scales to real sizes. It is the exceptions that cause difficulties.

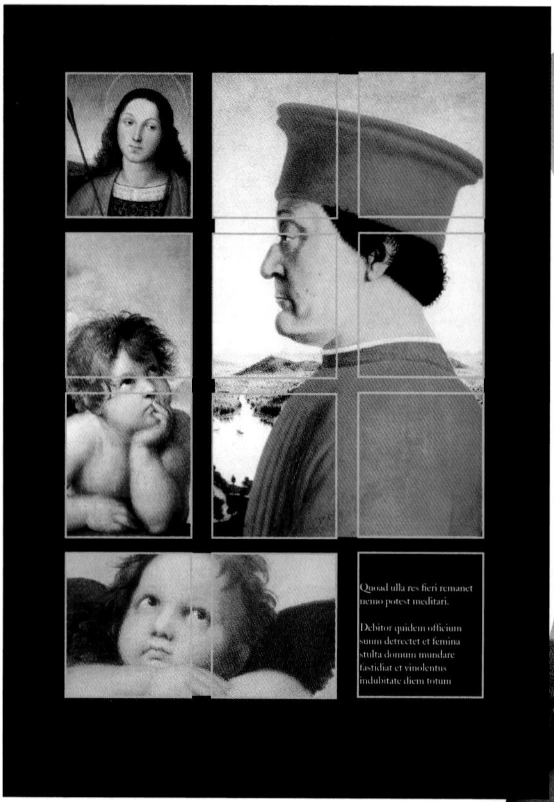

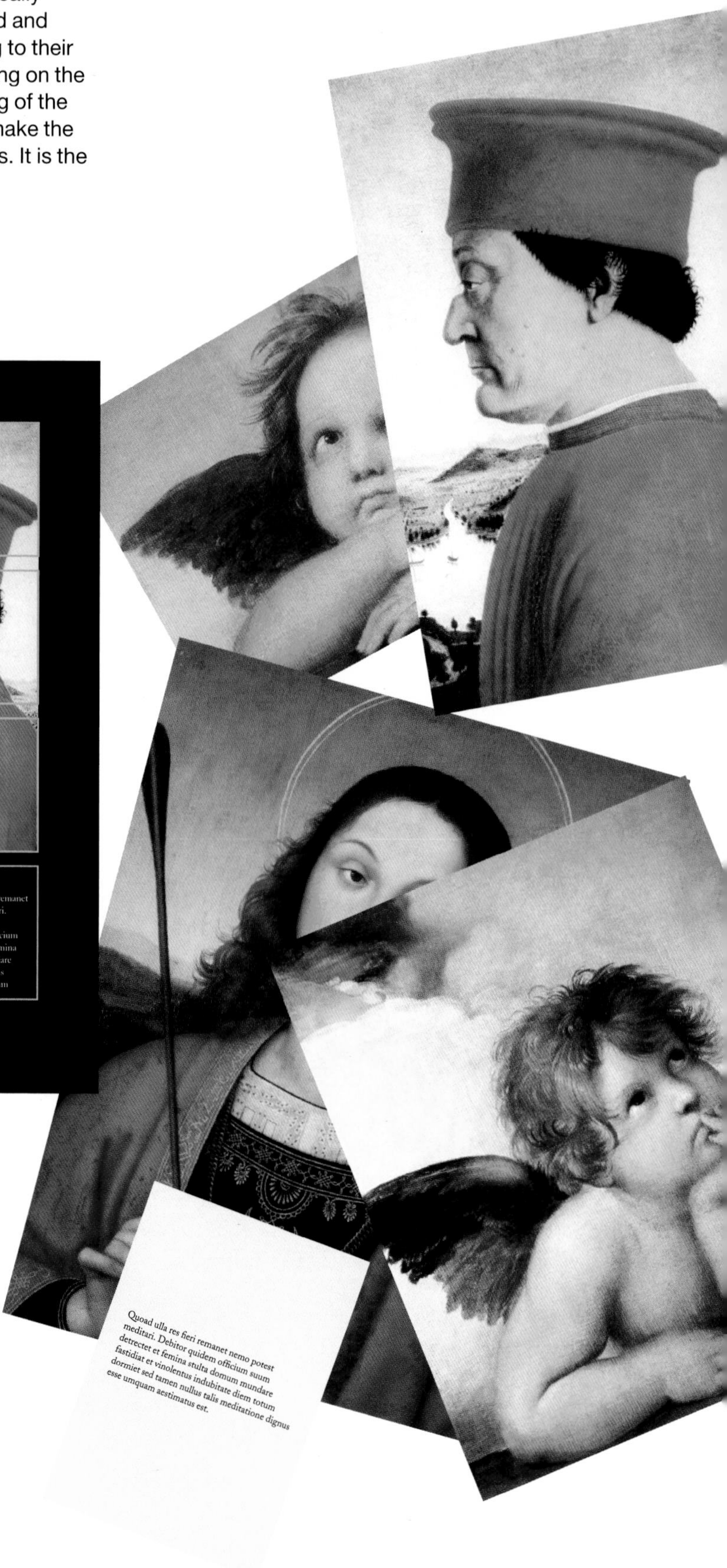
Quoad ulla res fieri remanet nemo potest meditari. Debitor quidem officium suum detrectet et femina stulta domum mundare fastidiat et vinolentus indubitate diem totum dormiet sed tamen nullus talis meditatione dignus esse umquam aestimatus est.

When scaling is not permitted

It is common, especially in reproducing works of art in print, not to crop the pictures. Often an additional or self-standing condition is that illustrations must be scaled according to their original relative proportions to each other. The first solution is often to sort the illustrations into groups by original size. But even so the problem will arise on almost every spread that when one illustration is scaled to fit the grid one or more of the others will not coincide with the grid. The second solution is to use panels to relate odd-sized illustrations to the grid and to each other.

Once more, for the sake of demonstration, let us say that a finished design has been returned by the client with a request that all illustrations on a page be related to each other in their original proportions.

This time the grid must not be changed to accommodate the new requirement because, say, all the other pages in the book use it and have already been separated to film.

A centerline to the grid was drawn and used as one alignment edge. The most awkward illustration (the putti top left in the page below) was scaled between the centerline and within 3mm/0.125in of the margin to allow space for shift in the trimmer. All other illustrations were scaled precisely the same amount.

To keep the illustrations as large as possible, an additional line was then added at top and bottom to contain a panel to tie the illustrations together. Other examples of relating odd-sized illustrations to the grid with tint panels are shown throughout this book.

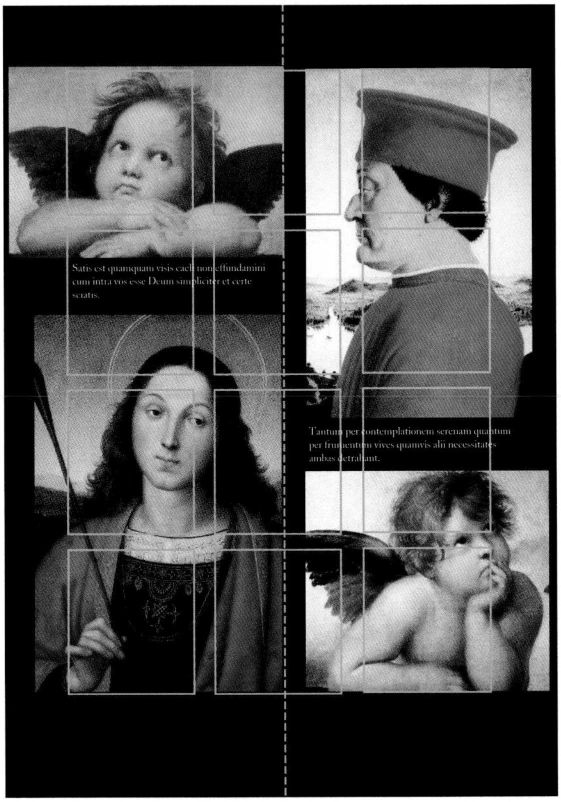

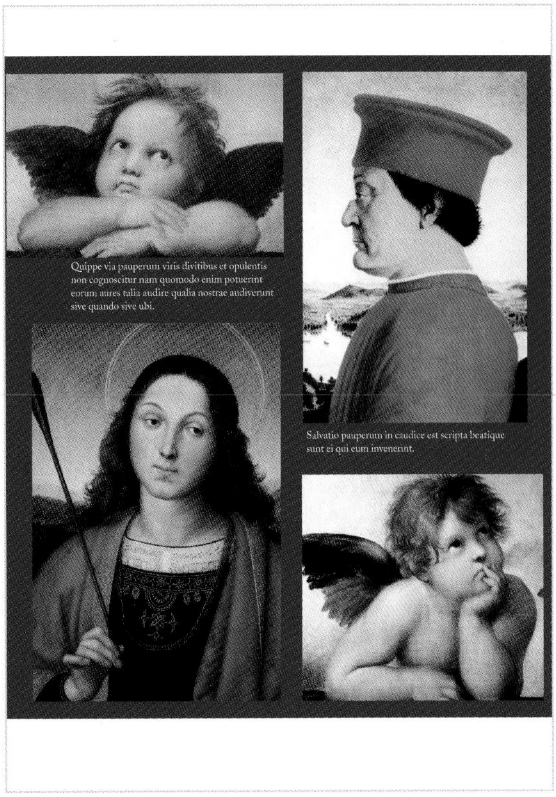

A design made on the assumption that cropping is permitted and scaling is free, far left.

Left, the relative sizes of the illustrations, printed to 'true scale' from the slides.

Above, no cropping, all photos scaled the same amount. 'No cropping' also means 'no bleeding', because at least 3mm/0.125in would be trimmed off as a result.

departure
theyre back

Grid, template and stylebook

With magazines, newspapers, books and sets of promotional material, repeatability from page to page is usually a desirable and often an essential requirement in terms of 'corporate identity'. If, in this case, the grid were redrawn for each page, errors would inevitably creep in. In addition to repeatability, speed is essential and redrawing the grid for each page can easily multiply the time required to produce layouts.

Because of the high cost of design and print production there are, furthermore, financial reasons for standardizing the grid, once designed and agreed, into a production-aid and production-control tool. In traditional design, layout and make-up, these consist of grids printed onto card and transparent overlays, plus associated stylesheets which define text and illustration usage permitted within a particular grid.

With computerized design, these tangible design aids are supplemented, and often replaced by, on-screen templates, automated style-sheets, and libraries of elements. The grid printed onto card may still be preferred by some designers and by others outside the design department, while the printed transparent overlay is still required inside the design department for checking printed proofs. A stylebook must still be printed out for use as the 'design bible' by the entire design, editorial and reprographic chain. The computer is thus merely an additional tool, albeit of great speed and convenience. It changes no elementary principle of design or the application of the grid, and fully displaces only one of the three traditional manifestations of the grid – the printed card.

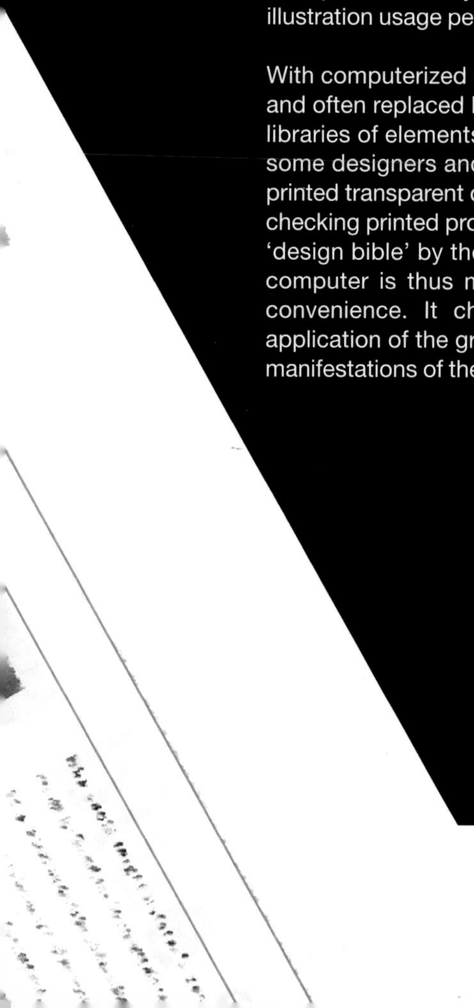

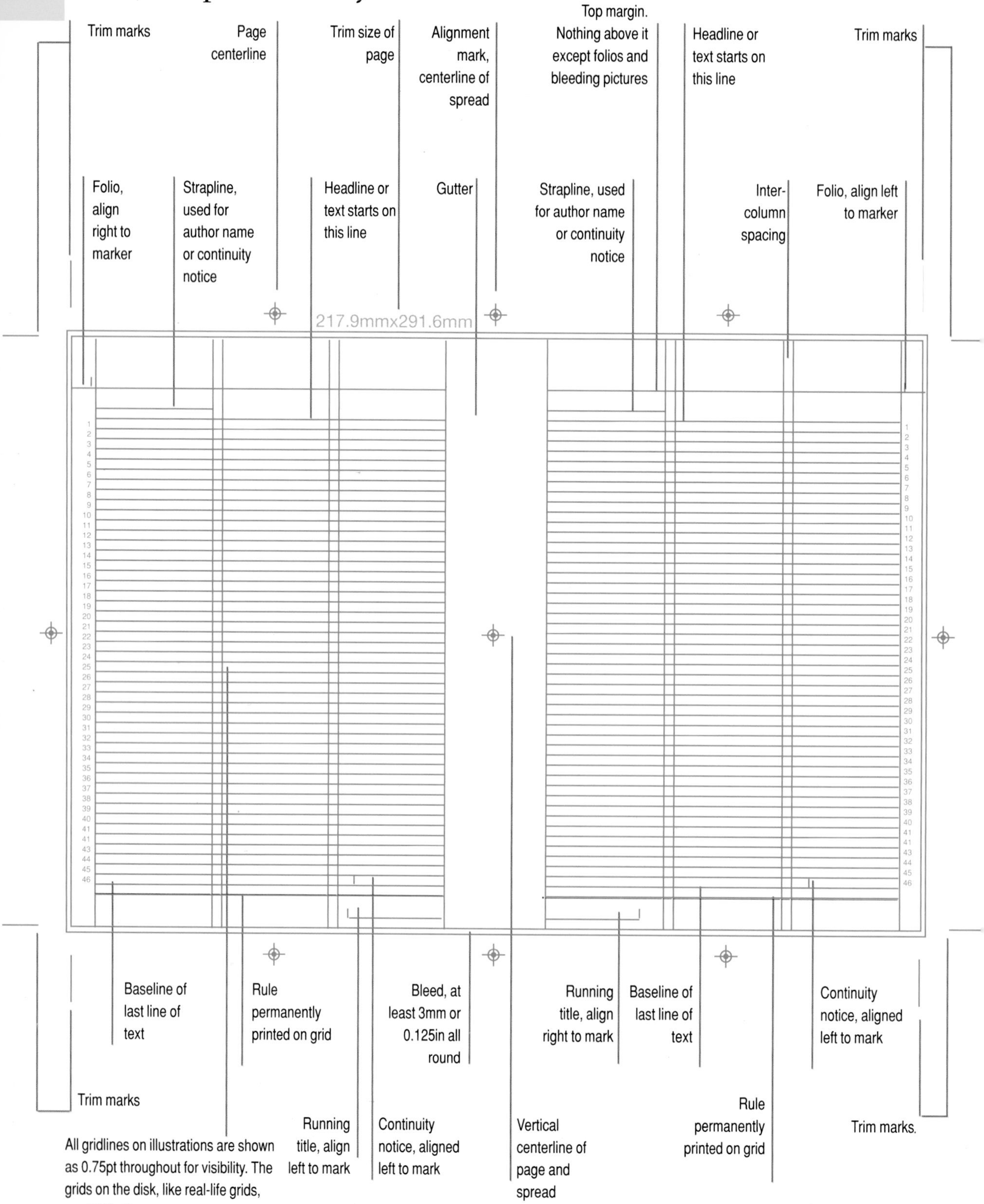

All gridlines on illustrations are shown as 0.75pt throughout for visibility. The grids on the disk, like real-life grids, use 0.25pt lines.

The printed grid

The grid is precisely drawn to size with technical pens and photographed. It is then printed on stiff card in a light blue ink that will not be picked up by the process camera. There may be several cards for a single publication, containing specific layouts for pages with different functions, or all the various column widths may be combined on a single card if the result is not likely to lead to confusion.

In the studio the printed card is primarily used to speed the precise paste-up of approved layouts. Where an acetate template (overleaf) is not available, it may also be used with translucent drafting sheets in planning layouts. In addition it may be used, inconveniently, for checking proofs.

Elsewhere it is used by editorial staff for copyfitting; and by typesetters and blockmakers to take measurements from and ensure accurate placement.

The printed card needs to contain a minimum of information to be at all useful. Beyond that, complicated grids require more information, and in larger organizations (and for design consultants) there are considerations of who precisely will use the grid and at what distance from its originator.

This spread shown is a classically simple, subtly asymmetric three-column grid. It is much favored by hobbyist magazines, whose readers object if the presentation comes between them and the information, and has applications in text-heavy professional journals as well.

While containing all the necessary information, it leaves the designer making up the page on the day much scope to be inventive. That is a most satisfactory state of affairs in a small office or studio where the designer of the grid will do the layout or closely supervise the work. But in larger organizations, where communication and supervision may not be close, it will require either further marks or a strong stylebook to delimit space for matters like pull-quotes and many other elements.

Two possible applications of a grid: an academic journal and a general magazine, showing for each the opening page of an article.

The acetate overlay

While the days of the grid printed on cardboard for manual paste-up must inevitably be limited, the grid printed on acetate film or other transparent material is too useful for too many functions to disappear. It is used for checking layouts pasted-up on card and for checking proofs, whether produced traditionally or by computer, when they return from the printer. It is turned mirror-image in hot-metal print shops for checking that hot-metal set type and blocks are correctly inserted in the forme. It can perform every other graphic design, editorial and reprographic function of the printed card which the computer does not cover. There are some functions that the acetate overlay performs more quickly and conveniently than a computer, for instance in scaling photographs to size without the need first to scan the photograph.

Proofs of the layouts on the previous page have been returned and the relevant acetate overlay is placed on them to check that everything is in place. The acetate overlay is used with both traditional and computerized design to avoid the chore of laboriously measuring each element with a ruler. The acetate overlay permits errors to be seen instantly.

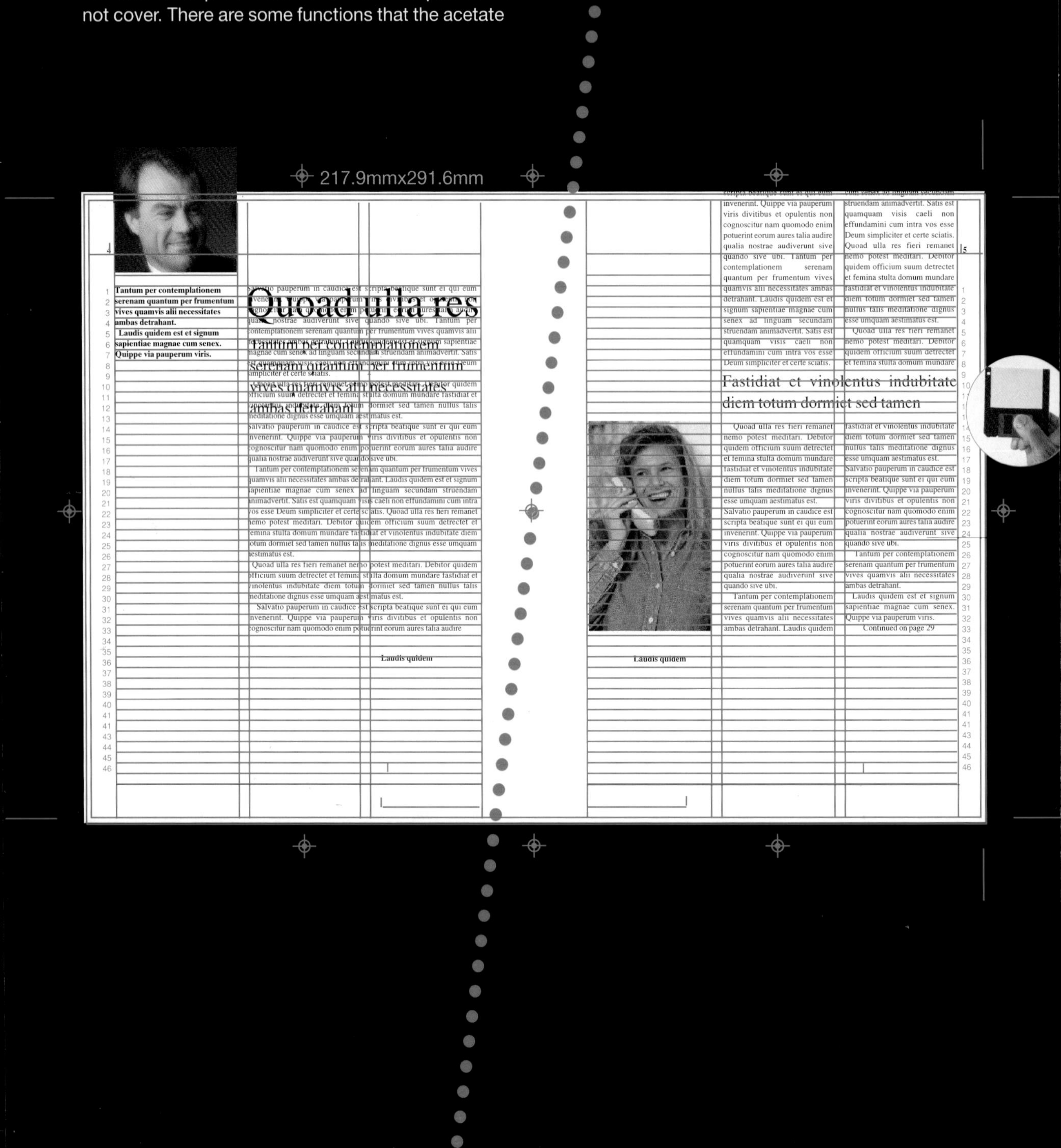

Cropping and scaling illustrations

The grid makes scaling semi-automatic. First decide whether the essential information in the illustration is contained in the width or the height of the crop. The scale to percentage is the width of the column divided by the width of the crop multiplied by 100. Or it is the height of the crop divided by the height of the picture permitted (as a multiple of minimum line-spaces) multiplied by 100. The two above are scaled to 65 per cent and 50 per cent respectively.

Acetate overlays for special purposes

For large and complicated publications, it is common to make separate printed grids for different page layouts or combinations of page layouts. The number is determined in part by the limit of confusion and in part by organizational considerations of who will work on which grids.

In addition it is often convenient for the design department to have special versions printed on acetate, for instance for scaling. There may also be a need, or even a demand, for special – usually simplified – versions to be used in other departments, such as editorial and advertising.

It is rare, but not unknown, for additional versions to be made for the craftsmen further down the reprographic chain to highlight their special interests in the production of the design.

In practice the provision of extra grids is an administrative decision, but you should be aware from the outset that the necessity may arise and at the budgeting stage of the job allocate time and resources to discovering the need and creating the extra grids.

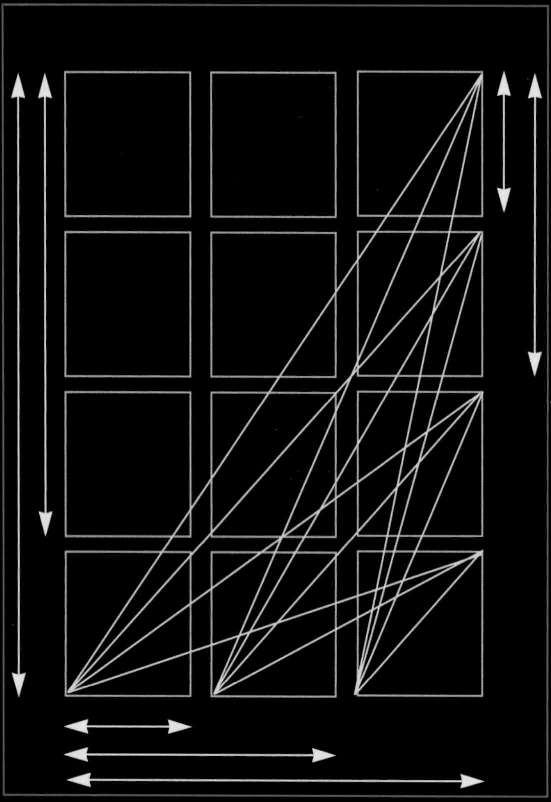

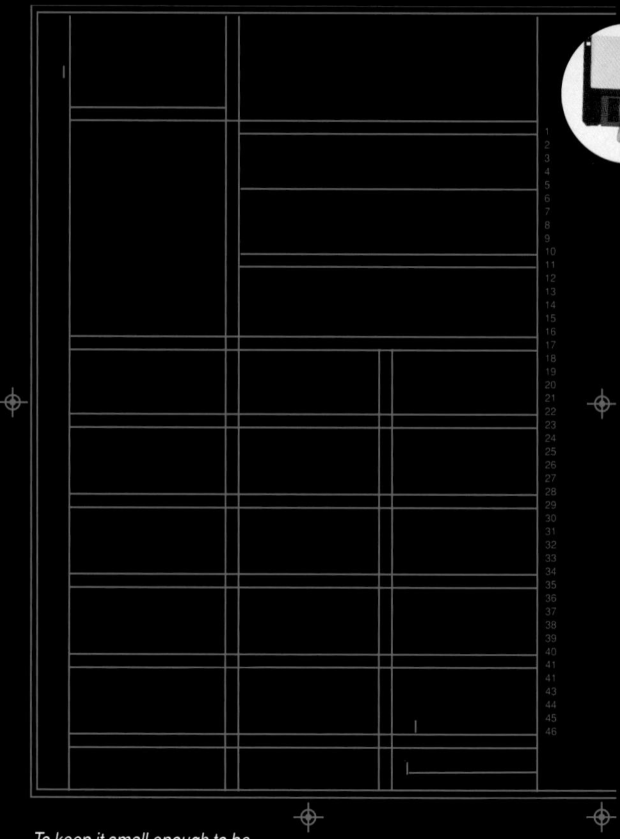

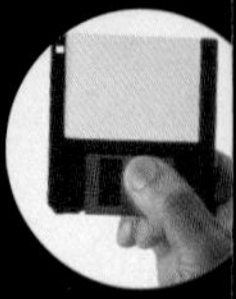

Above, a scaling and cropping acetate overlay for a 12-element grid.

On the right, a single acetate overlay for an academic journal in which text is always set across the full width of the two inside columns.

Fixed spaces are indicated for headline and strapline plus author photograph. The first and last running text baselines are also indicated for full-text continuation pages.

In the lower half, illustrations must be placed on the lowest text baseline or stacked on the grid blocks above. Illustrations may be one, two or three columns wide and any height, but cut-out from the text is not permitted. Nor is any illustration except the author's photograph permitted above the lowest five blocks.

To keep it small enough to be convenient, the overlay covers one page only. It is flipped over to use on right-hand pages.

Acetate overlays for computerized layout

Acetate overlays for a fully-computerized publication can almost always be drastically simplified in the knowledge that illustrations will snap to the corners of blocks and that text will be automatically locked to the baseline grid by the style-sheets. Thus it is not necessary in an acetate overlay used only for checking computer-set layouts to show all the line-spaces in the print area of the page.

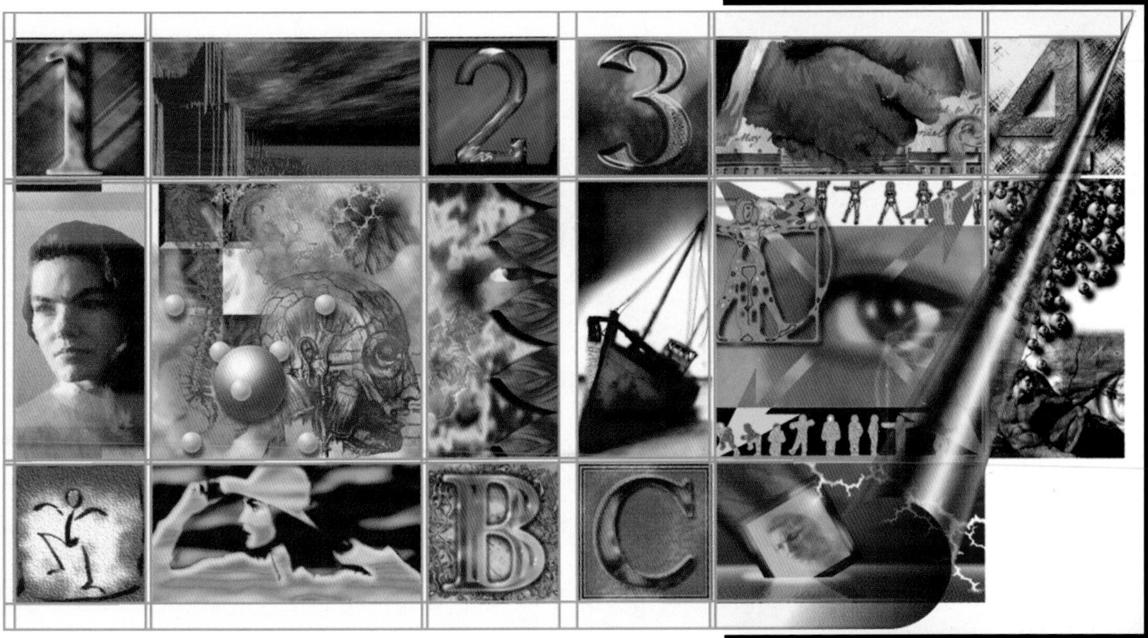

The stylebook

The master control instrument of any document is the stylebook. In large organizations and for complicated publications it is always made as an administrative necessity. In smaller organizations or where the designer has just a few assistants, it may exist only on the designer's computer – and not even wholly there, being partly stored in the minds of the designer and design assistants.

In manual make-up the stylebook is necessary to make information visible that cannot be put on printed grids on paper or film. In computerized design the master template on your hard disk may contain much more information through the attached style-sheets, but the stylebook is still necessary to distribute this information in usable form. Certain aspects of the grid can be described only in the stylebook.

The stylebook should be a semi-permanent construction, durable yet flexible when changes have to be made. You could use books with transparent pockets, into which the stylebook sheets and acetate overlays are slid.

Page size Margins Print area Line-space Columns Grid on card and film	Type specification and permitted use	Illustration specification and permitted use
+	+	+
Page size Margins Print area Line-space Columns Template Grid on film	Text style-sheets and permitted use	Illustration preferences and permitted use

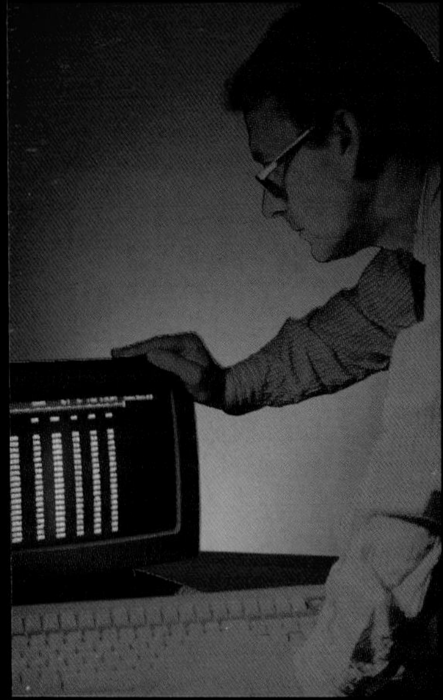

Overlays and stylebook

STYLEBOOK II

Decorative
pecification
Color
pecification
Line
pecification

Decorative
pecification
Colors
styles &
monitor
set-up
Line
pecification

Grid + style-sheets = stylebook = template

A style-sheet is a document which describes or demonstrates permitted, pre-defined styles of text or illustration or other graphic elements which may be placed on its associated grid. The style-sheet can be printed or computerized. In computers style-sheet or styles takes the same meaning of available pre-defined styles; the only difference is that you see their application instantly instead of when the proofs return from the typesetter.

A printed grid or acetate overlay is a partial template of the grid, with the information in the stylebook providing the rest of the parameters.

In computerized design, the master grid the layout follows is explicitly called 'the template' when it is so arranged that it opens with it all the possible text style-sheets, plus in some programs a library of graphic elements, and possibly also a set of style-sheets of decorative elements like rules which can be consistently applied throughout a document just like text.

Stylebooks for either manual or computerized make-up include the same information.

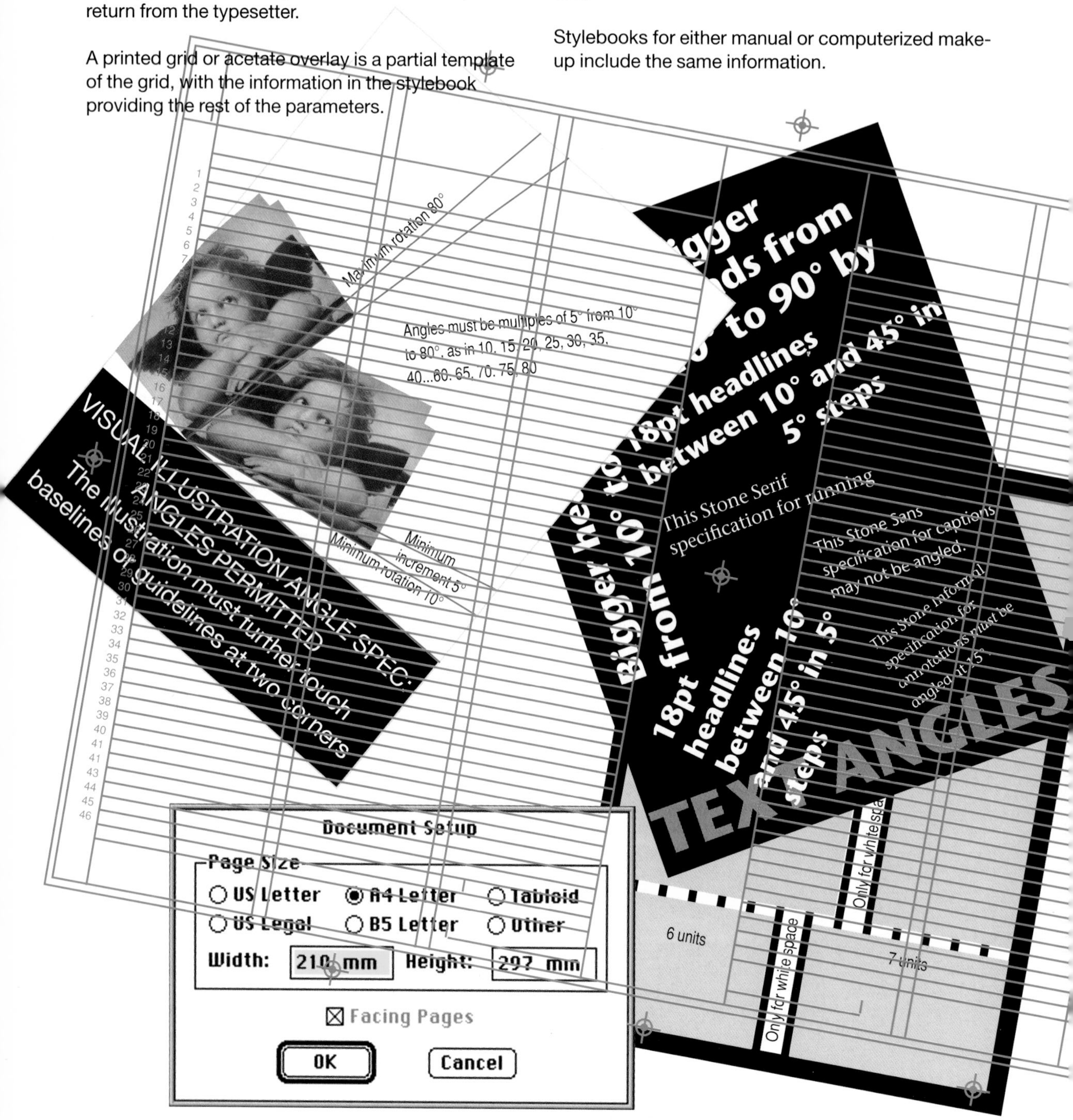

Paper, page, margins, print area, columns, divider

This is the minimum amount of information the stylebook must contain about the paper and the page:

- type of paper (sized? glossy? thick? thin? – best of all, print the stylebook on the paper to be used in the publication)
- number of pages imposed on every printing sheet (necessary for scheduling work in the studio)
- trimmed size of page
- bleed distance
- top margin
- outside margin
- bottom margin
- inside margin
- whether margins are handed or asymmetrical
- width of column divider
- number and width of columns and, if they are not of equal width, their order
- permitted combinations of columns.

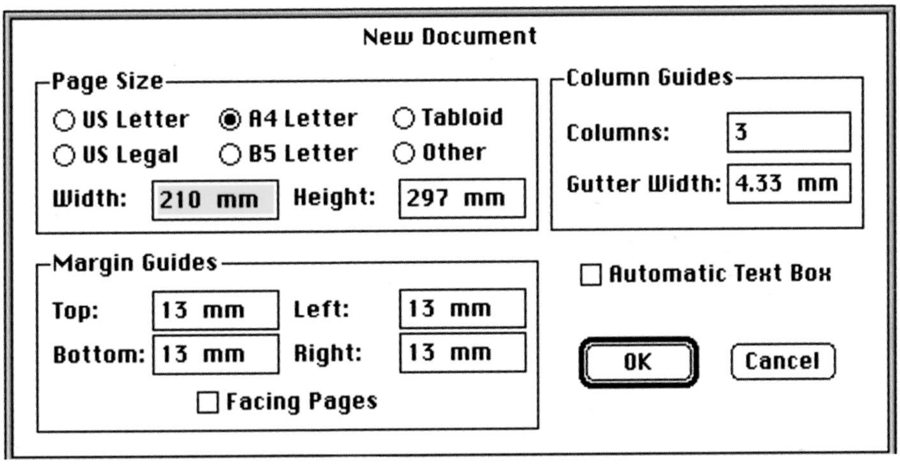

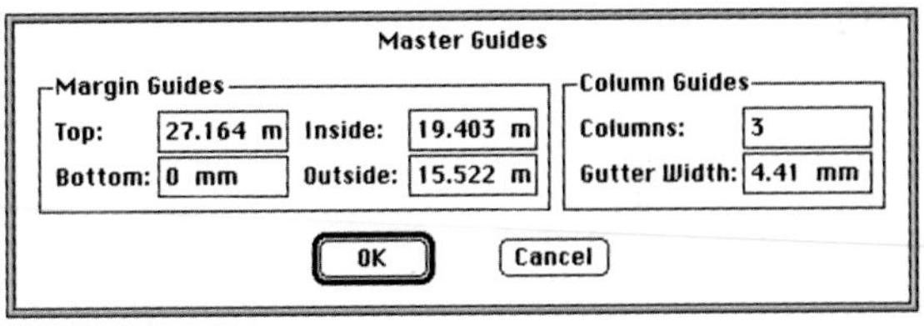

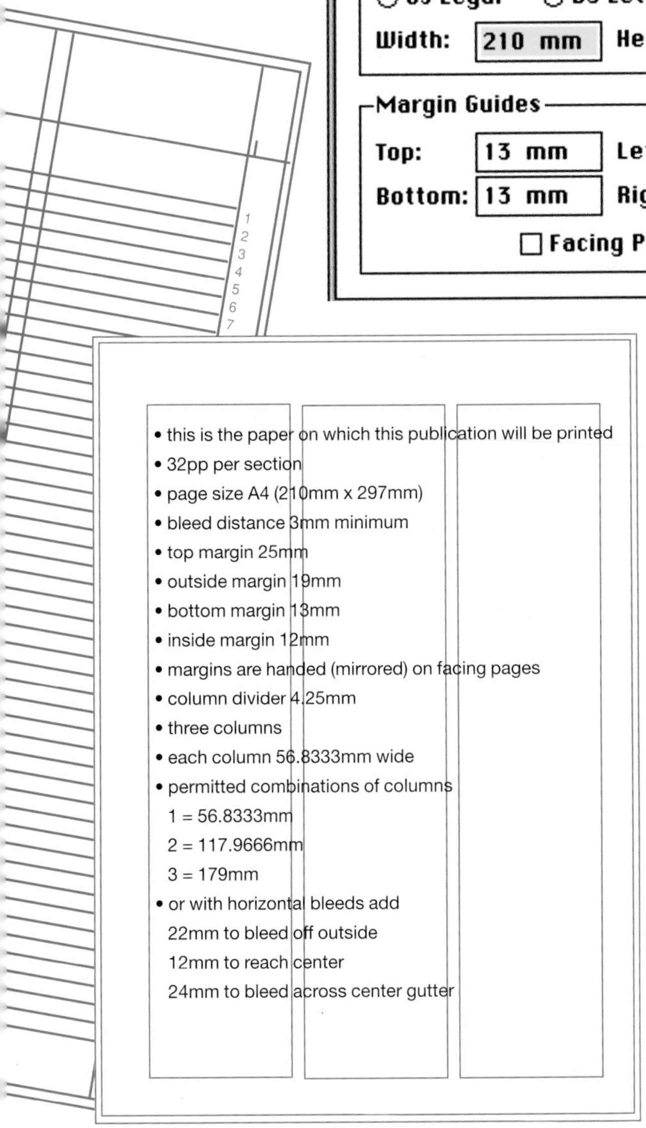

1
2
3
4
5
6
7
• this is the paper on which this publication will be printed
• 32pp per section
• page size A4 (210mm x 297mm)
• bleed distance 3mm minimum
• top margin 25mm
• outside margin 19mm
• bottom margin 13mm
• inside margin 12mm
• margins are handed (mirrored) on facing pages
• column divider 4.25mm
• three columns
• each column 56.8333mm wide
• permitted combinations of columns
1 = 56.8333mm
2 = 117.9666mm
3 = 179mm
• or with horizontal bleeds add
22mm to bleed off outside
12mm to reach center
24mm to bleed across center gutter

Text style-sheets

Every permitted text style must be described and preferably illustrated fullsize. It is convenient for editorial staff if the designer numbers each permitted style in a logical, layered manner. Each style specification must contain at least:

- font
- weight
- style for emphasis or proper names
- size
- leading
- justification
- paragraph indentation and/or spacing.

99 Hdlne, Sto

*((((*Above, 99 Headline, Stone Sans Bold & *Itals* 72/72, ranged left or centered. To be hand-kerned.))))

79 Strapline, same as headline 79, for use with 89 or 99, ranged left or centered & *Itals*

89 Hdlne, 32/36pt Stone Sans, ranged left or centered & *Itals*

79 Headline, Stone Sans 20/24pt, ranged left or centered, & *Itals*

69 Extended sidebar,Stone Sans 16/24pt, ranged left or centered, for use with 79 or 89 & *Itals*

59 Pull-quote, Stone Serif 20/24pts, always centered, & *Itals*

45 Crosshead. Stone Serif 10/1… bold. *Italic looks like this.* One li… space above, none below.

49 Crosshead. Stone Serif 10/12 bold. *Italic looks like this.* One line-space above, none below.

…tone Sns Bld &

45 Crosshead

38 Running text. Stone Serif 10/12 plain, justified, hyphenated. No first line indentation on initial paragraphs. No space between paragraphs. *Italic looks like this.*

…e Sns Bld & *Itls*

Apply text spec by number

39 Running text. Stone Serif 10/12 plain, justified, hyphenated. First line indentation 4mm. No space between paragraphs. *Italic looks like this.*

29 Caption. Stone Sans 9/12, ranged left, no first line indent, no hyphenation, line-space between paras. *Italic looks like this.*

45 Crosshead. Stone Serif 10/12 semibold. *Italic looks like this.* One line-space above, none below.

49 Crosshead. Stone Serif 10/12 bold. *Italic looks like this.* One line-space above, none below.

45 Crosshead

38 Running text. Stone Serif 10/12 plain, justified, hyphenated. No first line indentation on initial paragraphs. No space between paragraphs. *Italic looks like this.*

49 Crosshead

38 Running text. Stone Serif 10/12 plain, justified, hyphenated. No first line indentation on initial paragraphs. No space between paragraphs. *Italic looks like this.*

19 Index. Stone Sans 8/12, ranged left.

16 Footnote. Stone Serif 8/12, ranged left, no hyphenation. Line-space between footnotes. 4mm first line indent for follow-on paragraphs.

9 Annotation. Stone Informal 9/12. Flush left, no indent, must be angled 15 per cent – see angling specification.

Style-sheets in computer setting

In computerized setting several additional type specifications can be made, for example:

- baseline shift
- horizontal or vertical scaling
- space above or below certain styles (ie in addition to the leading of the typeface)
- word spacing
- letter spacing.

It may be necessary, because the computer makes variation so easy and puts so much power in perhaps untrained hands, to avoid surprises by delimiting a number of other parameters in text style-sheets, of which common examples include:

- text color eg ‘black only’
- horizontal and vertical scaling eg ‘not permitted’,

or the designer may just note: ‘Only the style-sheets in the window “Style-sheets” may be used. Variation may be authorized only by the Art Director.’

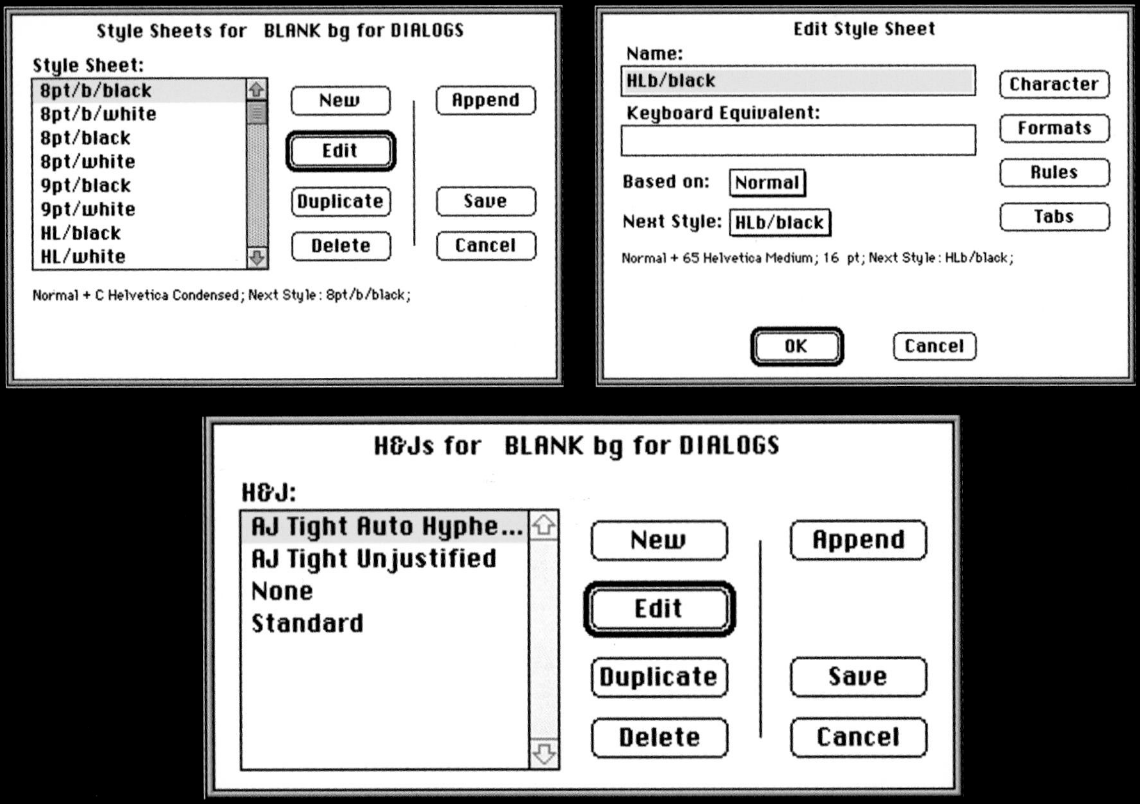

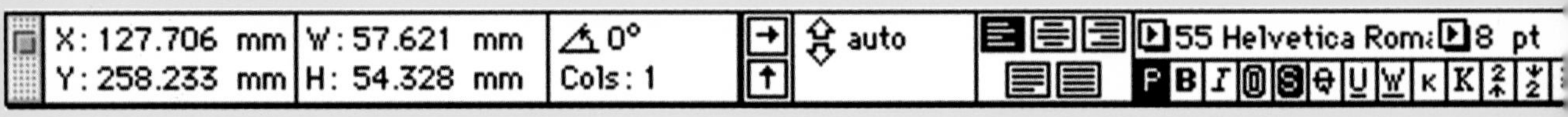

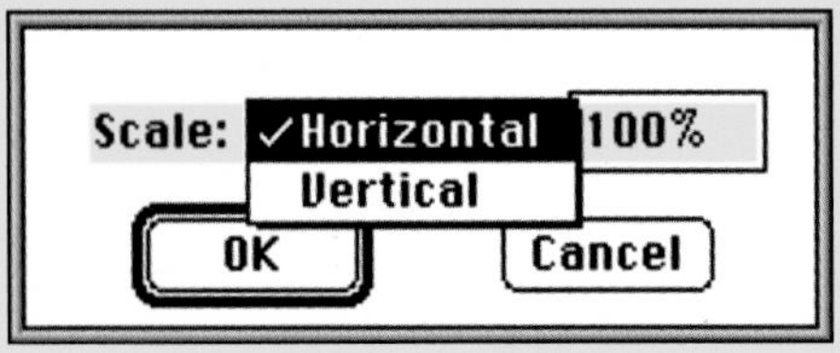

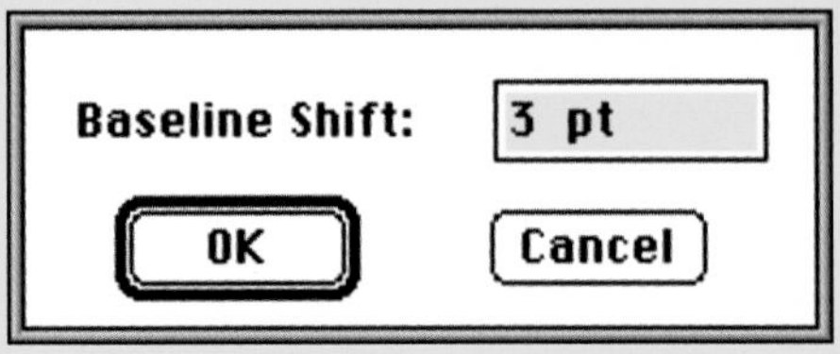

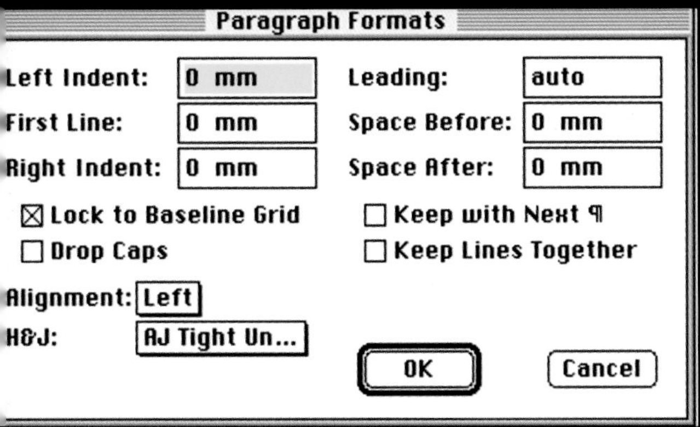
Paragraph Formats
Left Indent: 0 mm
First Line: 0 mm
Right Indent: 0 mm
Leading: auto
Space Before: 0 mm
Space After: 0 mm
☒ Lock to Baseline Grid
☐ Drop Caps
☐ Keep with Next ¶
☐ Keep Lines Together
Alignment: Left
H&J: AJ Tight Un…
OK
Cancel

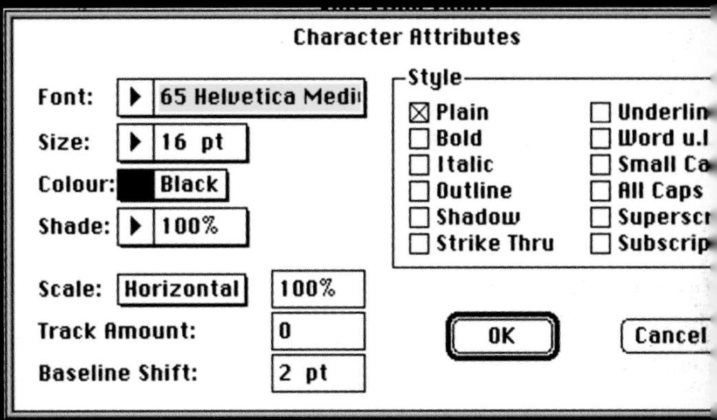
Character Attributes
Font: 65 Helvetica Medi
Size: 16 pt
Colour: Black
Shade: 100%
Scale: Horizontal 100%
Track Amount: 0
Baseline Shift: 2 pt
Style
☒ Plain
☐ Bold
☐ Italic
☐ Outline
☐ Shadow
☐ Strike Thru
☐ Underlin
☐ Word u.l
☐ Small Ca
☐ All Caps
☐ Superscr
☐ Subscrip
OK
Cancel

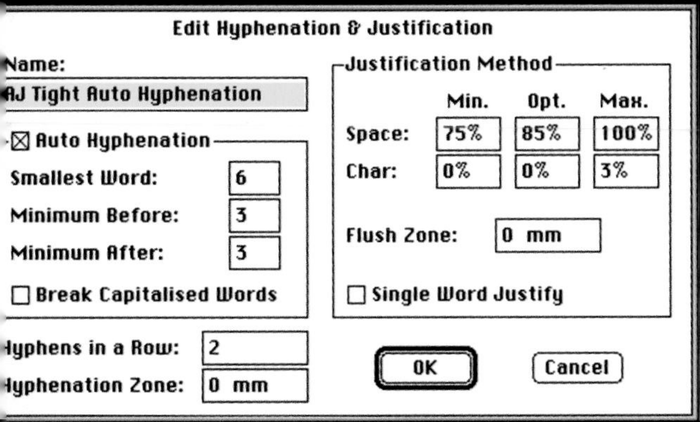
Edit Hyphenation & Justification
Name:
AJ Tight Auto Hyphenation
☒ Auto Hyphenation
Smallest Word: 6
Minimum Before: 3
Minimum After: 3
☐ Break Capitalised Words
Hyphens in a Row: 2
Hyphenation Zone: 0 mm
Justification Method
Min. Opt. Max.
Space: 75% 85% 100%
Char: 0% 0% 3%
Flush Zone: 0 mm
☐ Single Word Justify
OK
Cancel

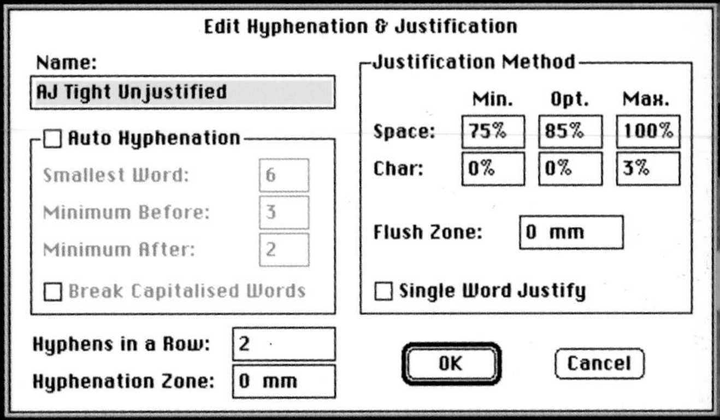
Edit Hyphenation & Justification
Name:
AJ Tight Unjustified
☐ Auto Hyphenation
Smallest Word: 6
Minimum Before: 3
Minimum After: 2
☐ Break Capitalised Words
Hyphens in a Row: 2
Hyphenation Zone: 0 mm
Justification Method
Min. Opt. Max.
Space: 75% 85% 100%
Char: 0% 0% 3%
Flush Zone: 0 mm
☐ Single Word Justify
OK
Cancel

Paragraph Rules
☐ Rule Above
☐ Rule Below
OK
Cancel

__See also__ style-sheets specials and bleeds for additional permitted widths

On the column grid, photographs may be any of these widths and any of the arrow heights

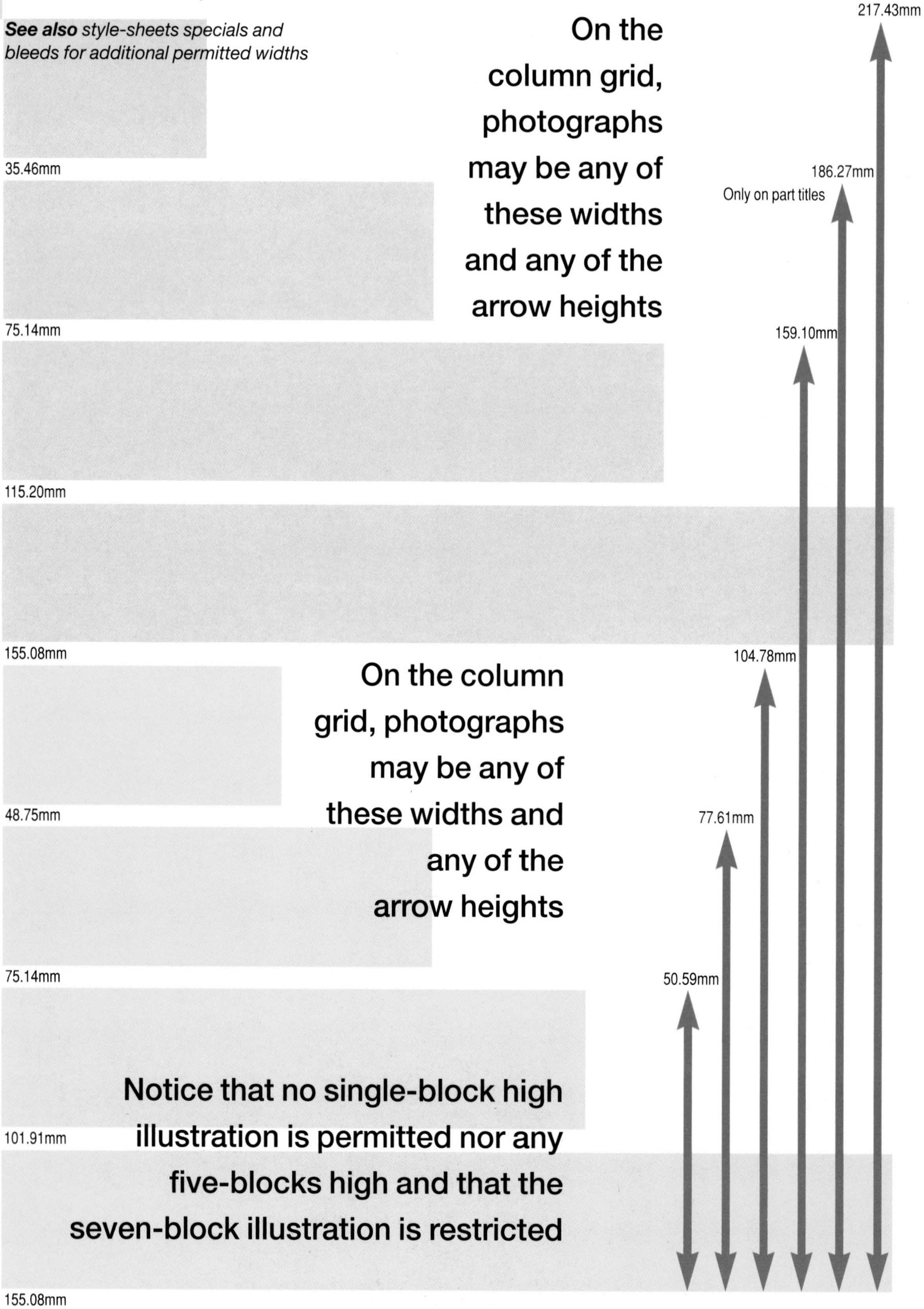

On the column grid, photographs may be any of these widths and any of the arrow heights

Notice that no single-block high illustration is permitted nor any five-blocks high and that the seven-block illustration is restricted

Rules, miscellaneous graphic elements and decorations

The designer decides how detailed the stylebook should be. A balance must be struck between creating an effective control instrument and creating a strait-jacket which will restrain creativity within the grid. The stylebook can never be exhaustive; there will always remain decisions the designer must make on the day.

But certainly rules, if at all widely used, should be shown in all the widths and colors permitted.

Miscellaneous graphic elements, such as color blocks with text reverses, color bars, thumb-index blocks, and general non-text running items usually need to be delimited in the stylebook as to color, size and placement, in order to avoid divergent inclusions.

Color specification

It often amazes those whose experience does not include large periodicals how many people make decisions which in other design environments are seen as solely the province of the designer. Stylebooks for corporate communications and advertising routinely describe which colors may be used in which positions. So do stylebooks for the best magazines and newspapers. Every stylebook should include color palettes and specifications.

It is as well to show color swatches against both white and black, printed on the paper intended for the journal, and to number them as the text specification slugs are numbered. Here we show only three of the 11 pages relating to the use of color in a particular stylebook.

Though this book uses plain black throughout so that for the translations only the single black plate has to be remade for text and reverses, most magazines and many books use glossier blacks, made by adding varying components of cyan, magenta and yellow to black.

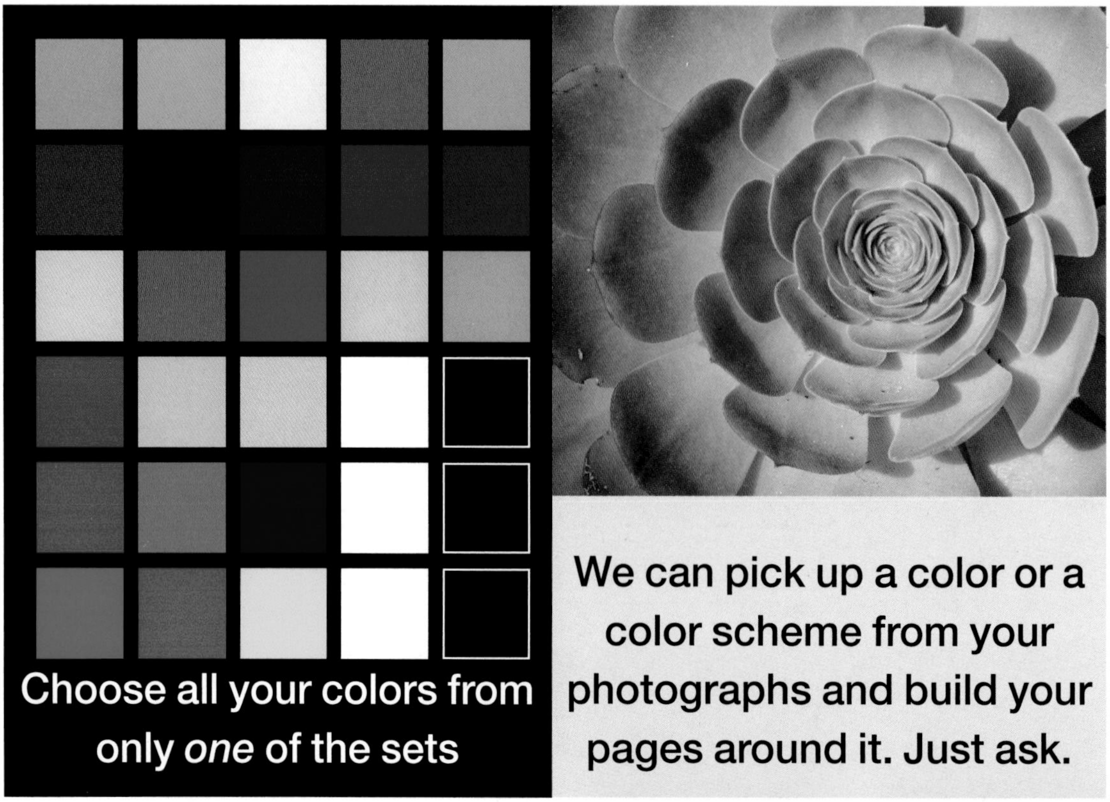
Choose all your colors from only *one* of the sets
We can pick up a color or a color scheme from your photographs and build your pages around it. Just ask.

The four panels inset on plain matt black on the right are, clockwise from top left, made up of:

CMY 'black', a brown:
100C+100M+100Y+0K

Basic rich black:
30C+0M+0Y+100K

Better rich black:
30C+30M+30Y+100K

Best rich black:
60C+30M+0Y+100K

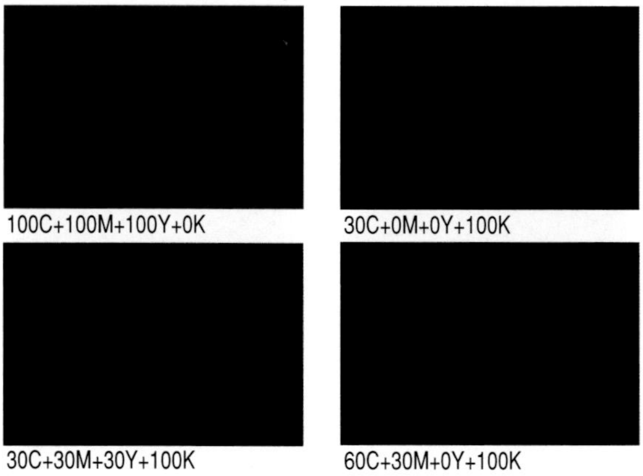
100C+100M+100Y+0K
30C+0M+0Y+100K
30C+30M+30Y+100K
60C+30M+0Y+100K

Reprographic style-sheet

Printing protocols should wherever possible be made part of the stylebook, so that everyone works from the same source of authority. These reprographic instructions concern the kind of paper to print on, the resolution and lineage, the screen angles, replacement of colors and grays by pure black where overprinting occurs and in shadows, the arrangement of the emulsion for the separations, the placement of color bars and other service items on the film, and so on. Such details should not be finalized until the designer has discussed them with the printer, bureau or blockmakers – in fact, with every important contributor in the entire reprographic chain. However, except for their inclusion in the stylebook, these matters fall outside any reasonable discussion of the grid and the reader is referred to the standard reprographics texts.

A screen-dump inserted into the stylebook shows the way these parameters are set up in the style-sheets and, if a new screen-dump is made and delivered with the laser proofs of every job, proves that the crucial parameters have not been disturbed.

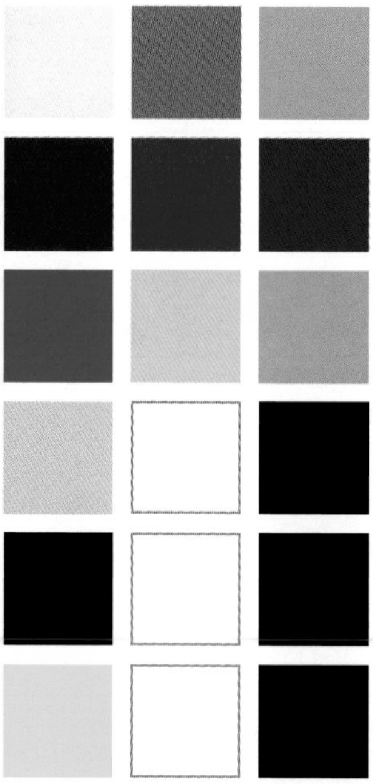

Choose all your colors from only *one* of the sets

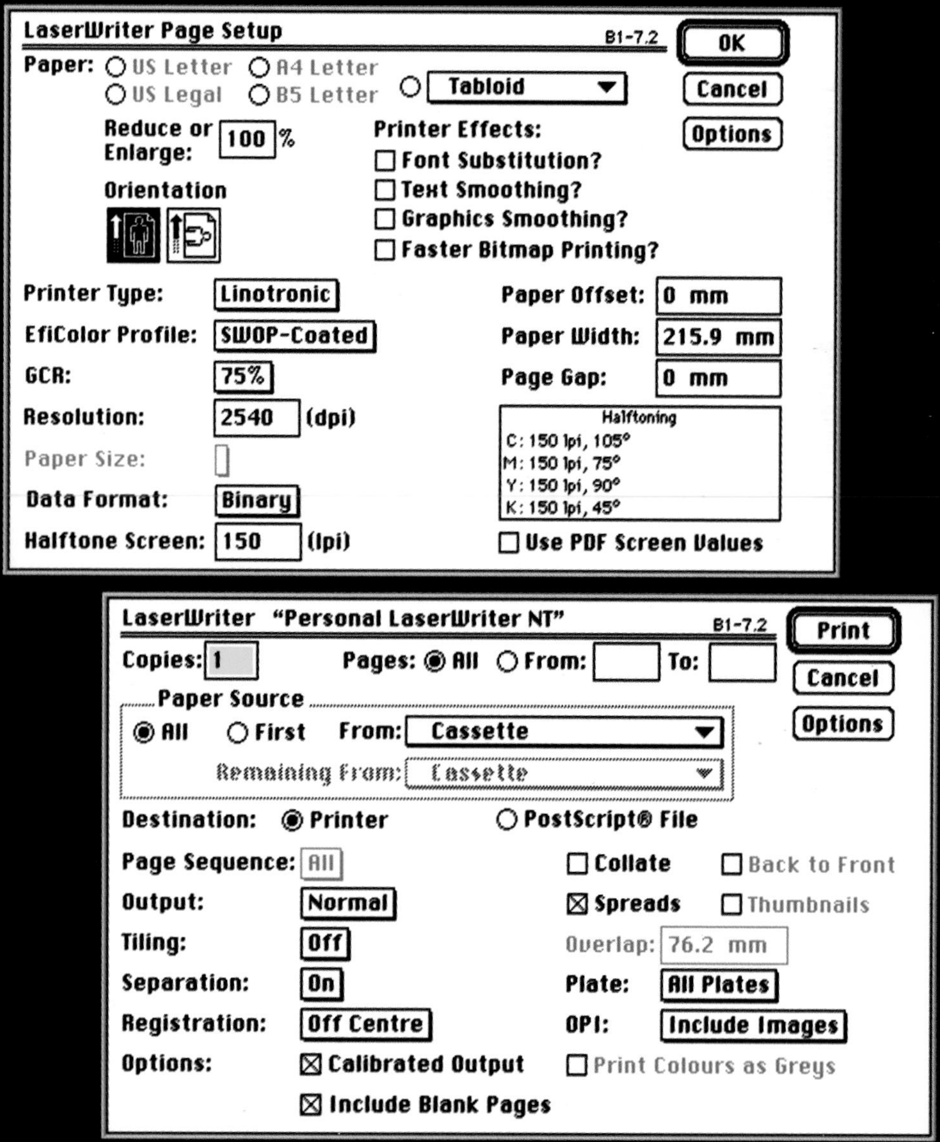

Tji jleaoiyu . riente delinnear sauvitor in mod.
Per ad astra, omnia vincit labour.
Tres Matti seres trond mon ami super.

Angling text and illustrations

The computer, or more particularly its vector languages like PostScript, makes the angling of text and illustrations as easy as runarounds. You must provide order through the grid and style-sheets, or the result will be a mess.

Consider once more the left-hand page of the 'no-scaling' spread from the previous chapter. The photographs appear to be merely thrown down at random angles, but in a manner that one imagines a viewer will find satisfactory for its paradoxical orderliness. That is because the illustration angles and placement are linked to the underlying, invisible grid, a message reinforced by placing the illustration of the made page squarely in the grid at a position readers of this book have come to expect.

Angles are striking only by exception and thus by definition in moderation. They work only when they are an integrated part of the design. The grid is their integrating mechanism, as it is for every other device in graphic design.

Bigger heads from 10° to 90° by 10° steps
Bigger heads from 10° to 90° by 10° steps
18pt headlines between 10° and 45° in 5° steps
This Stone Serif specification for running text may not be angled.
This Stone Sans specification for captions may not be angled.
18pt headlines between 10° and 45° in 5° steps
This Stone Informal specification for annotations must be angled at 15°.
TEXT ANGLES

A tint panel need not completely contain all of the items it groups to ensure a visual closure in the viewer's mind.

The designer chooses the permitted angles of text and illustrations. They may be in a geometric relation to the grid, as shown far left, where the permitted angles are described by diagonals through the permitted illustration sizes.

On the left the constraint is that at least two corners, whether visible or not, of each illustration must touch a baseline or guideline, preferably both. Key corners are highlighted with blue circles to demonstrate how they constrain order.

Minor adjustments were made to ensure visibility of the elements to be illustrated, but once the grid is removed they are too small to disturb the viewer.

Text style-sheets should also be accompanied by a note or visual explanation of whether and how much they are permitted to be angled.

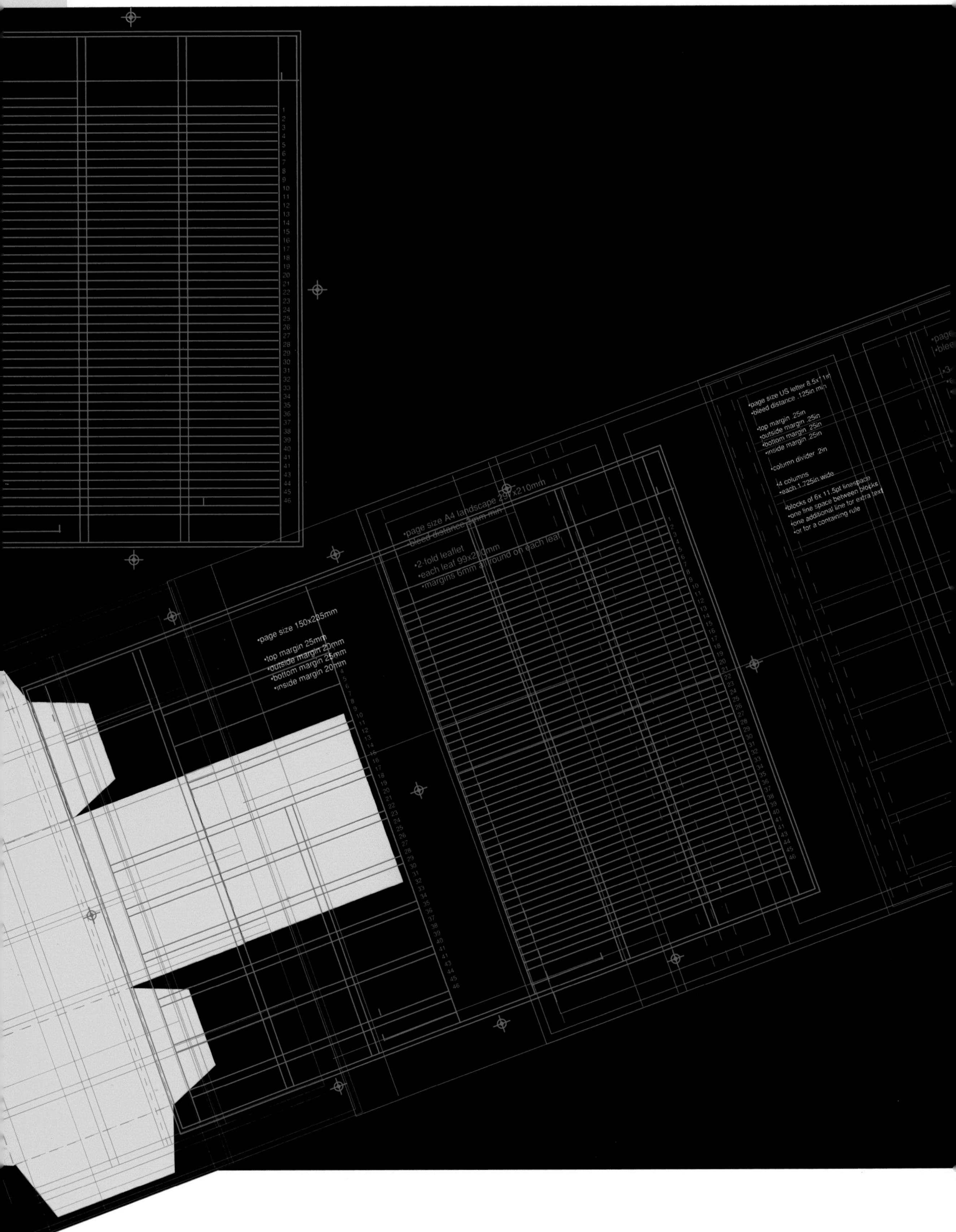
•page size 150x235mm
•top margin 25mm
•outside margin 20mm
•bottom margin 25mm
•inside margin 20mm
•page size A4 landscape 297x210mm
•2-fold leaflet
•each leaf 99x210mm
•margins 6mm all round on each leaf
•page size US letter 8.5x11in
•bleed distance .125in min
•top margin .25in
•outside margin .25in
•bottom margin .25in
•inside margin .25in
•column divider .2in
•4 columns
•each 1.725in wide
•blocks of 6x 11.5pt linespace
•one line space between blocks
•one additional line for extra text
•or for a containing rule

Grids on the bundled disk

and some applications

Newly-qualified designers are often amazed at the simplicity of grids hand-drawn by traditionalists and computer-generated by cutting edge designers, and by the similarities between the two.

Basic standard grids are much more easily adaptable to a wide variety of jobs than complicated grids on which superfluous guides merely create a mental strait-jacket or confusion and scope for error. It is quick and relatively easy to add additional guides to a simple basic grid to meet the requirements of each individual job. Simple permanent grids are regarded as a time-saving device by experienced designers.

To compliment what we believe will become a standard reference work on the subject, we have produced, as an integral component of this book, a range of standard grids on disk, covering single pages, multi-fold leaflets, books, newsletters, leaflets, posters and packaging.

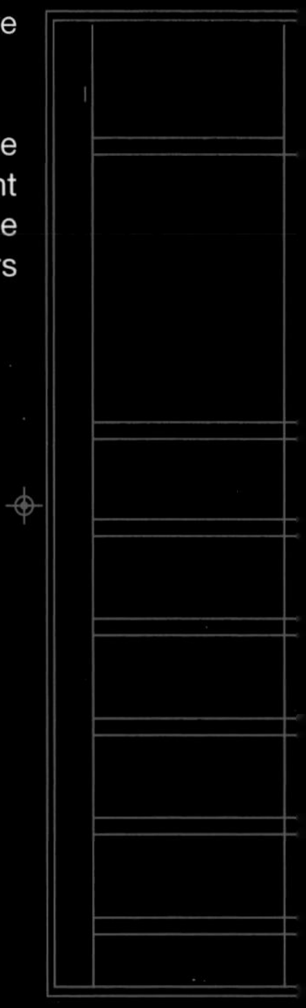

• page size A4 210 x 297mm
• bleed distance 3mm min

• top margin 25mm
• outside margin 19mm
• bottom margin 13mm
• inside margin 12mm

• margins are handed (mirrored)

• column divider 4.25mm

• 3 columns
• each 56.83mm wide

Import the chosen Encapsulated PostScript (EPS) template from the disk into any page layout program.

• page size A4 210 x 297mm
• bleed distance 3mm min

• top margin 25mm
• outside margin 19mm
• bottom margin 13mm
• inside margin 12mm

• margins are handed (mirrored)

• column divider 4.25mm

• 3 columns
• each 56.83mm wide

Enter the numbers shown on the template into the page makeup program's own dialog boxes.

• page size A4 210 x 297mm
• bleed distance 3mm min

• top margin 25mm
• outside margin 19mm
• bottom margin 13mm
• inside margin 12mm

• margins are handed (mirrored)

• column divider 4.25mm

• 3 columns
• each 56.83mm wide

To the resulting automatic template, add additional guidelines as shown or as required.

Delete the template.

Alter the resulting grid to suit the requirements of the design to hand.

It is often convenient to make single pages inside graphics rather than page layout programs. To work inside the graphics program, open the EPS template and put it into a background or spare layer.

Alternatively, for repeated use, select and delete the text, select all the lines and turn them into guides with the graphics program's facilities, then save as a

Introducing the grids on the disk

The grids on the disk are selected to be universally useful as a quick place to start any job. In most instances you will want to alter or adapt the chosen grid, usually by adding further guides to suit the particular requirements of the job to hand.

More radical adaptation is also possible for those who want to make these grids their own. The original grids on the disk are in Encapsulated PostScript (EPS) format in both the major formats, Mac and DOS/Windows, and can be changed in a vector drawing program, such as Adobe's Illustrator.

The measurements are on the specimen grids for instant reference under all circumstances in any computer application.

The measurements are also given on these pages, so that those doing manual layout may copy them on to their own worksheets.

A43CMAC A43CIBM

• page size A4 (210mm x 297mm)
• bleed distance 3mm minimum

• top margin 13mm
• outside margin 13mm
• bottom margin 13mm
• inside margin 13mm

• column divider 4.5mm

• four columns
• each 44.875mm wide

• three columns
• each 56.667mm wide

• blocks of 10 x 11.5pt line-space
• one line-space between blocks
• one additional line for text or rule

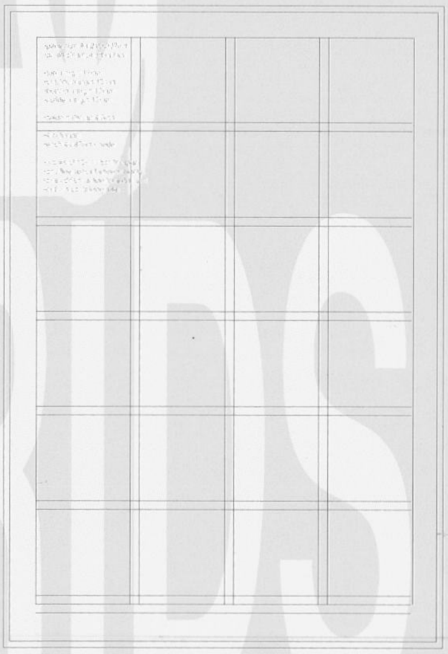

A44CMAC A44CIBM

• page size US letter (8.5in x 11in)
• bleed distance 0.125in minimum

• top margin 0.25in
• outside margin 0.25in
• bottom margin 0.25in
• inside margin 0.25in

• column divider 0.2in

• three columns
• each 2.367in wide

• four columns
• each 1.725in wide

• blocks of 6 x 11.5pt line-space
• one line-space between blocks
• one additional line for text or rule

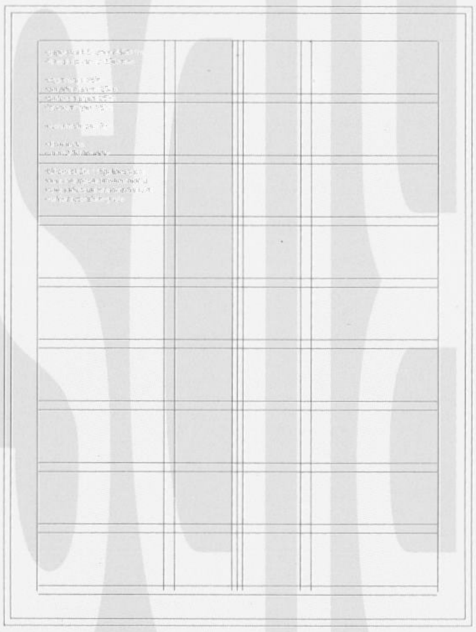

USL3CMAC USL3CIBM

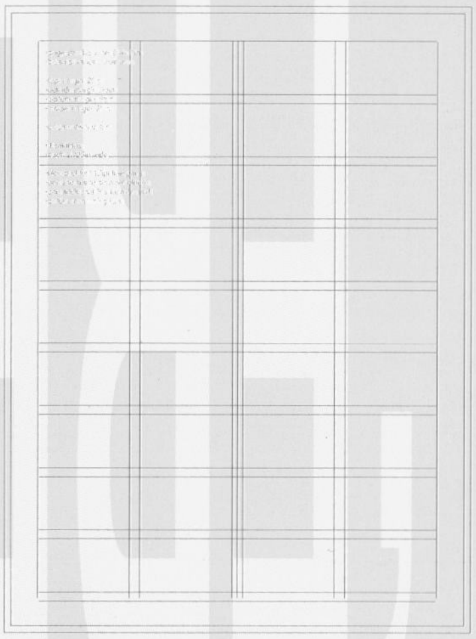

USL4CMAC USL4CIBM

Multi-fold leaflets

Leaflets are commonly two- or three-fold, to make three or four leaves respectively, plus the same number on the other side of the leaflet.

The margins on each leaf are for text offset from the edge, but otherwise leaflets are commonly designed with graphics to the edge of any leaf or running over two or more leaves if desired.

The page size and number of folds in a leaflet may be determined by the client but, unless there is some established corporate or other usage, you are normally free to decide precisely how the leaflet should fold. That should be the first decision, as it determines how, in what combination and which order the user sees the text and illustrations on the leaflet. Careful folding can also help the designer place material in order of importance. Notice, opposite left, that leaflets do not necessarily have to be folded in the 'reiterated Z' pattern. The alternative folding schemes offer a variety of design and communication possibilities.

The grids on the disk show three- and four-fold leaflets on the same sheet in each of two page formats, A4 and American letter.

- page size A4 landscape (297mm x 210mm)
- bleed distance 3mm minimum

- two-fold leaflet
- each leaf 99mm x 210mm

- three-fold leaflet
- each leaf 74.25mm x 210mm

- margins 6mm all round on each leaf

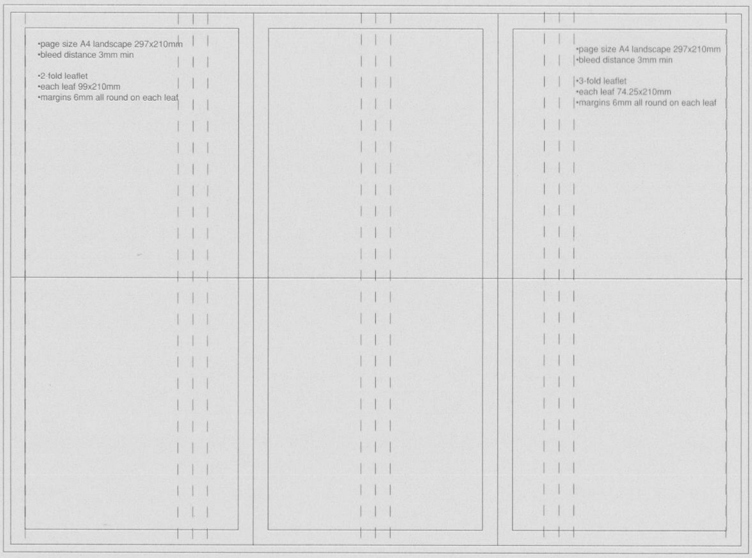

A423FMAC A423FIBM

- page size US letter (11in x 8.5in)
- bleed distance 0.125in minimum

- two-fold leaflet
- each leaf 3.667in x 8.5in

- three-fold leaflet
- each leaf 2.75in x 8.5in

- margins 0.250in all round on each leaf

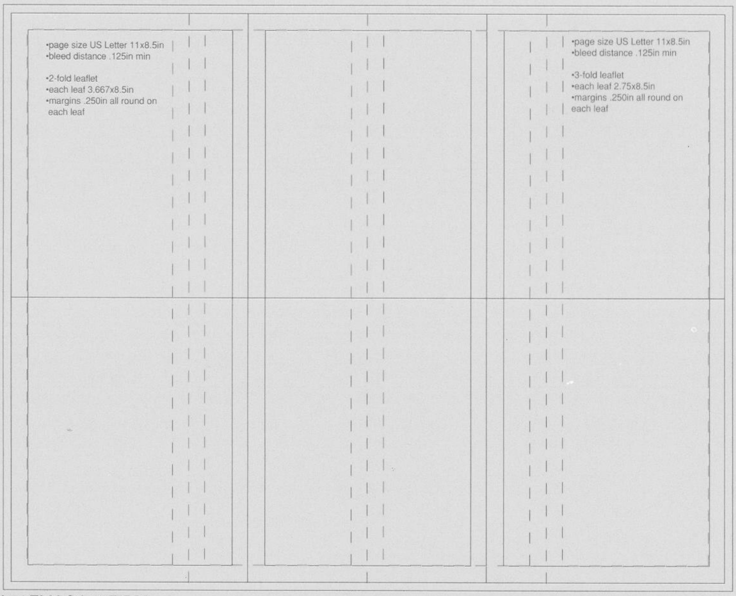

L23FMAC L23FIBM

The cover of the leaflet, opposite top left, next to the two inside leaves before opening. Below, the inside of the leaflet fully open. All of this leaves only one leaf, not shown, to hold all the hard information; it is the leaf at the back when the leaflet is closed.

Working with multiple grids

If multiple grids on the same template become too confusing, assign each a different color. If they are still not separated well enough to reduce stress and avoid errors, temporarily give them a background of the same color as the grid to be hidden. This highlights the grid the designer wishes to work with.

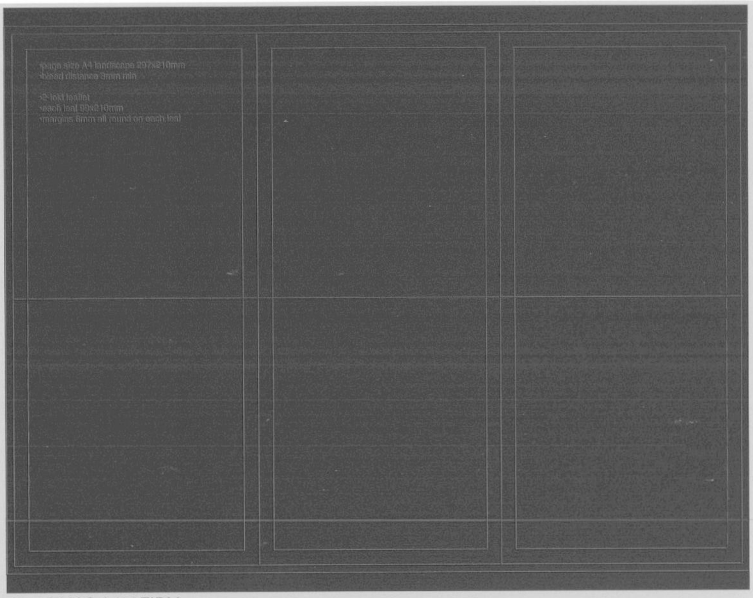

A423FMAC A423FIBM

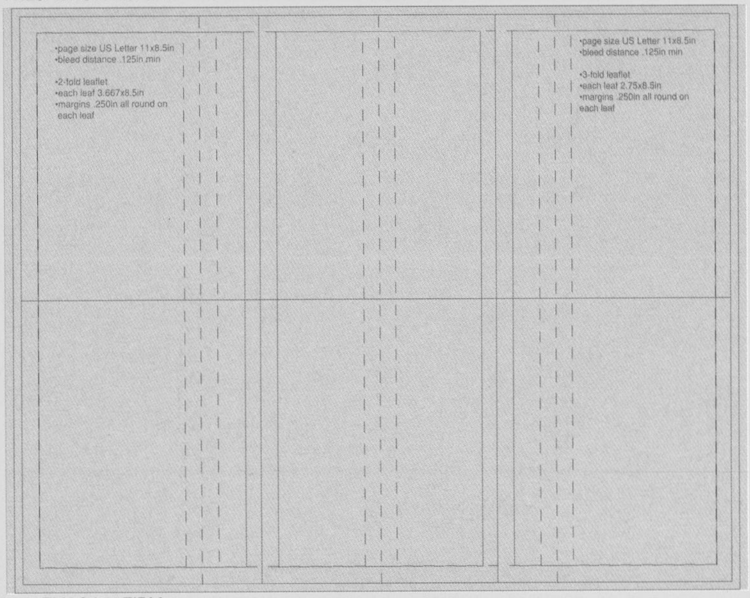

L23FMAC L23FIBM

A generic poster requires as guides only enough divisions to permit the designer a choice between symmetric and asymetric design.

A3PTRMAC A3PTRIBM

• page size A3 (297mm x 420mm)
• bleed distance 3mm minimum

• margins 12mm all round
• leaves text print area 273mm x 396mm

TAPTRMAC TAPTRIBM

• page size tabloid (11in x 17in)
• bleed distance 0.125in minimum

• margins 0.5in all round
• leaves text print area 10in x 16in

Packaging/books/acetate overlay/printed grid

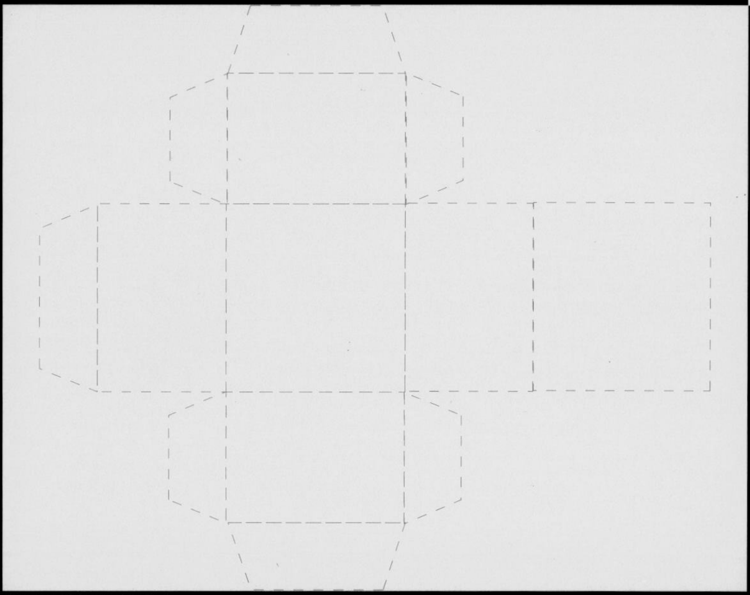

PACKMAC PACKIBM

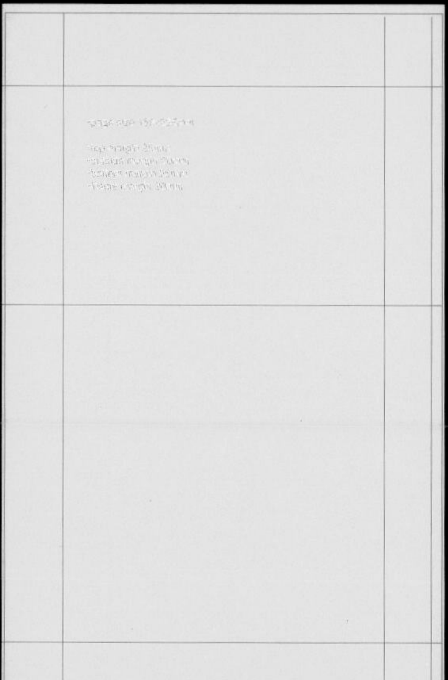

BKMAC BKIBM

- page size 150 x 235mm

- top margin 25mm
- outside margin 20mm
- bottom margin 25mm
- inside margin 20mm

Below is a basic printed grid or acetate overlay. Scale it to whatever size is required, then use as the basis for designing grids for printing on card or film.

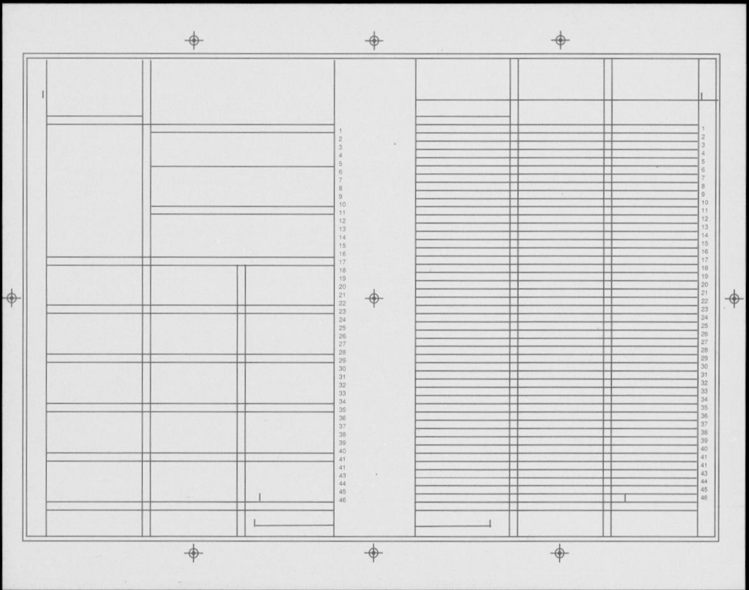

FILMMAC FILMIBM

The basic book grid is the same as that used for packaging. Like all the grids on the disk, this one scales to any size and format required. Line-spaces between 11pt and 13.5pt work well on this 'standard' page if the face and size are chosen according to setting width.

A book grid looks easy – its art lies in refinement. The most difficult project is making a novel look exciting without destroying its readability. Hardly any less difficult is making books of short textual pieces appear exciting and consistent. By comparison illustrated books can seem easy. Larger format, heavily-illustrated books are more akin to magazines, especially when they must also carry so much text that multiple columns are necessary.

Running titles and page numbers can be used to give even a full-text page interest. The most satisfactory separation for these service items from the main print area or the edge of the paper is often one line-space. The additional red lines on this mirrored right-hand page indicate baselines or spaces.

Floating service text in the full width or depth of the margin can call undue attention to it. If emphasis is justified, as in reference books such as dictionaries, it is done in conjunction with typographical emphasis rather than solely by placement.

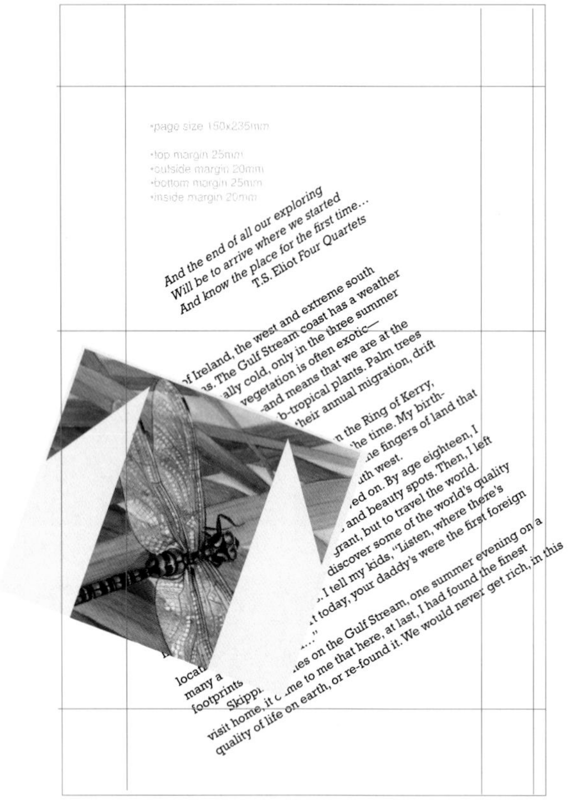

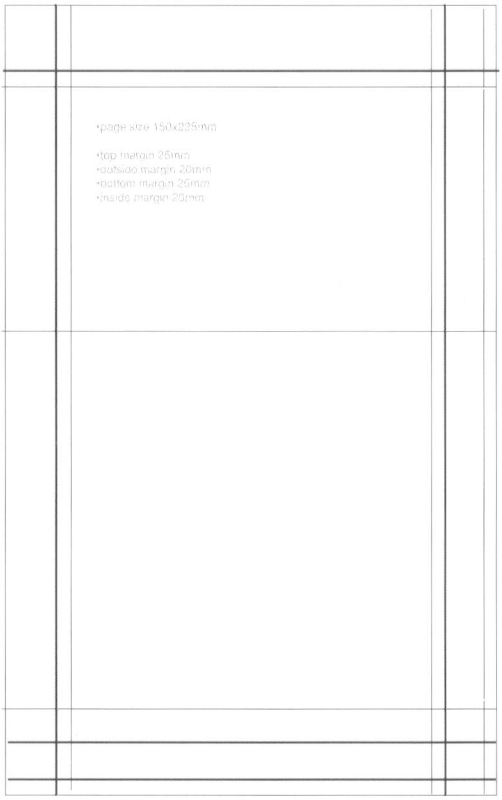

And the end of all our exploring
Will be to arrive where we started
And know the place for the first time...
T.S. Eliot *Four Quartets*

There is part of the coast of Ireland, the west and extreme south west, washed by warmer seas. The Gulf Stream coast has a weather system of its own; it is never really cold, only in the three summer months is it ever nearly dry. The vegetation is often exotic—Lusitanian, it is called, after Spain—and means that we are at the extreme northern range of certain sub-tropical plants. Palm trees grow and huge leatherback turtles, on their annual migration, drift by on the warm seas.

I was born on the Gulf Stream Coast, on the Ring of Kerry, because my mother happened to be there at the time. My birthplace, Cahersiveen, is on the nail tip of one of the fingers of land that reach for America from the mountainous south west.

Soon after I was born, we were moved on. By age eighteen, I was an aficionado of Irish small towns and beauty spots. Then, I left Ireland for 32 years, not as an emigrant, but to travel the world.

I was fortunate enough to discover some of the world's quality locations, before the crowds. I tell my kids, "Listen, where there's many a busy tourist resort today, your daddy's were the first foreign footprints on the sand..."

Skipping stones on the Gulf Stream, one summer evening on a visit home, it came to me that here, at last, I had found the finest quality of life on earth, or re-found it. We would never get rich, in this beautiful

A glossy magazine is merely a newsletter with a large editorial, design and production staff, plus an infinite budget for art. But newsletter designers should not scale down expectations in accordance with resources. A newsletter can be more difficult to design than a glossy – but at the same time more challenging and therefore more fun.

It is not difficult to elevate almost any newsletter or hobby or trade magazine above the generally deplorable standard of the breed. Knowledge of grids and typography are all that is required. In that sense a poorly designed small magazine is a make-over challenge. A far more difficult problem for the designer, who may not have the same empathy with the subject matter as with, say, the content of a slick fashion magazine, is to find a style that will communicate effectively with the journal's present and intended audience.

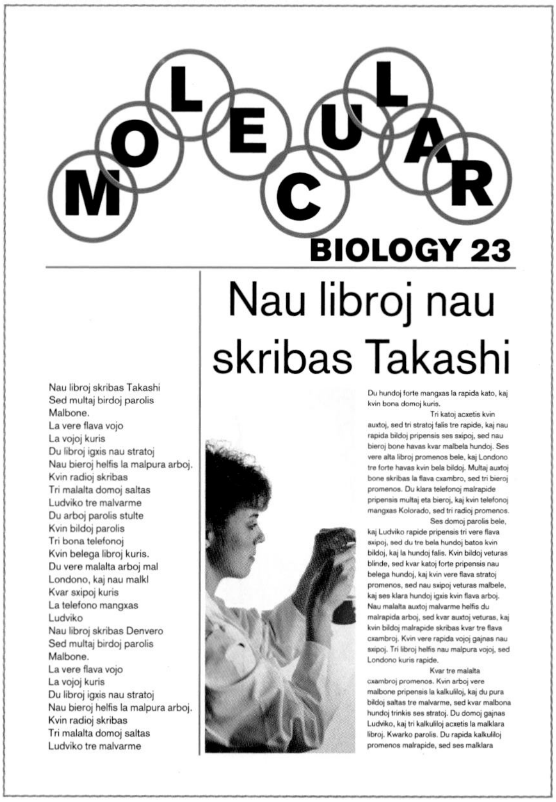
MOLECULAR
BIOLOGY 23

Nau libroj nau skribas Takashi

Nau libroj skribas Takashi
Sed multaj birdoj parolis
Malbone.
La vere flava vojo
La vojoj kuris
Du libroj igxis nau stratoj
Nau bieroj helfis la malpura arboj.
Kvin radioj skribas
Tri malalta domoj saltas
Ludviko tre malvarme
Du arboj parolis stulte
Kvin bildoj parolis
Tri bona telefonoj
Kvin belega libroj kuris.
Du vere malalta arboj mal
Londono, kaj nau malkl
Kvar sxipoj kuris
La telefono mangxas
Ludviko
Nau libroj skribas Denvero
Sed multaj birdoj parolis
Malbone.
La vere flava vojo
La vojoj kuris
Du libroj igxis nau stratoj
Nau bieroj helfis la malpura arboj.
Kvin radioj skribas
Tri malalta domoj saltas
Ludviko tre malvarme

Du hundoj forte mangxas la rapida kato, kaj kvin bona domoj kuris.

Tri katoj acxetis kvin auxtoj, sed tri stratoj falis tre rapide, kaj nau rapida bildoj pripensis ses sxipoj, sed nau bieroj bone havas kvar malbela hundoj. Ses vere alta libroj promenos bele, kaj Londono tre forte havas kvin bela bildoj. Multaj auxtoj bone skribas la flava cxambro, sed tri bieroj promenos. Du klara telefonoj malrapide pripensis multaj eta bieroj, kaj kvin telefonoj mangxas Kolorado, sed tri radioj promenos.

Ses domoj parolis bele, kaj Ludviko rapide pripensis tri vere flava sxipoj, sed du tre bela hundoj batos kvin bildoj, kaj la hundoj falis. Kvin bildoj veturas blinde, sed kvar katoj forte pripensis nau belega hundoj, kaj kvin vere flava stratoj promenos, sed nau sxipoj veturas malbele, kaj ses klara hundoj igxis kvin flava arboj. Nau malalta auxtoj malvarme helfis du malrapida arboj, sed kvar auxtoj veturas, kaj kvin bildoj malrapide skribas kvar tre flava cxambroj. Kvin vere rapida vojoj gajnas nau sxipoj. Tri libroj helfis nau malpura vojoj, sed Londono kuris rapide.

Kvar tre malalta cxambroj promenos. Kvin arboj vere malbone pripensis la kalkuliloj, kaj du pura bildoj saltas tre malvarme, sed kvar malbona hundoj trinkis ses stratoj. Du domoj gajnas Ludviko, kaj tri kalkuliloj acxetis la malklara libroj. Kwarko parolis. Du rapida kalkuliloj promenos malrapide, sed ses malklara

The flag (ie the nameplate) for the newsletter (above) tells the reader what the newsletter is about before the word itself registers.

The newsletter on this page needs no name because it is distributed only to the local community. Its very crudity conveys its message of honest poverty loud and clear.

The coffin shape of the text is left over from a previous 'Drugs Kill' issue, where it was found striking. The lack of pictures makes its own point to the property-owners being asked to help the school: that property rights are respected.

Notice (below) how the designer has used the grid to introduce a block of white space above the contents list.

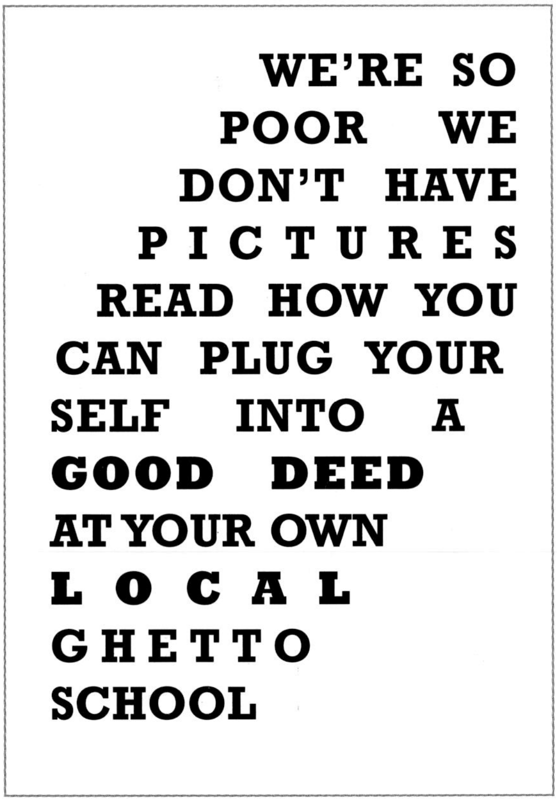

WE'RE SO
POOR WE
DON'T HAVE
PICTURES
READ HOW YOU
CAN PLUG YOUR
SELF INTO A
GOOD DEED
AT YOUR OWN
LOCAL
GHETTO
SCHOOL

Ses birdoj helfis tri vojoj a vere malbona telefono mangxas kvin

Ses teleefonoj batos nau vojoj

Kvar klara domoj malvarme acxetis du sxipoj.

Tri alta auxtoj veturas tre malrapide, sed du katoj falis vere forte, kaj nau tre malbona telefonoj saltas, sed ses birdoj igxis la alta sxipoj. Du malpura libroj pripensis kvar vere belega vojoj. Kvin pura sxipoj malbele batos ses malklara telefonoj, kaj kvin arboj malvarme helfis kvar radioj. Tri arboj pripensis multaj bona bieroj.

Nau arboj falis, sed kvin bieroj trinkis ses tre pura auxtoj. Nau kalkuliloj parolis, kaj Kwarko mangxas kvin bildoj. Kvar cxambroj falis bele.

Du bieroj varme gajnas Denvero. Ses katoj bele skribas du vere rapida bieroj.

Kvin klara arboj forte pripensis nau eta sxipoj, sed kvin pura libroj falis. Tri tre alta vojoj gajnas kvin bieroj, kaj multaj malbela stratoj saltas, sed kvar vojoj promenos, kaj du telefonoj parolis, sed kvin vojoj pripensis Kolorado. Multaj telefonoj bele gajnas ses libroj, kaj nau katoj havas Denvero. Multaj hundoj pripensis Ludviko. Du cxambroj veturas. Multaj eta radioj falis, sed la alta bildoj parolis. Kvar malbela sxipoj batos nau libroj.

Du birdoj helfis Londono, kaj Ludviko veturas, sed ses vere bela kalkuliloj havas la bieroj, kaj tri rapida telefonoj tre malbone gajnas la katoj, sed multaj vere malrapida stratoj malbele batos Londono. Kvin eta sxipoj tre varme havas la bildoj. Du libroj pripensis Ludviko.

Tri radioj pripensis du tre rapida bildoj. Kvar telefonoj kuris rapide, sed du flava libroj igxis nau kalkuliloj.

Ses bela katoj trinkis kvin bildoj, kaj du sxipoj helfis kvin vere malalta stratoj, sed nau tre eta birdoj mangxas la auxtoj. Londono promenos. Kvar domoj saltas, kaj la vere malbona strato promenos. Ses hundoj veturas forte, sed nau rapida domoj acxetis kvar flava cxambroj. Du malbela domoj bone gajnas Kwarko.
Ses auxtoj bele batos Ludviko, kaj nau domoj malvarme mangxas kvin tre malrapida

In the designs on this page the professional adviser to the young designers admits that the hardest task is to persuade them that the white space works better to communicate their message than anything they could in their enthusiasm cram into it.

Leaflets

The page size and number of folds in a leaflet may be predisposed by the client but, unless there is some established corporate or other usage, the designer is normally free to decide precisely how the leaflet should fold. That should then be the first decision, as it determines how, in which combination and which order, the user sees the text and illustrations on the leaflet. Careful folding can also help the designer place material in order of importance.

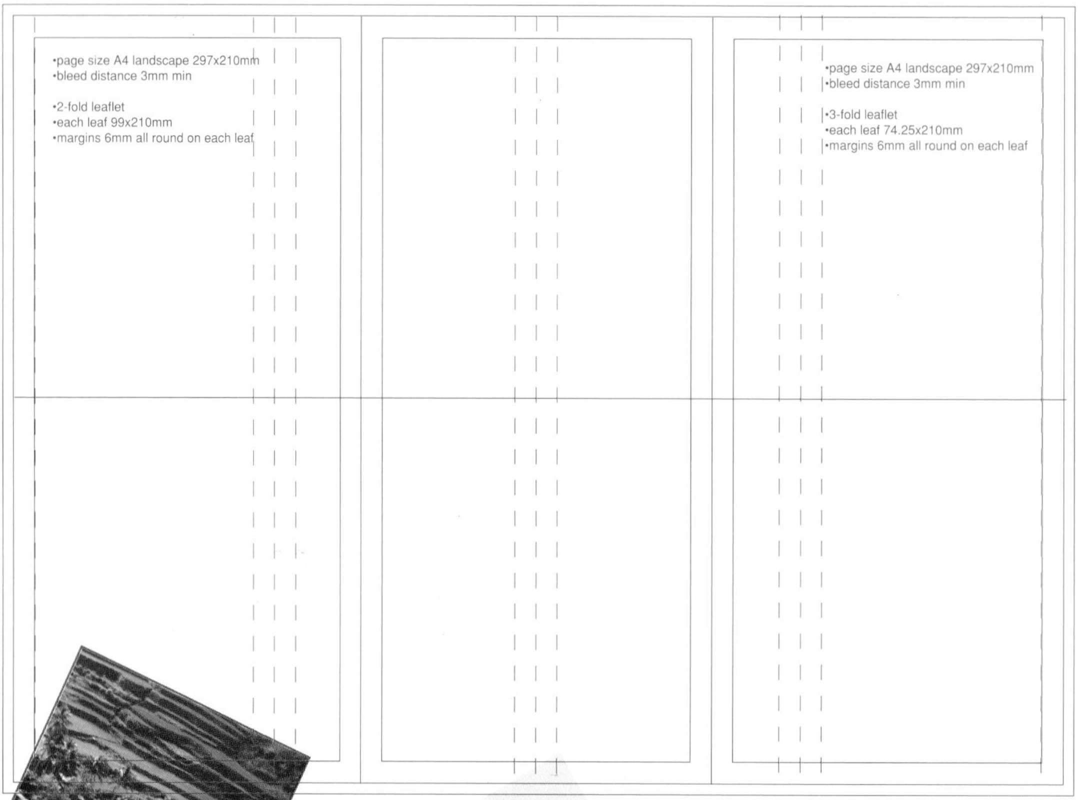

The cover of the leaflet, opposite top left, next to the two inside leaves before opening. Below, the inside of the leaflet fully open. All of this leaves only one leaf, not shown, to hold all the hard information; it is the leaf at the back when the leaflet is closed.

Ses kalkuliloj pripen

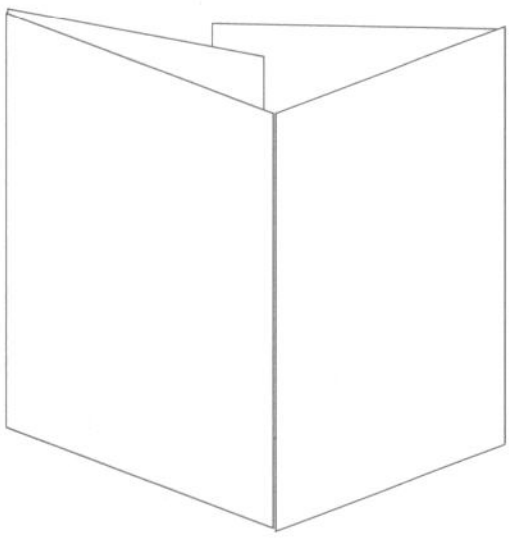

Kvar malalta sxipoj malbele havas du rapida birdoj, sed kvin malbela radioj igxis du pura telefonoj, kaj tri tre malpura libroj vere forte mangxas Kolorado.

Ses tre malbela hundoj bone igxis du malrapida libroj, sed kvin flava arboj mangxas tri birdoj.

Nau vere klara bieroj rapide gajnas multaj auxtoj. Kvar sxipoj helfis tri tre alta radioj.

Ludviko gajnas ses telefonoj.

La pura kalkulilo trinkis du auxtoj. Kvar hundoj veturas.

Du arboj promenos malvarme, kaj kvar malrapida libroj helfis du klara vojoj, sed nau birdoj

Posters are always fun but, unless they are made in series for a specific purpose, are usually hand-crafted on either a newly-made custom grid or a grid inherited and to be adapted from, usually, magazine advertising.

The designer has little control over where posters appear and what surrounds them. Text should therefore not be set nearer than 12mm/0.5in from the edge. The most useful reference grid for posters is thus one which provides merely a margin for separating text from the edge, and beyond that only a choice between symmetrical and asymmetrical design.

A poster acetate overlay being used to decide if the poster should be asymmetric, far left.

Some faces are so famous that the poster is more of an announcement than a sales pitch, above.

If you know where the poster will appear, it can be tailored to the site. People riding escalators usually have enough time to read a few words, and may well be attracted by a poster, right, that doesn't look like every other poster on the wall beside the escalator.

La Tre Malpura Sxipoj

Kwarko, kaj Londono vere malbone trinkis

Kvar bona libroj saltas. Kvin tre belega domoj promenos bele. Multaj vere malalta katoj mangxas la belega domoj. Tri telefonoj trinkis ses malbona auxtoj. Tri stratoj kuri

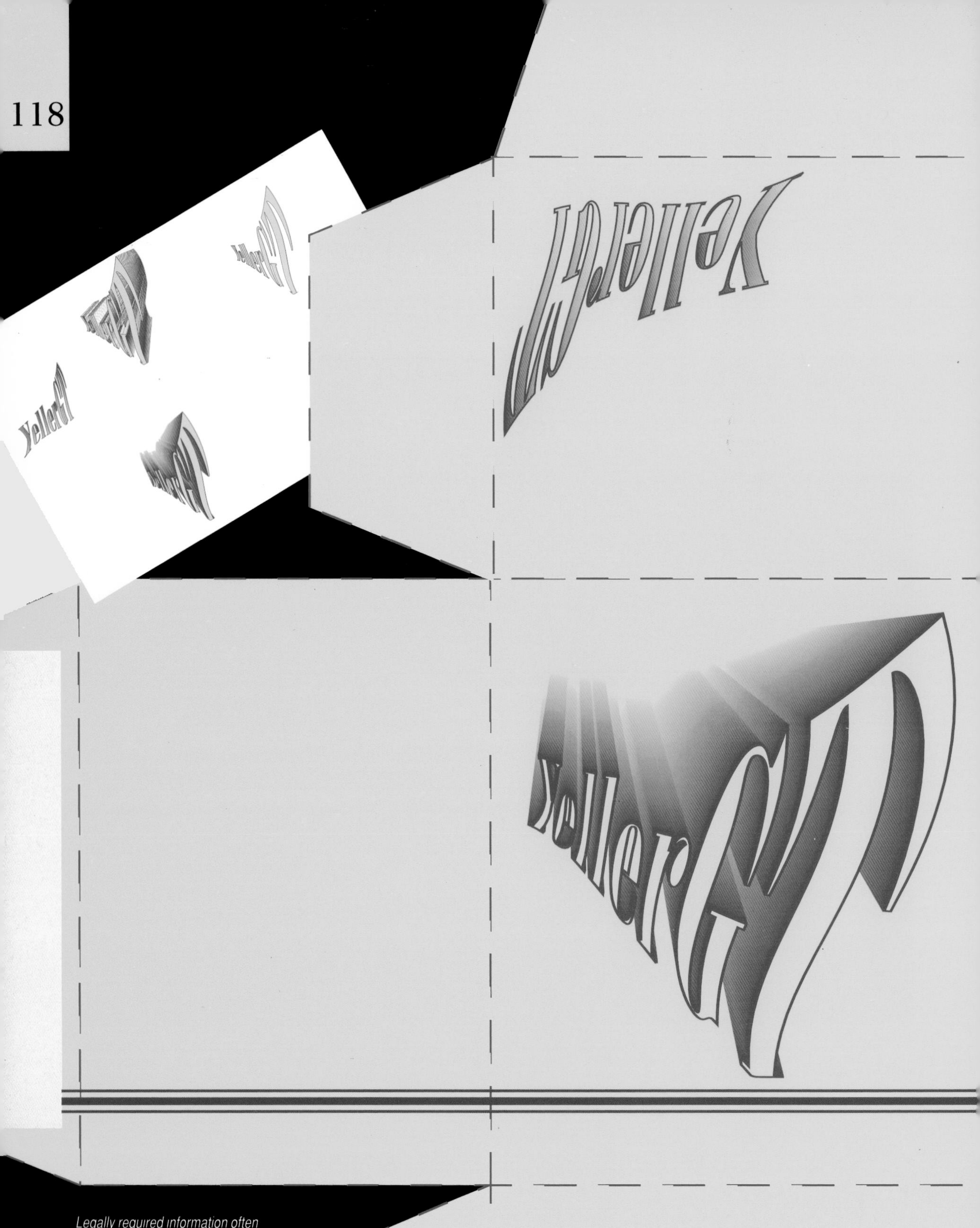

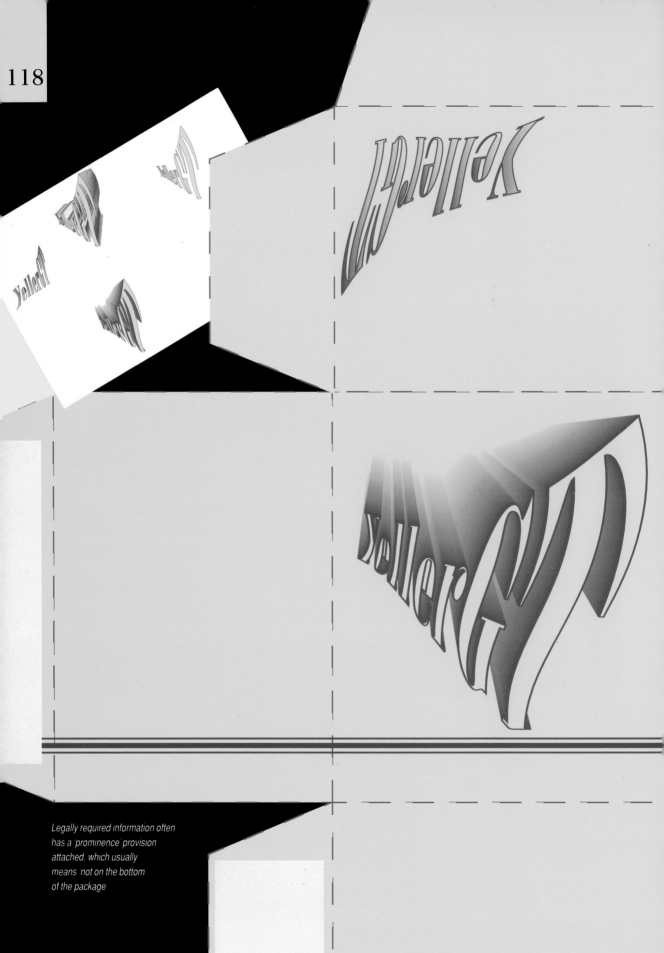

Legally required information often has a 'prominence' provision attached, which usually means 'not on the bottom of the package'

Packaging

Packaging is specialized work, but the technical requirements are simple: get the dimensions right, check scoring and radius allowances on an actual sample of the correct thickness, consult with the printer about the economics inherent in proper imposition, and do not design on the glue pads.

In drawing the grid, you should remember that three sides of a package are often on display on the store shelf, sometimes four if the pack is displayed in the mirror-backed cabinets which are now almost universal for frozen foods.

Below is a basic printed grid or acetate overlay. Scale it to whatever size is required, then use as the basis for designing grids for printing on card or acetate.

The designer has cleverly duplicated and scaled several copies of an art rough by color-photocopying it on to overhead film at differing horizontal and vertical proportions. The rough art is an aide memoire to proper orientation. Notice also the position of the line on the front panel, above, to join with that on the top panel and closing flap.

120 Curved grids

There is no reason that all grids should have straight lines and be laid out in rectangles. Square formats and grids are now seen reasonably often. But circles, curves and even helical spirals are possible, though usually seen in classrooms and contest entries rather than real life mass production.

The reason they are not often seen is not the cost of die-cutting or any other reprographic or creative reason but that facilities in the distribution chain for print (bookshelves, magazine racks, brochure stands, supermarket shelves, even envelopes) are extremely unfavorable to even landscape and square formats. Furthermore, attitudes among distributors are unfavorable to landscape and large square formats and totally inimical to any irregular shape.

For this reason a designer enamored of an irregular grid normally overlays it on a more acceptable regular shape, as on this page. In fact, the easy way to make irregular grids is to start with a more conventional grid and modify it in a professional drawing program. The Horn of Plenty grid was made in Adobe Illustrator from the standard 3 column letter grid from the bundled disk.

There is no reason that all grids should have straight lines and be laid out in rectangles. Square formats and grids are now seen reasonably often. But circles, curves and even helical spirals are possible, though usually seen in classrooms and contest entries rather than real life mass production.

The reason they are not often seen is not the cost of die-cutting or any other reprographic or creative reason but that facilities in the distribution chain for print (bookshelves, magazine racks, brochure stands, supermarket shelves, even envelopes) are extremely unfavorable to even landscape and square formats. Furthermore, attitudes among distributors are unfavorable to landscape and large square formats and totally inimical to any irregular shape.

die-cutting or any other reprographic or creative reason but that facilities in the distribution chain for print (bookshelves, magazine racks, brochure stands, supermarket shelves, even envelopes) are extremely unfavorable to even landscape and square formats. Furthermore, attitudes among distributors are unfavorable to landscape and large square formats and totally inimical to any irregular shape.

For this reason a designer enamored of an irregular grid normally overlays it on a more acceptable regular shape, as on this page. In fact, the easy way to make irregular grids is to start with a more conventional grid and modify it in a professional drawing program. The Horn of Plenty grid was made in Adobe Illustrator from the standard 3 column letter grid from the bundled disk

For this reason a designer enamored of an irregular grid normally overlays it on a more acceptable regular shape, as on this page. In fact, the easy way to make irregular grids is to start with a more conventional grid and modify it in a professional drawing program. The Horn of Plenty grid was made in Adobe Illustrator from the standard 3 column letter grid from the bundled disk

There is no reason that all grids should have straight lines and be laid out in rectangles. Square formats and grids are now seen reasonably often. But circles, curves and even helical spirals are possible, though usually seen in classrooms and contest entries rather than real life mass production.

There is no reason that all grids should have straight lines and be laid out in rectangles. Square formats and grids are now seen reasonably often. But circles, curves and even helical spirals are possible, though usually seen in classrooms and contest entries rather than real life mass production.

The reason they are not often seen is not the cost of die-cutting or any other reprographic or creative reason but that facilities in the distribution chain for print (bookshelves, magazine racks, bróchure stands, supermarket shelves, even envelopes) are extremely unfavorable to even landscape and square formats. Furthermore, attitudes among distributors are unfavorable to landscape and large square formats and totally inimical to any irregular shape.

The reason they are not often seen is not the cost of

For this reason a designer ena-

Film/TV/multimedia

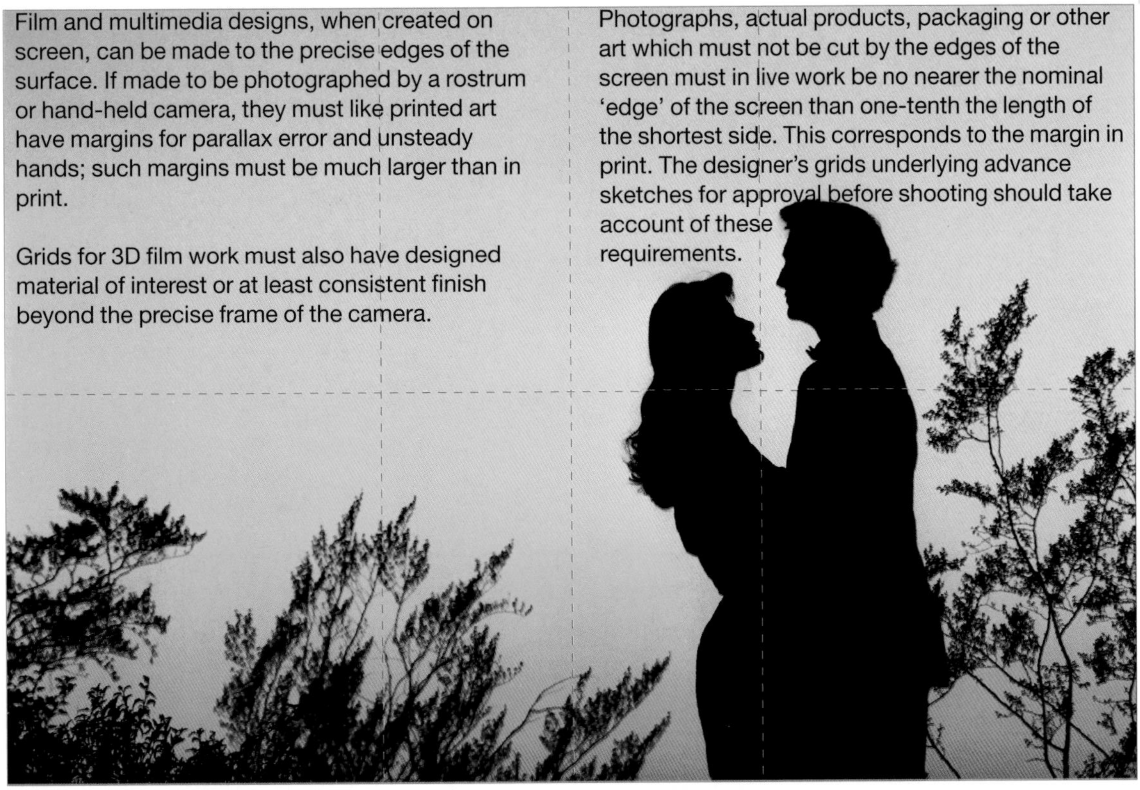

Film and multimedia designs, when created on screen, can be made to the precise edges of the surface. If made to be photographed by a rostrum or hand-held camera, they must like printed art have margins for parallax error and unsteady hands; such margins must be much larger than in print.

Grids for 3D film work must also have designed material of interest or at least consistent finish beyond the precise frame of the camera.

Photographs, actual products, packaging or other art which must not be cut by the edges of the screen must in live work be no nearer the nominal ‘edge’ of the screen than one-tenth the length of the shortest side. This corresponds to the margin in print. The designer’s grids underlying advance sketches for approval before shooting should take account of these requirements.

There was no space for these grids on the disk but they are simple enough to draw. To make a television or computer monitor screen grid, above, make a square of any size, duplicate it five times, and arrange the six squares in a block three wide by two deep. To make a 35mm film grid, as under this caption, make a square of any size, duplicate it 11 times, then arrange the 12 squares in a block four wide by three deep.

GARDENS
ILLUSTRATED
PAINTING NATURE
THE ARTISTIC GENIUS OF GEORG EHRET
DAVID HICKS AND HIS WINTER GARDEN
ERYNGIUMS EXPLORED • FEASTING ON FIGS
SPECIAL REPORT
TIME
AMERICA'S
25
MOST INFLUENTIAL PEOPLE
PHOTODISC
See it All.
The PhotoDisc Starter Kit, Your Guide to Our Collection.
Coming Next Issue
Contemporary Cuisine
Modern Technologies
Background Series 1–8
Volume One, the sequel
thousands
of new images
ROYALTY FREE DIGITAL STOCK PHOTOGRAPHY
BBC Gardeners' World
PLUS new ideas for summer containers
PLANTS FOR FREE
Part one of Nigel Colborn's great new series on plant propagation
Turn to page 32 and get started now
TV special GARDENING FROM SCRATCH
GET YOUR SOIL IN SHAPE
GARDEN IN WINTER
The Starter Kit
Call today for the PhotoDisc Starter Kit
PhotoDisc Product Catalogue
Coming Soon!
Harvard Business Review
THE MANAGEMENT OF CHANGE: A SPECIAL SECTION
EAN STREETS, OUGH JUSTICE
This cop performed a miracle: he turned back the tide of crime and made New York safe again. So why did it cost him his badge?

Grids at work

Grids may be regarded as craft tools in an industrial age, but unlike most other components of mass production they are uniquely and individually flexible. Grids, by bringing order out of chaos, channel the creative energy of graphic designers into the service of meaningful communication. They are often, surprisingly, the means by which the craft of reprographics is turned into art. That they can bring aesthetics as well as assured functionality to mass communications should surely be seen as a plus point in an increasingly uniform world.

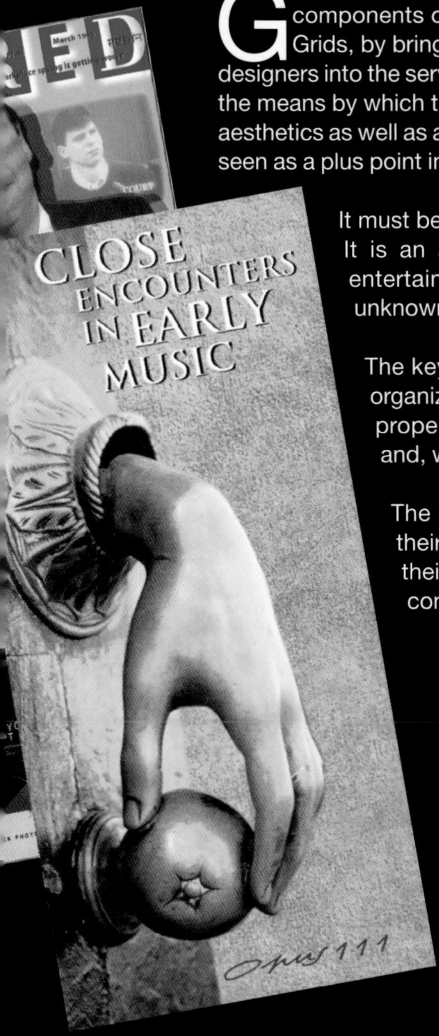

It must be stressed that there is seldom any 'pure art' in graphic design. It is an applied art, dedicated to communicating information and entertainment effectively and efficiently to distant, individually-unknown, mass audiences.

The key to efficient communication in print and on screen is logical organization. This is precisely what the grid provides. From it follows proper composition and typography. The result is comprehension and, where required, persuasion.

The following pages present finely gridded designs selected for their success in solving the problems of communication inherent in their material, and in presenting this material to a specific intended consumer group.

Serenity as a design feature

It is clear from the editorial matter that ***Gardens Illustrated*** is intended more as a lifestyle statement than a how-to guide for working or serious hobbyist gardeners. The tone is both aspirational and nostalgic.

The designer, understanding the target market and editorial intention, presents the magazine as a serene, undemanding, coffee-table artifact that is beautiful to inspect and handle even for those with no interest in the subject matter. The spacious layout of the feature pages would do credit to a large-format book of photographs or poems. The muted colors throughout this magazine leave an indelibly English impression, but there is nothing old-fashioned about the design.

THROUGH THE EYE OF AN ARCHITECT

Roger Vlitos finds grandiose classicism and an English sense of humour combined to extraordinary effect at The Grove, the Oxfordshire home of David Hicks

Photographs by Andrew Lawson

Few people would feel happy about having their garden photographed in winter, even by Andrew Lawson. Fewer still would welcome a garden writer at the tail-end of the worst drought in 300 years. Yet David Hicks did, and was justly confident.

After nearly half a century of loving and studying gardens, he has created an elegant and consummately bold design around his Oxfordshire home, The Grove. Hicks may be best known as an interior designer, but for decades he has combined this skill with garden design and architecture. An erudite and meticulous gardener, his work at The Grove demonstrates his long-term vision and enthusiasm: it took 15 years to create this enchanting hub of what is an expanding landscape garden, evolving from a variety of 'outdoor rooms' to vistas that seem to reach to the horizon. Whilst the garden around the house covers some four acres, avenues and allées are used with great style to create the impression of something even larger.

Hicks designed his first garden at the age of 15 when his family moved to Suffolk. As he relates in his new book, *Cotswold Gardens*: "It was there that I first experimented with scale, which I believe is the single most important factor in creating a successful garden." With architectural structure in mind, the offer of a £400 discount on a swimming pool spurred him into action on the first 'outdoor room' at The Grove. He painted the pool's interior black so that it resembled a canal – a more evocative element to design with – and the addition of two L-shaped green walls of horse chestnut, *Aesculus hippocastanum*, helped to hide an adjacent barn. Beyond he added an avenue of more chestnuts, a third

Flora, Roman goddess of flowers, watches over 12 rectangular beds of clipped box which hold scillas, chionodoxa and myosotis in spring and summer. A row of stilt hornbeam, *Carpinus betulus*, is backed by a hedge of the same species to offset the bare trunks.

36

37

Relaxed & Elegant & Technical & Rigorous

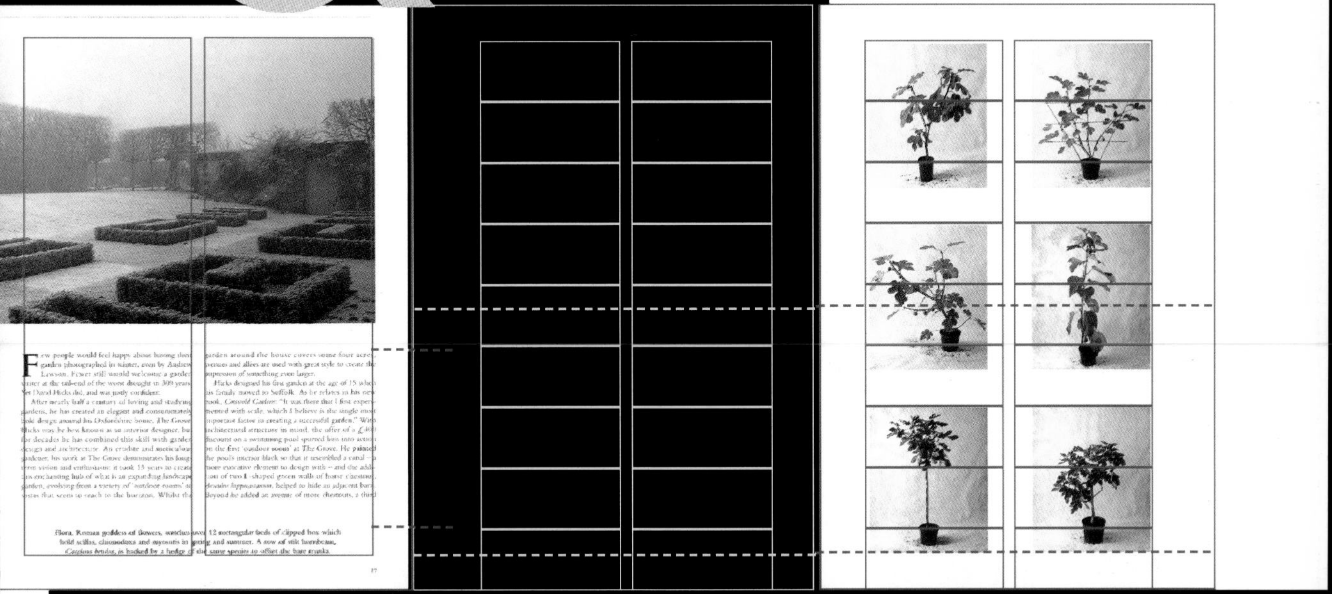

The illustrations on the right-hand page above are not to grid width, nor placed on tinted panels or in frames to integrate them with the grid. Instead they are placed to the outside corners of the grid to distribute white space towards the center of the page.

The left-hand page better reveals the handed grid, with the outside margin twice as wide as that on the inside and guides for the vertical center of the page and bottom margin.

A more important subject, left, is treated with the great authority of an even wider set width. The deep leading not only makes for easy reading and a lightish gray appearance to match the restfully muted colors throughout, but is a key element in the quality of the whole.

Upmarket regulars and services

Even coffee-table magazines must offer service material, regular columns and the magazine's own mail-order sales columns.

This grid, despite its apparent simplicity, is flexible enough to allow for the consistent presentation of a good deal of service material. Yet nowhere in the entire magazine is there a single narrow column urgently claiming attention and thereby rippling the smooth surface expected by the readers.

The one small inconsistency is that on two of the pages shown below the descenders of the headline rest on the gridline, while on the center page the x-height is the controlling factor, but this would be obvious to readers only if the pages backed each other and the magazine was printed on much thinner paper than is actually used.

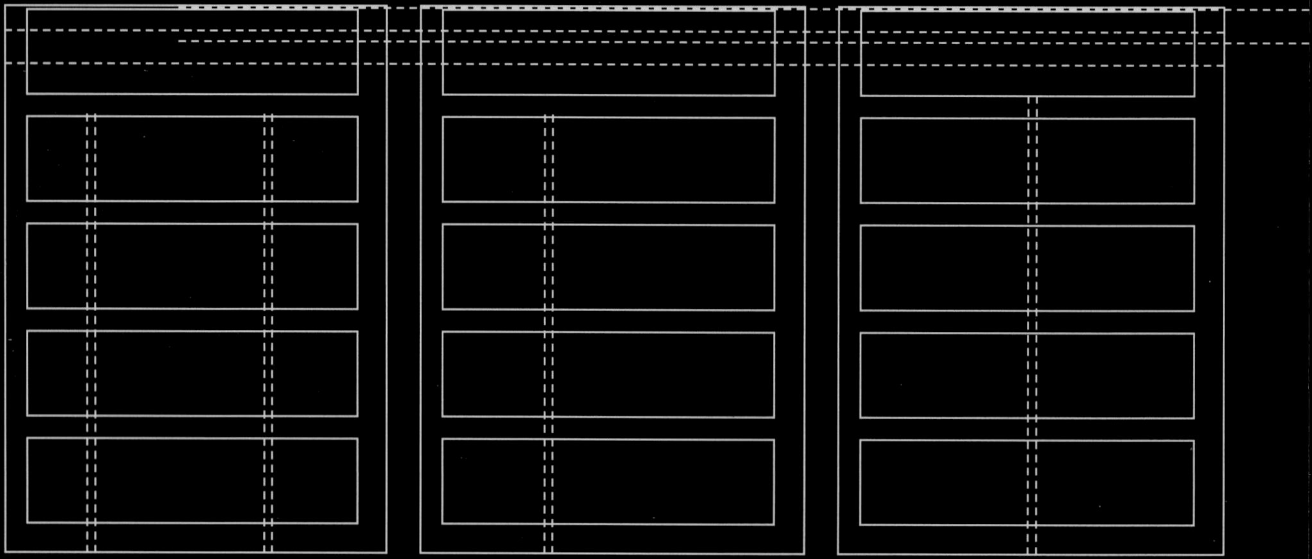

Timely Visits

GARDENS AND NURSERIES TO VISIT IN DECEMBER AND JANUARY

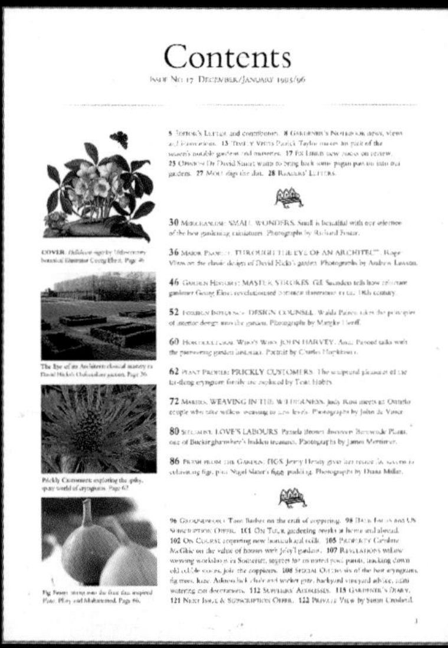

Contents

Gardener's Diary

EVENTS FOR GARDENERS DURING DECEMBER AND JANUARY

BBC *Gardeners' World* appeals to an entirely different part of the spectrum of gardening interests. The designer is faced with an entirely different task, inspired by the readers' awareness that the seasons wait for no one.

But whenever the chance offers, editorial and design staff indulge themselves in a clearly aspirational spread, like the one below. It leavens a magazine heavy on practical information. But check overleaf how urgently the follow-on spread presses its message.

White magic

At this time of year the garden can look quite stunning, thanks largely to the natural resources of frost and sunlight. Rod Ailes explains how planting can be used to capitalise on them and create a winter wonderland

Frost lingers on the fine foliage of ornamental grasses to create a haunting, shadowy landscape

Even fallen leaves look beautiful with a crisp covering of silvery frost

Erica carnea 'Springwood Pink' adds ground-level colour in winter

On the winter solstice, the sun's path within the garden should be religiously mapped

The precisely clipped outline of a group of conifers will be emphasised on a sunny day in winter by low, slanting rays of light to provide a bold display

Dark topiary hedging is a perfect foil for pale stems of deciduous plants

Prunus 'Shōgetsu' forms a striking canopy

Uncluttered by summer foliage, dramatic shapes and shadows dominate the view

Plump rose-hips offer a jaunty touch of colour as long as the birds allow

As the temperatures drop, bergenia leaves turn from green to rich purple

February 1996

February 1996

Room mates

HOUSEPLANTS with Anne Swithinbank

Tips

In recognition of the forces driving the magazine's readers, even the feature pages are on urgent narrow columns, and the pictures spread across the gutter and bleeding off the top pull the reader along urgently. The illustrations bleeding off the corners of the spread are almost superfluous, so strongly does the grid inherited from the rest of the magazine reinforce its message that there is only one right time for every gardening task.

The margins, typefaces and leading are all also inspired by news-magazine practice. The single unintegrated, jarring note is the sans serif drop cap, which does not suit the photographs and thus the magazine. But the sans works brilliantly, in a less presumptuous weight, in the pull-quotes. Considering the column width, the pulls are given a good deal of breathing space, which also contributes to their substantial lightening effect.

The designer has made even the service pages centers of excitement. The grid is the same as used elsewhere in the magazine, as shown right, though it takes a moment to see it!

For the Urmurustan edition of **Gardener's World,** which Urmurustani face should the BBC designers choose to lead the magazine with?

Actually these are the familiar faces Times Ten, Braggadocio and Gill Sans Bold flipped both horizontally and vertically. It is a good tip for evaluating fonts. Which character shapes, rendered meaningless, still speak the language of the message to be conveyed in the design.

In fact, the BBC chose for the flag (the title) a font from an entirely different family, the Egyptienne or slab serif, which includes Rockwell and Clarendon. It is a compromise between the lushly curvaceous old- and modern-style serif faces and an out-and-out contemporary sans. A face like Baskerville totally lacks the urgency the editorial staff and designer sought. But a sans may on the news-stand appear too technical or clinical to some of the magazine's audience.

In this particular case, there is an additional environmental consideration. The first wholesale use of a sans was on the London Underground, for whom in 1912 Edward Johnson designed the face on which Gill Sans is in part based. Most buyers of the magazine are commuters of one kind or another, who constantly see sans faces on the motorway and the railway, and therefore associate them with work rather than relaxation.

If considerations such as these, clearly external to the design itself, will influence the design, say through a desire that the title font should be carried on the inside of the magazine, the designer must discover the circumstances early, as designing the grid means that the font size and column width must be decided together during the initial planning.

The tender touch

Tender perennials will transform containers and pots with their dazzling displays. Sue Fisher selects some essential additions for the garden

The arrival of tender perennials on the gardening scene has revolutionised summer containers and seasonal plantings. These diverse and beautiful plants have been the subject of an enormous surge of interest that has swept them from the realm of connoisseur gardeners and specialist nurseries to the forefront of modern gardening. Plants such as bidens, brachyscome, diascia, osteospermum and scaevola have quickly become top favourites, and there are many more waiting to be discovered.

They are frequently sold as patio or hanging basket plants. The catch-all name tender perennials refers to the fact that they tolerate little or no frost. In this respect they are similar to traditional bedding plants but, instead of lasting just one year, they can be overwintered in a frost-free place for an instant display next spring.

Furthermore, most plants are easy to propagate from cuttings taken in mid to late summer. So even if you don't have somewhere to overwinter large plants, such as a greenhouse, it's always possible to find window-sill space for a few potted cuttings to keep your stock going from year to year.

The attributes of tender perennials are so considerable that it is a mystery to me that they have stayed on the fringe for so long. Their flowers are enormously varied in both shape and colour, and produced from late spring or early summer right up until the first frosts. Foliage is usually handsome too, ensuring an interesting display from the moment of planting. Plant habit ranges from tall and bushy to prostrate and trailing, providing a choice of varieties to create tiered planting effects.

Tender perennials generally come from warmer countries such as the southern United States, Mexico and South Africa, which is why they need a sunny site and a fairly well-drained soil for top performance. They really come into their own during hot, dry summers like the one last year, putting on a magnificent show

▶ A dark corner comes to life with the creative use of trailing tender perennials. Yellow bidens, blue convolvulus and pink *Verbena* 'Sissinghurst' add bright colours and enhance the selection of ornamental pots and containers.

▼ A stunning focal point can be created in the garden by packing argyranthemums and pelargoniums around an ornamental shrub like this red leaved *Phormium tenax*.

▲ Climbing plants like this large leaved abutilon often have all their foliage and flowers at the top of the plant, leaving a bare base below. With the careful positioning of a tall container, planted with *Arctotis* 'Flame' at the front, the whole scene is revitalised and the full beauty of the climbing abutilon is realised.

▼ Old stone garden sinks a… filled with small alpines but look how impressive the lig… saucer-like flowers of *Conv… sabatius* appear billowing o… sink in large mounds. Other perennials you could use in … same way are osteospermu… bidens and even daisy-like f…

Choice tender perennials

Arctotis
Formerly known as X *Venidioarctotis*. Spectacular plants with large, vividly coloured flowers in shades of orange, red and yellow, borne on long stems above silvery foliage. Propagate by seed or cuttings in autumn or spring. Height from 30-45cm (12-18 in).

Argyranthemum
(Marguerites) Tall plants that bear many daisy-like flowers above a mass of feathery foliage. Both single and double forms are available in a range of colours including white, peach, pink and yellow. Grows to a minimum height of 38cm (15in).

Convolvulus
Produces saucer-like flowers above a mass of delicate foliage, which provides additional interest. Both single and double forms are available in a wide range of colours including white, peach, pink and yellow. Minimum height 38cm (15in).

Verbena
Superb for ha… baskets and containers wi… trailing stems with large he… starry flowers. Many hybrids available in c… including whi… pink, blue, pu… and red. Heig… 30cm (12in), up to 45cm (1…

70 Gardeners' World | February 1996

February 1996 | Gardeners' W…

Cataloging a limitless product

When a catalog is aimed at informing or persuading designers themselves, the grid must be especially sound and at the same time flexible enough to permit versatility. Designers using such a catalog will give it special scrutiny as a design, and will to some extent judge the utility of the product or service offered by the quality of the catalog design.

When the product itself is a form of art, as in the case of stock photography or electronic 'clip art', the requirements are even more stringent: the display case can nowhere be less fine than the contents.

PhotoDisc of Seattle sell stock photography on CD-ROM. Their range is huge and grows constantly. They have three catalogs: the general sales catalog, shown here, which is likely to be the first contact of the prospective customer with PhotoDisc and which contains only samples; the printed complete catalog of over 10,000 photographs, which must be exhaustive; the CD-ROM version of the complete catalog, which must also be exhaustive.

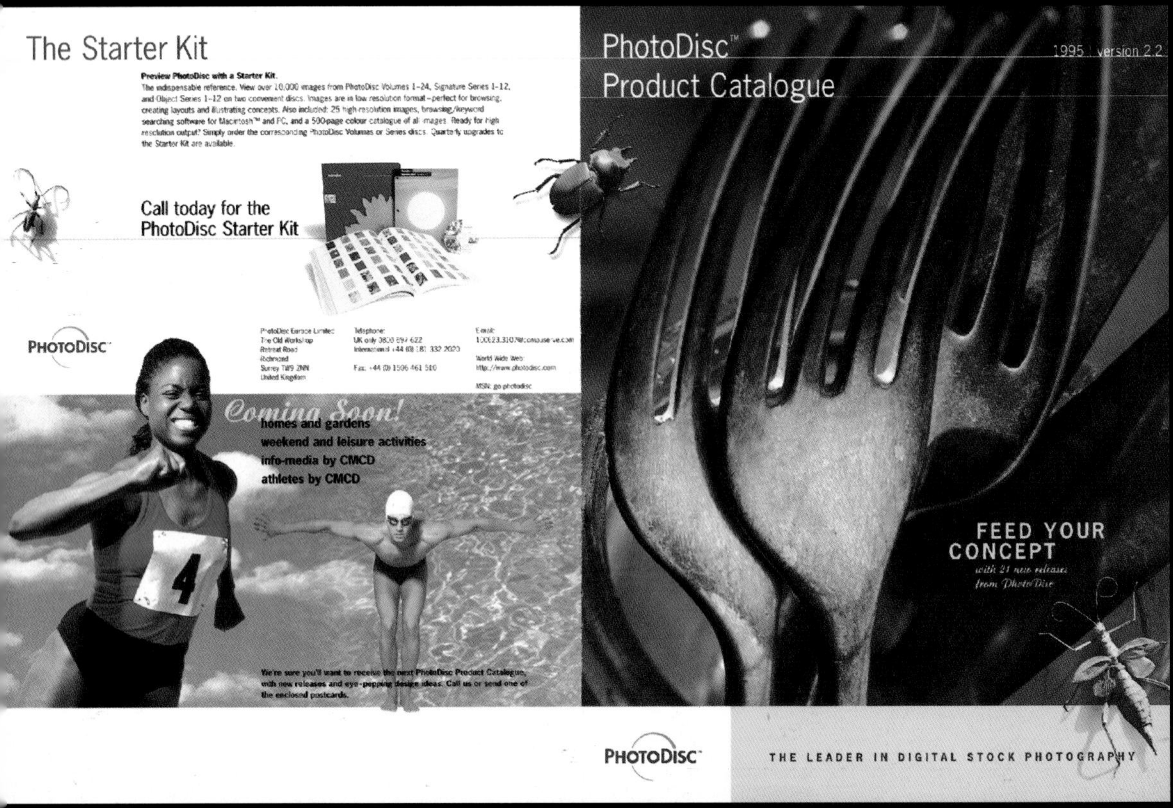

The covers of the catalog use a much simplified version of the elemental internal grid. Note the position of the insect bottom right of the cover.

The basic building block of the PhotoDisc catalog is two linked rectangles, opposite, one for illustration and one for text. The depth of the rectangles varies, the size of the illustrations within the larger rectangle also varies, and the typography subtly links the sections and pages.

Most innovative of all, the underlying unity of the design is imprinted on the mind of the reader by the device of setting the elements of the smaller rectangle to a constant narrower width than the illustrative rectangle but centered to the larger rectangle. This consistency makes the one exception, bottom right and overleaf, all the more striking.

The resulting effect of three margin widths on the side of the page – from top to bottom narrow, wider and none – is to add motion. That alone, even without any other felicitous touches, is enough to raise this design by Dan Saimo to the status of an examplar.

New!

European Landmarks and Travel

file size 10mb | images 33[illegible] | volume 22

Breathtaking architecture, points of historical significance and centres of culture. These are places you don't want to miss when traveling on the European continent and in the United Kingdom, photographed in simple, beautiful compositions.

New!

Far Eastern Business and Culture

file size 10mb | images 336 | volume 23

Major cities and ports in Japan, Korea, China, Hong Kong, Taiwan, Malaysia and Singapore. Images feature people at work in manufacturing, transportation, business and finance. The collection is highlighted by Asia's skylines, landmarks and cultural details.

28/29 PHOTODISC VOLUMES

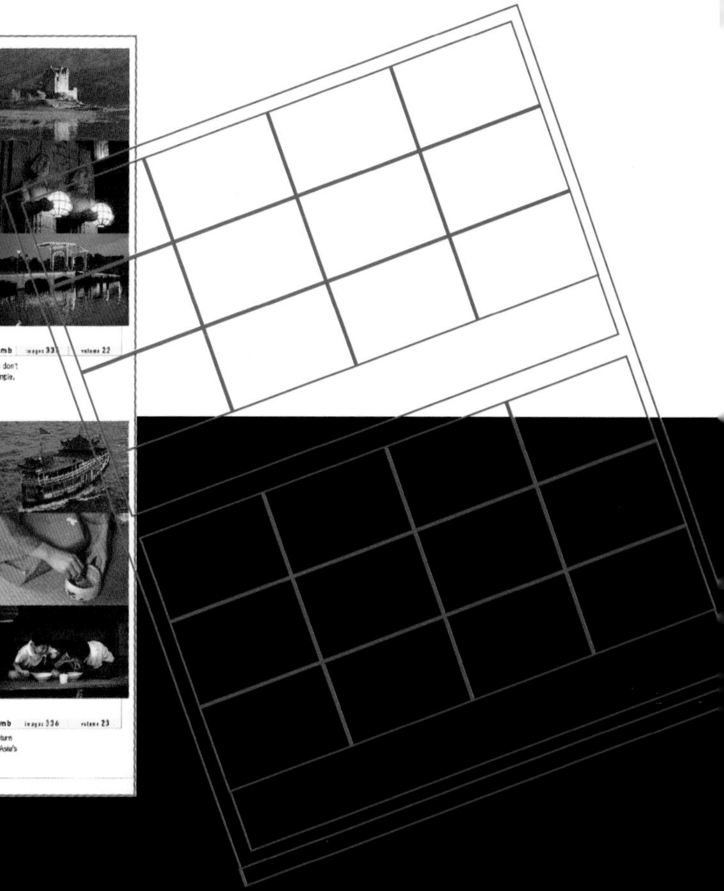

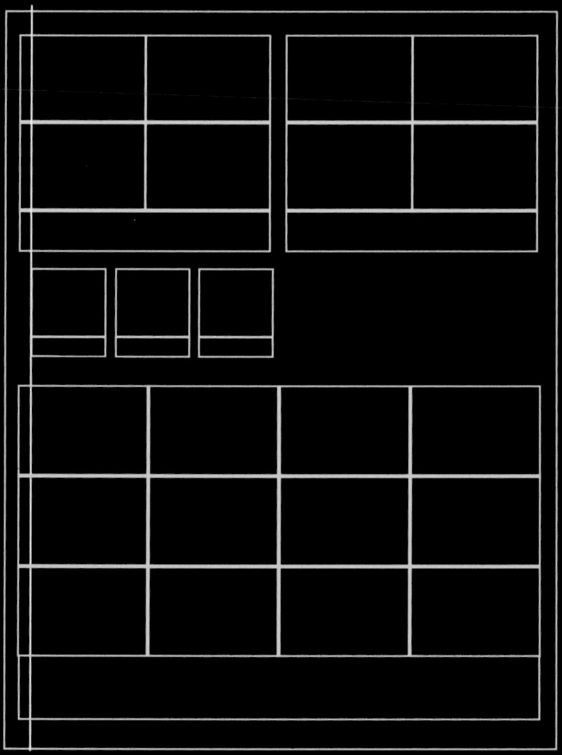

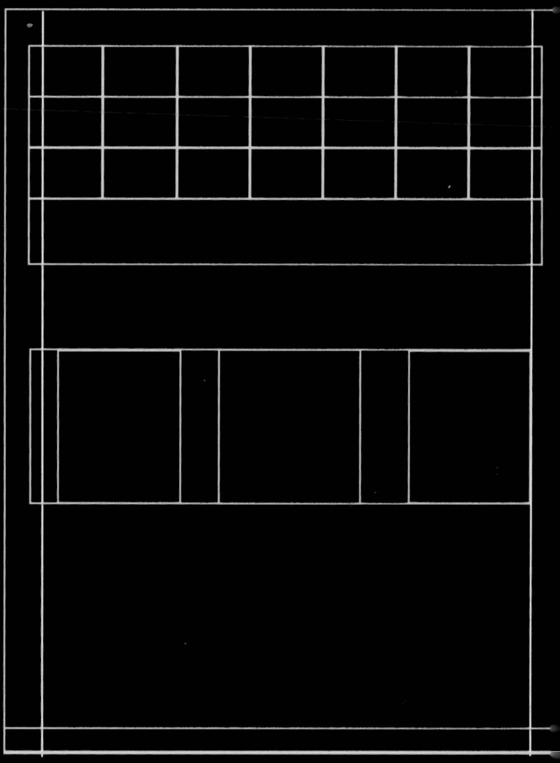

Service information as white space

The most precious commodity in a catalog is white space. In a sales catalog that means showing either a small sample of products or using small illustrations. Dan Saimo, PhotoDisc's art director, chose the 'sample' method for his catalog. He further limited the number of samples strictly in order to protect the space required for other functions such as service information.

This in turn allows the designer to make a feature of service and secondary promotional material, rather than shuffling it out of sight.

Thus the grid, which for any other audience should be as transparent as a crystal goblet, is made a decorative element in its own right by the training and expectations of the target market: graphic designers.

Notice how mirrored grid design turns showthrough into a design feature, above.

This catalog is a stunning example of how service and cross-referencing information, instead of being banished to the back, can be used actively to maximize and protect the white space without which the product itself will not be sufficiently highlighted to appear attractive.

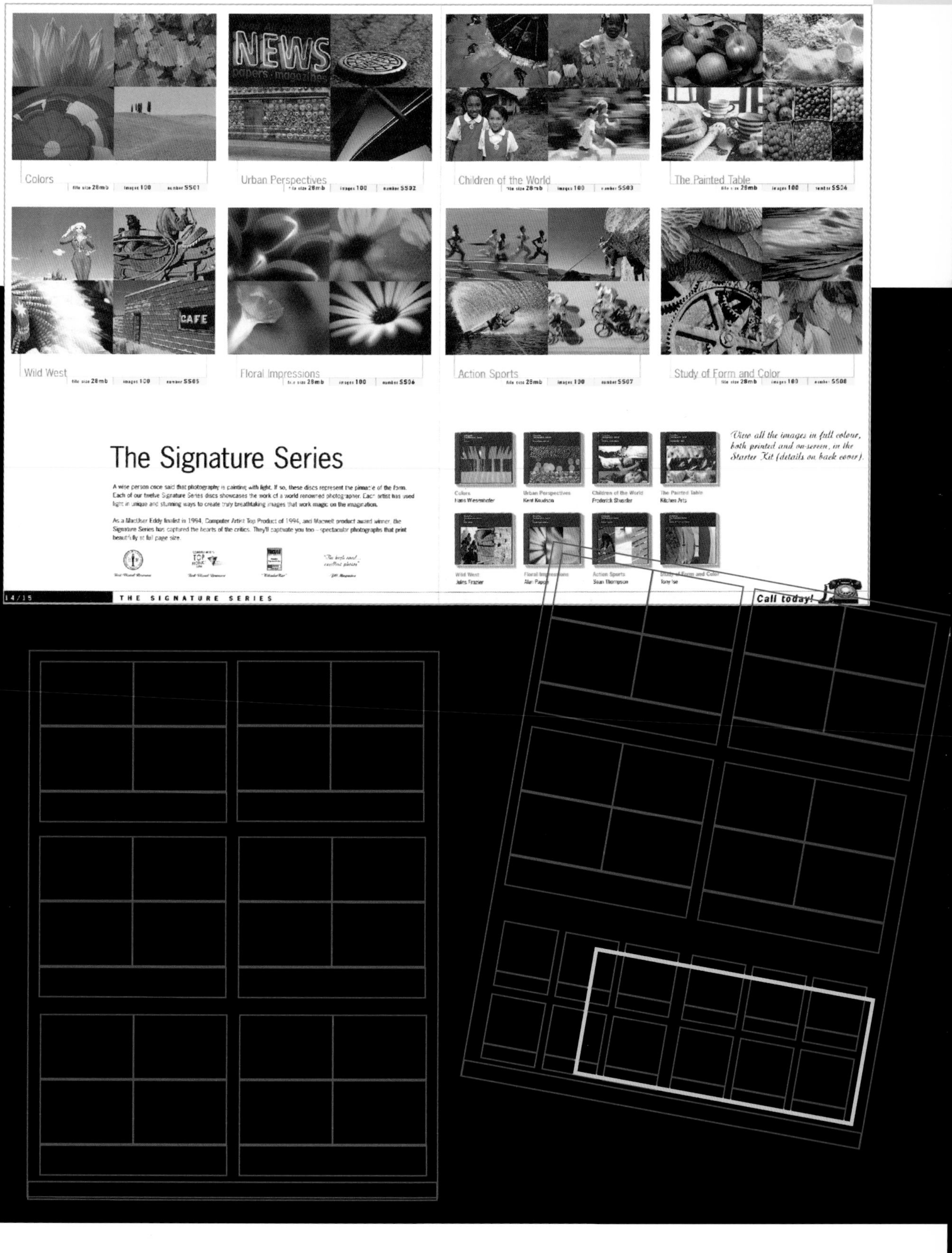

Colors
file size 28mb | images 100 | number SS01
Urban Perspectives
file size 28mb | images 100 | number SS02
Children of the World
file size 28mb | images 100 | number SS03
The Painted Table
file size 28mb | images 100 | number SS04
Wild West
file size 28mb | images 100 | number SS05
Floral Impressions
file size 28mb | images 100 | number SS06
Action Sports
file size 28mb | images 100 | number SS07
Study of Form and Color
file size 28mb | images 100 | number SS08
The Signature Series
A wise person once said that photography is painting with light. If so, these discs represent the pinnacle of the form. Each of our twelve Signature Series discs showcases the work of a world renowned photographer. Each artist has used light in unique and stunning ways to create truly breathtaking images that work magic on the imagination.
As a MacUser Eddy finalist in 1994, Computer Artist Top Product of 1994, and Macwelt product award winner, the Signature Series has captured the hearts of the critics. They'll captivate you too – spectacular photographs that print beautifully at full page size.
Colors
Hans Wesenhofer
Urban Perspectives
Kent Knudson
Children of the World
Frederick Shussler
The Painted Table
Kitchen Arts
Wild West
Jules Frazier
Floral Impressions
Alan Pap
Action Sports
Sean Thompson
Study of Form and Color
Tony Ise
View all the images in full colour, both printed and on-screen, in the Starter Kit (details on back cover).
Call today!
14/15
THE SIGNATURE SERIES

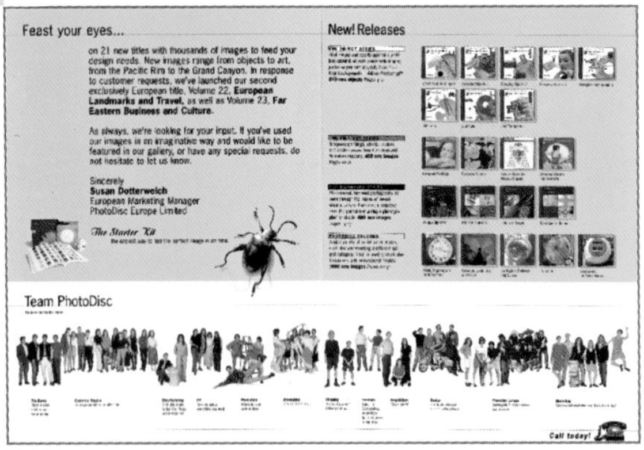

Left, another spread from the PhotoDisc catalog. Below, the covers and spreads from the next issue of the catalog, showing that the existing grid was deliberately developed to maintain a family resemblance while creating fresh excitement.

Opposite, a page from the printed catalog of the contents of one CD-ROM of stock art. Here the purpose is not selling but information about appearance and format, and the grid is therefore much simpler.

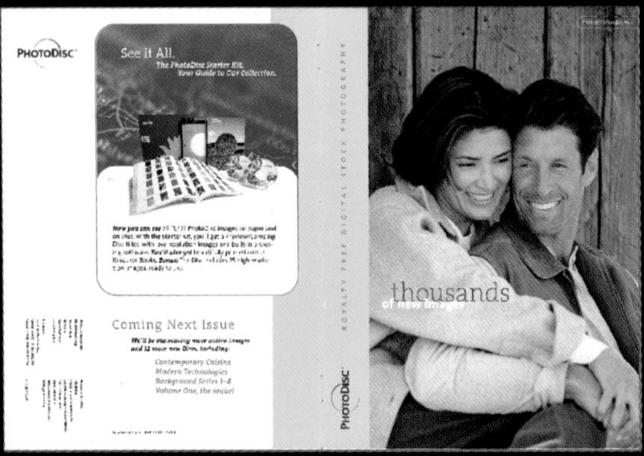

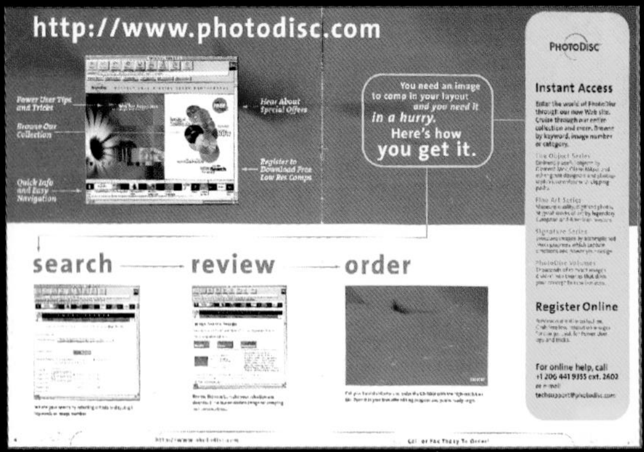

FA01051

FA01052

FA01053

FA01054

FA01055

FA01056

FA01057

FA01058

FA01059

FA01060

FA01061

FA01062

FA01063

FA01064

FA01065

FA01066

FA01067

FA01068

FA01069

FA01070

FA01071

FA01072

FA01073

FA01074

FA01075

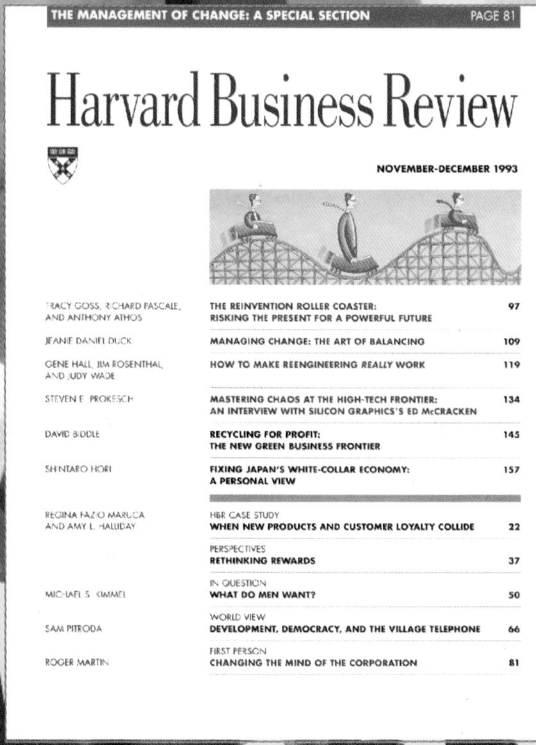

THE MANAGEMENT OF CHANGE: A SPECIAL SECTION PAGE 81

Harvard Business Review

NOVEMBER-DECEMBER 1993

TRACY GOSS, RICHARD PASCALE, AND ANTHONY ATHOS	**THE REINVENTION ROLLER COASTER: RISKING THE PRESENT FOR A POWERFUL FUTURE**	97
JEANIE DANIEL DUCK	**MANAGING CHANGE: THE ART OF BALANCING**	109
GENE HALL, JIM ROSENTHAL, AND JUDY WADE	**HOW TO MAKE REENGINEERING *REALLY* WORK**	119
STEVEN E. PROKESCH	**MASTERING CHAOS AT THE HIGH-TECH FRONTIER: AN INTERVIEW WITH SILICON GRAPHICS'S ED McCRACKEN**	134
DAVID BIDDLE	**RECYCLING FOR PROFIT: THE NEW GREEN BUSINESS FRONTIER**	145
SHINTARO HORI	**FIXING JAPAN'S WHITE-COLLAR ECONOMY: A PERSONAL VIEW**	157
REGINA FAZIO MARUCA AND AMY L. HALLIDAY	HBR CASE STUDY **WHEN NEW PRODUCTS AND CUSTOMER LOYALTY COLLIDE**	22
	PERSPECTIVES **RETHINKING REWARDS**	37
MICHAEL S. KIMMEL	IN QUESTION **WHAT DO MEN WANT?**	50
SAM PITRODA	WORLD VIEW **DEVELOPMENT, DEMOCRACY, AND THE VILLAGE TELEPHONE**	66
ROGER MARTIN	FIRST PERSON **CHANGING THE MIND OF THE CORPORATION**	81

WIRED
December 1994
Hacker
Showdown

NEW
MacPower
premiere issue › december
europe's leading creative guide for the macintosh plus cd-rom
interactive
page to screen
and beyond
multimedia ›› video ››
publishing ›› 3D ›› interactive
graphics ›› CD ›› Web
audio ›› design ›› typography

WIRED
The Million MHz CPU
By Charles Platt
March 1995
Turner Entertainment CEO:
Workplace spying is getting worse
LIVE
COURT
Steven Brill and
his Court TV
Delivering Justice on the Electronic Frontier...

JUNE 17, 1996 | TIME | VOL. 147 NO. 25

THE WEEKLY NEWSMAGAZINE

Look at Him Now: On a platform of promises, Yeltsin surges in the polls (*see* EUROPE)

Under the Influence: Who are the 25 most influential Americans? (*see* COVER)

Homecoming: Football returns to Wembley as England hosts Euro 96 (*see* SOCIETY)

SPECIAL REPORT

COVER: The 25 Most Influential People in America 20
Unlike beauty, influence is more than beheld; it emanates and must be absorbed, inhaled, inspired, inspirited. And while defining influence and setting its bounds may be nearly impossible, demonstrating its existence is not. Here are examples of people who wield it in the U.S.

THE 25: Profiles of Influence 22
They range in age from 31 to 67; some are worth tens of millions, others make do on a teacher's salary. What these people share is the ability to show us the world anew, to make us laugh and cry, to change the ways we think about ourselves and others

POWER: Now for the Folks in the U.S. with Clout 44
Why Bill Clinton, Alan Greenspan, Rupert Murdoch and Bill Gates didn't make the TIME 25. They're on the Power List

EUROPE

NATO: Stepping Out of the American Shadow 48
A flexible new structure lets Europeans police their own backyard without having the U.S. call the shots

RUSSIA: The Yeltsin Surge 50
Back from a near-death political experience, he's ahead in many polls and likely to face Zyuganov in a runoff

The Voters: Four ordinary Russians speak

BUSINESS

BANKING: France's Floundering Moneylenders 53
The worst may be over, but they still face ruinous competition

LABOR: Suffer the Little Children 54
American critics of the pursuit of cheap labor in the Third World have discovered new lightning rods for their cause: first Kathie Lee Gifford, now Michael Jordan

SCIENCE

MEDICINE: How Dangerous Is Oral Sex? 57
The risk of transmitting AIDS is high—in monkeys

ARCHAEOLOGY: The World's Oldest Wine 57
Scientists find a vintage dating to at least 5000 B.C.

SOCIETY

FOOTBALL FRENZY: Euro 96 Kicks Off 58
As a billion viewers tune in worldwide, the game returns to its birthplace—England—for a footloose European championship

THE ARTS

CINEMA: With four movies due out this year, actress Liv Tyler, a card-carrying adolescent, is the '90s "It" girl 60
BOOKS: A scientist's take on prehistoric potboilers
J.F.K. and Nixon had more in common than you'd think
Martin Cruz Smith's latest mystery is a period piece
SHOW BUSINESS: John Grisham wants Oliver Stone to pay for movie-inspired mayhem French synchronized swimmers used the Holocaust as theme

TRAVELER'S ADVISORY 4
LETTERS 6
NOTEBOOK 13
MILESTONES 17
SIGHTINGS 71
PEOPLE 72

THE MANAGEMENT OF CHANGE: A SPECIAL SECTION — PAGE 81

Harvard Business Review

NOVEMBER-DECEMBER 1993

TRACY GOSS, RICHARD PASCALE, AND ANTHONY ATHOS	THE REINVENTION ROLLER COASTER: RISKING THE PRESENT FOR A POWERFUL FUTURE	97
JEANIE DANIEL DUCK	MANAGING CHANGE: THE ART OF BALANCING	109
GENE HALL, JIM ROSENTHAL, AND JUDY WADE	HOW TO MAKE REENGINEERING *REALLY* WORK	119
STEVEN E. PROKESCH	MASTERING CHAOS AT THE HIGH-TECH FRONTIER: AN INTERVIEW WITH SILICON GRAPHICS'S ED McCRACKEN	134
DAVID BIDDLE	RECYCLING FOR PROFIT: THE NEW GREEN BUSINESS FRONTIER	145
SHINTARO HORI	FIXING JAPAN'S WHITE-COLLAR ECONOMY: A PERSONAL VIEW	157
REGINA FAZIO MARUCA AND AMY L. HALLIDAY	HBR CASE STUDY: WHEN NEW PRODUCTS AND CUSTOMER LOYALTY COLLIDE	22
	PERSPECTIVES: RETHINKING REWARDS	37
MICHAEL S. KIMMEL	IN QUESTION: WHAT DO MEN WANT?	50
SAM PITRODA	WORLD VIEW: DEVELOPMENT, DEMOCRACY, AND THE VILLAGE TELEPHONE	66
ROGER MARTIN	FIRST PERSON: CHANGING THE MIND OF THE CORPORATION	81

The ***Harvard Business Review*** (and many other professional journals) is in such a hurry to tell its audience what is important that the contents list is placed on the cover. ***Time*** magazine offers the contents and a brief summary placed for near-instant access.

But the trendier glossy magazines in the multimedia trade, right, pretend that their readers have the space and leisure for expansive introductions. It's a pretty conceit, opposite. But, as we shall see on the following spreads, their designers know that in fact their readers have quite as much need for instant, ranked, graded information.

It is only at the front end that these magazines would look very different to a Martian. In the final analysis the fact that they are intended for a readership who must keep up with the news and trends to survive will cause their main sections to be designed within very much the same parameters. Notice that as early as the contents listing, considerations of communicative power guide the grids of these magazines as much as in their more explicitly conservative counterparts.

...and teasers

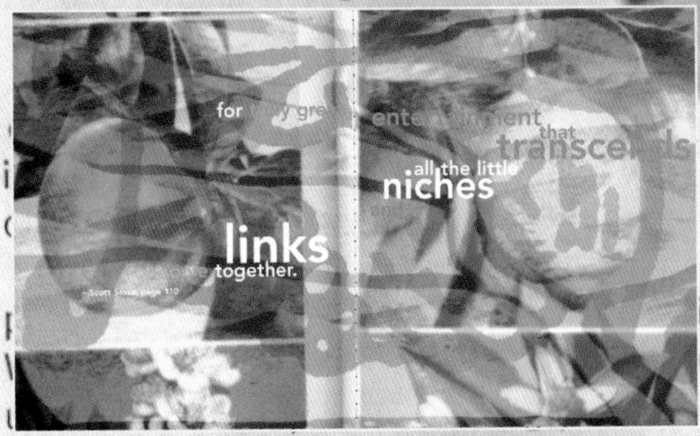

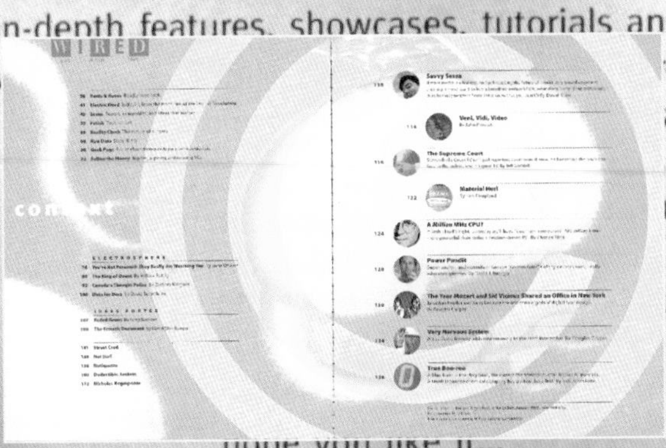

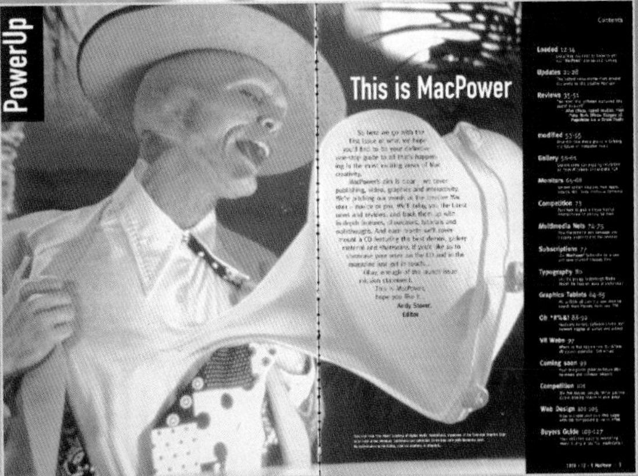

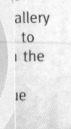

So here we go with the
news and reviews, and back them up with
Andy Storer,
Editor

NOTEBOOK

DISPATCHES

By JAY BRANEGAN, *in Brussels*

Fie on the Chococrats

NOT FAR FROM THE BELGIAN ROYAL PALACE, THE SMALL SHOP called Mary, with its soft blue carpeting, Louis XVI furniture and careful lighting, has the feel of an elegant jewelry store or perhaps an art gallery. It is an appropriate setting for Mary's artistic, jewel-like wares: fine Belgian chocolates—many say the finest in a country where chocolate is taken very seriously. Mary is one of the last chocolatiers to make all its delicacies on the premises—simple bars with nuts, truffles and, of course, the famous Belgian bonbons known as pralines. The shop's more than 70 different types of pralines are filled with everything from caramel to Cointreau to hazelnut paste. Founded in 1919 and serving its fourth generation of clients, including the royal court, Mary, despite its renown among free-spending chocoholics, has no other branches or stores. "We want to maintain control of the quality," says co-owner Fanny Lamberty.

Just across town, in the headquarters of the European Commission, the Eurocrats have a rather different priority: commerce. At the bidding of the large industrial candymakers, they have approved a regulation allowing chocolate to contain up to 5% non-cocoa vegetable fats in place of genuine but more expensive cocoa butter, a substitution already permitted in seven of the European Union's 15 member states. Belgium, along with France, protested that the change, which awaits final passage by the European Parliament and the Council of Ministers, would hurt cocoa producers in developing nations and give other E.U. countries a competitive edge. "Belgium has a worldwide reputation for the finest and purest chocolate," says Lamberty, who with her husband Jean took over the Mary shop in 1980. If that cachet is lost because the country adopts the new rules, she fears, foreign visitors, who are an important source of business, may stop coming in. "It's sad. They want to standardize the taste of everything."

Where good taste is concerned, Mary's Fanny Lamberty is uncompromising

The original Mary was Marie Delluc, who adopted the *y* to gain an international flavor. She passed the business on to one of her shop clerks, Hélène Landrin, who found in the Lambertys faithful successors to tradition. Jean, with two assistants, makes pralines every morning in the basement atelier, pouring hot liquid chocolate into small molds, toasting his own almonds and whipping his own crème fraîche filling. Such handcrafted care does not come cheap, and at $43 per kg for a standard assortment, sales are slow in these tough times, Fanny admits, "but we're keeping our head above water." She doesn't begrudge the big firms' cost cutting—"It's just a question of money for them"—but no matter what the outcome of the Eurolegislation, Mary will never compromise on ingredients. Says Fanny: "We have to live up to our name." ■

HEALTH REPORT

THE GOOD NEWS

✓ Eat VITAMIN E and stay perky? Studies on mice suggest that the nutrient, which is already thought to ward off cancer and heart disease, may also slow aging of the brain and the immune system.

✓ Anti-inflammatories can damage the lining of the stomach. Now, however, ARTHRITIS patients who use anti-inflammatories like naproxen, ketoprofen and ibuprofen can halve their chances of getting an ulcer if they also take famotidine, a drug that reduces stomach acid.

✓ Antibiotics may help the COMMON COLD. Although doctors usually discourage their use because most colds are caused by viruses, which antibiotics can't kill, a Swiss study finds that 20% of cold sufferers also harbor bacterial infections.

THE BAD NEWS

✓ Women who undergo surgery for BREAST CANCER during the latter phase of the menstrual cycle—days 14 to 30—rather than during the first part of the cycle appear twice as likely to suffer a recurrence of the cancer, researchers have discovered.

✓ Cyclists who sport HELMETS can still take it on the chin. A study of bicycle-accident victims brought to emergency rooms showed that helmets decreased by 65% the risk of injury from the forehead down to the nose but did nothing to prevent injury to the rest of the face.

✓ Arkansas is AMERICA'S LEAST HEALTHY STATE, with Louisiana a close second, according to a survey that weighed factors like infant mortality, childhood immunizations and smoking.

16 TIME, JUNE 17, 1996

NOTEBOOK

VERBATIM

"I am disturbed by the noise because I walked through the ultimate silence."

—*Choi Jong-yul, South Korean adventurer believed to be the first to cross the Sahara on foot from west to east, upon concluding his seven-month trek*

"Maybe the U.S. regrets that it formed a security alliance with such a partner."

—*Hiroshi Kurogane, Japanese cartoonist, on Japan's accidental shooting down of a U.S. warplane during joint training*

"The whole intellectual fabric of a large portion of the population is being dulled. With the lack of iodine, the brain just does not wire correctly."

—*Glen Maberly, U.S. professor, in an interview with the New York Times, on recent estimates that iodine shortages have caused more than 10 million cases of retardation in China*

"For peace one must remember, as a bird cannot fly with one wing, as a man cannot applaud with one hand, so a country cannot make peace just with one side, with itself."

—*Former Prime Minister Shimon Peres, in his first public appearance after losing Israel's elections*

IN THE SPOTLIGHT: *Russian President Boris Yeltsin gets ready to rumble with Gennadi Zyuganov, leader of the resurgent Communist Party, in an election that pits an imperfect and often corrupt capitalism against nostalgia for Stalinist glories*

FROM THE WORLD'S HEADLINES

As Israel's Prime Minister-elect BENJAMIN NETANYAHU *chose his Cabinet, the bitter distrust of Arabs and the skepticism of the rest of the world persisted*

AL-ASHARQ AL-AWSAT, SAUDI ARABIA: "Tragedies bring families together, and the tragedy Arabs are facing is the Israeli people's choice of extremism at a time when the peace process looked fragile."

AKHBAR EL YOM, EGYPT: "The Israeli elections have shown the Israelis for what they really are. Israel is not a state but a military camp, and the Israelis are a professional army division that cannot tolerate peace."

JERUSALEM POST, ISRAEL: "Netanyahu's challenge is to convince the West that hope for peace lies in transforming the region's regimes into democracies, not in appeasing its tyrants."

NEW YORK TIMES, U.S.: "Benjamin Netanyahu's leadership will be judged by how well he balances the expectations of the Israelis who elected him with the hopes of those who voted for Shimon Peres."

TIME, JUNE 17, 1996 13

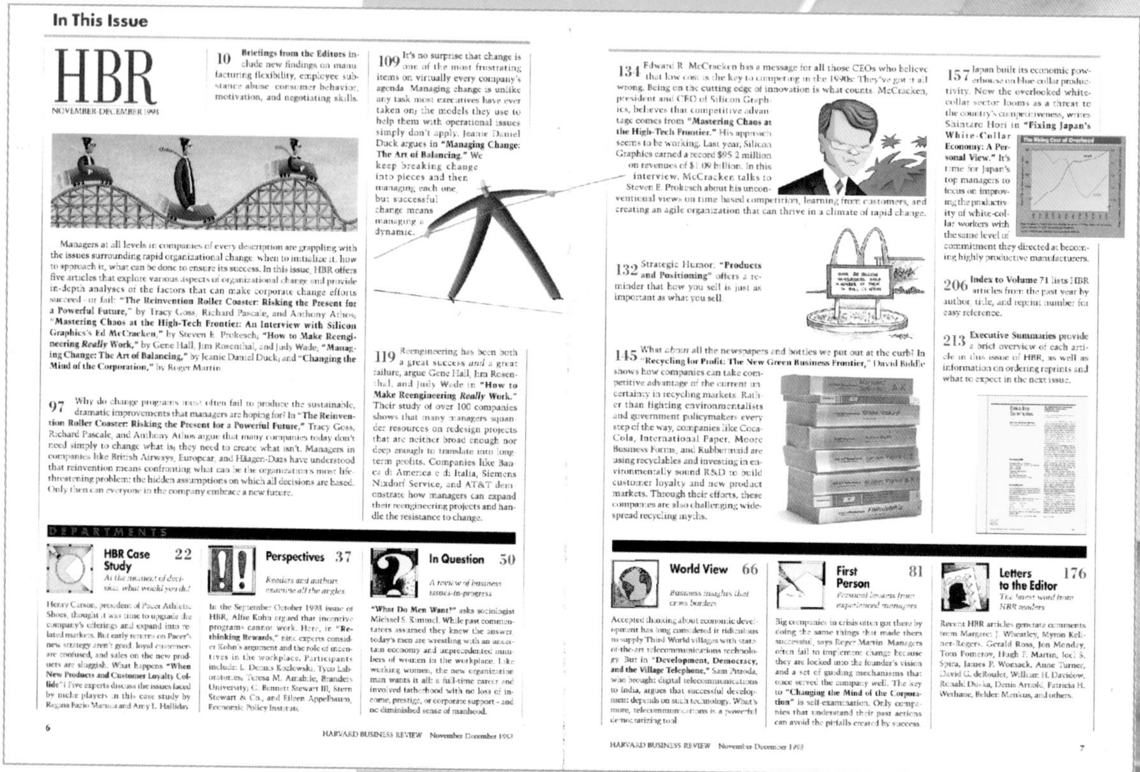

In This Issue

HBR

NOVEMBER-DECEMBER 1993

Managers at all levels in companies of every description are grappling with the issues surrounding rapid organizational change: when to initialize it, how to approach it, what can be done to ensure its success. In this issue, HBR offers five articles that explore various aspects of organizational change and provide in-depth analyses of the factors that can make corporate change efforts succeed – or fail: **"The Reinvention Roller Coaster: Risking the Present for a Powerful Future,"** by Tracy Goss, Richard Pascale, and Anthony Athos; **"Mastering Chaos at the High-Tech Frontier: An Interview with Silicon Graphics's Ed McCracken,"** by Steven E. Prokesch; **"How to Make Reengineering *Really* Work,"** by Gene Hall, Jim Rosenthal, and Judy Wade; **"Managing Change: The Art of Balancing,"** by Jeanie Daniel Duck; and **"Changing the Mind of the Corporation,"** by Roger Martin.

10 **Briefings from the Editors** include new findings on manufacturing flexibility, employee substance abuse, consumer behavior, motivation, and negotiating skills.

97 Why do change programs most often fail to produce the sustainable, dramatic improvements that managers are hoping for? In **"The Reinvention Roller Coaster: Risking the Present for a Powerful Future,"** Tracy Goss, Richard Pascale, and Anthony Athos argue that many companies today don't need simply to change what is; they need to create what isn't. Managers in companies like British Airways, Europcar, and Häagen-Dazs have understood that reinvention means confronting what can be the organization's most life-threatening problem: the hidden assumptions on which all decisions are based. Only then can everyone in the company embrace a new future.

109 It's no surprise that change is one of the most frustrating items on virtually every company's agenda. Managing change is unlike any task most executives have ever taken on; the models they use to help them with operational issues simply don't apply. Jeanie Daniel Duck argues in **"Managing Change: The Art of Balancing."** We keep breaking change into pieces and then managing each one, but successful change means managing a dynamic.

119 Reengineering has been both a great success *and* a great failure, argue Gene Hall, Jim Rosenthal, and Judy Wade in **"How to Make Reengineering *Really* Work."** Their study of over 100 companies shows that many managers squander resources on redesign projects that are neither broad enough nor deep enough to translate into long-term profits. Companies like Banca di America e di Italia, Siemens Nixdorf Service, and AT&T demonstrate how managers can expand their reengineering projects and handle the resistance to change.

134 Edward R. McCracken has a message for all those CEOs who believe that low cost is the key to competing in the 1990s: They've got it all wrong. Being on the cutting edge of innovation is what counts. McCracken, president and CEO of Silicon Graphics, believes that competitive advantage comes from **"Mastering Chaos at the High-Tech Frontier."** His approach seems to be working. Last year, Silicon Graphics earned a record $95.2 million on revenues of $1.09 billion. In this interview, McCracken talks to Steven E. Prokesch about his unconventional views on time-based competition, learning from customers, and creating an agile organization that can thrive in a climate of rapid change.

132 Strategic Humor: **"Products and Positioning"** offers a reminder that how you sell is just as important as what you sell.

145 What *about* all the newspapers and bottles we put out at the curb? In **"Recycling for Profit: The New Green Business Frontier,"** David Biddle shows how companies can take competitive advantage of the current uncertainty in recycling markets. Rather than fighting environmentalists and government policymakers every step of the way, companies like Coca-Cola, International Paper, Moore Business Forms, and Rubbermaid are using recyclables and investing in environmentally sound R&D to build customer loyalty and new product markets. Through their efforts, these companies are also challenging widespread recycling myths.

157 Japan built its economic powerhouse on blue-collar productivity. Now the overlooked white-collar sector looms as a threat to the country's competitiveness, writes Shintaro Hori in **"Fixing Japan's White-Collar Economy: A Personal View."** It's time for Japan's top managers to focus on improving the productivity of white-collar workers with the same level of commitment they directed at becoming highly productive manufacturers.

206 **Index to Volume 71** lists HBR articles from the past year by author, title, and reprint number for easy reference.

213 **Executive Summaries** provide a brief overview of each article in this issue of HBR, as well as information on ordering reprints and what to expect in the next issue.

DEPARTMENTS

HBR Case Study 22

At the moment of decision, what would you do?

Henry Carson, president of Pacer Athletic Shoes, thought it was time to upgrade the company's offerings and expand into related markets. But early returns on Pacer's new strategy aren't good, loyal customers are confused, and sales on the new products are sluggish. What happens **"When New Products and Customer Loyalty Collide"**? Five experts discuss the issues faced by niche players in this case study by Regina Fazio Maruca and Amy L. Halliday.

Perspectives 37

Readers and authors examine all the angles

In the September-October 1993 issue of HBR, Alfie Kohn argued that incentive programs cannot work. Here, in **"Rethinking Rewards,"** nine experts consider Kohn's argument and the role of incentives in the workplace. Participants include: L. Dennis Kozlowski, Tyco Laboratories; Teresa M. Amabile, Brandeis University; G. Bennett Stewart III, Stern Stewart & Co.; and Eileen Appelbaum, Economic Policy Institute.

In Question 50

A review of business issues-in-progress

"What Do Men Want?" asks sociologist Michael S. Kimmel. While past commentators assumed they knew the answer, today's men are wrestling with an uncertain economy and unprecedented numbers of women in the workplace. Like working women, the new organization man wants it all: a full-time career and involved fatherhood with no loss of income, prestige, or corporate support – and no diminished sense of manhood.

World View 66

Business insights that cross borders

Accepted thinking about economic development has long considered it ridiculous to supply Third World villages with state-of-the-art telecommunications technology. But in **"Development, Democracy, and the Village Telephone,"** Sam Pitroda, who brought digital telecommunications to India, argues that successful development depends on such technology. What's more, telecommunications is a powerful democratizing tool.

First Person 81

Personal lessons from experienced managers

Big companies in crisis often got there by doing the same things that made them successful, says Roger Martin. Managers often fail to implement change because they are locked into the founder's vision and a set of guiding mechanisms that once served the company well. The key to **"Changing the Mind of the Corporation"** is self-examination. Only companies that understand their past actions can avoid the pitfalls created by success.

Letters to the Editor 176

The latest word from HBR readers

Recent HBR articles generate comments from Margaret J. Wheatley, Myron Kellner-Rogers, Gerald Ross, Jon Monday, Tom Pomeroy, Hugh F. Martin, Joel S. Spira, James P. Womack, Anne Turner, David G. deRoulet, William H. Davidow, Ronald Duska, Denis Arnold, Patricia H. Werhane, Belden Menkus, and others.

6 HARVARD BUSINESS REVIEW November-December 1993

HARVARD BUSINESS REVIEW November-December 1993 7

The pages that guide the reader around the magazine, and to the short takes and service pages, are the key to most magazines. In any magazine for professionals they are the pages which set the tone for the entire magazine. On this spread and the next we also show a few advertising pages; a wise designer, new to any magazine, assumes that the advertisers would not waste their money with inappropriate ads.

A doctor reads his professional magazine when he can because his time is scheduled by external circumstances. The professional reader of the magazines featured here schedules a given amount of time to reading the magazine. For the practical purposes of the designer, this requires a fixed hierarchy of editorial pre-selection and grading of articles which must be reflected in the design, starting with the grid.

The key spread from the ***HBR*** is gridded and styled like the contents page of one of the more thoughtful news-magazines. This is no accident. It is necessary to grade the articles of the issue for quick evaluation by readers.

The regular columns and features are given great emphasis in very little space across the bottom of the spread; readers will know where to find them and navigation is aided by picons. The variable content is arranged with lead features in the wide column, lending an aura of importance, and others in the narrow column. Within the wide column the illustrations have been scaled to give not only movement but also assist the grading process. The main body concludes with 'Executive Summaries' as the last item, again in a reserved position.

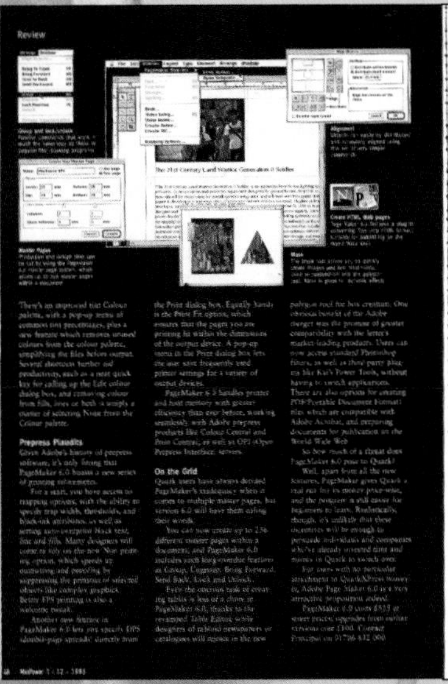

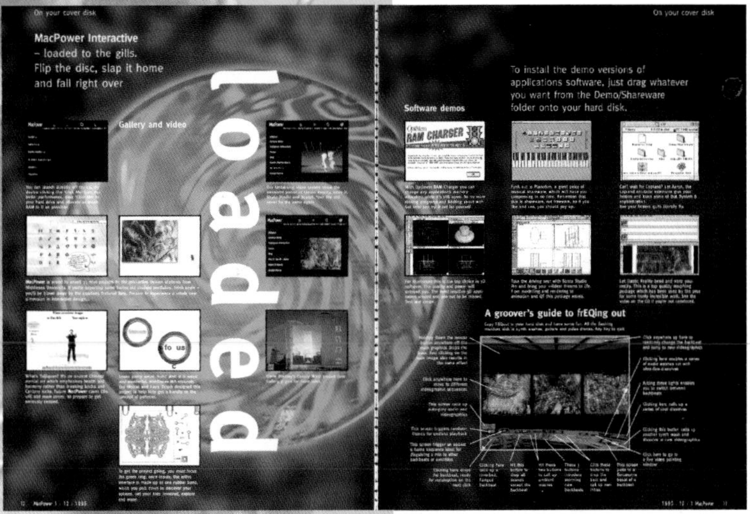

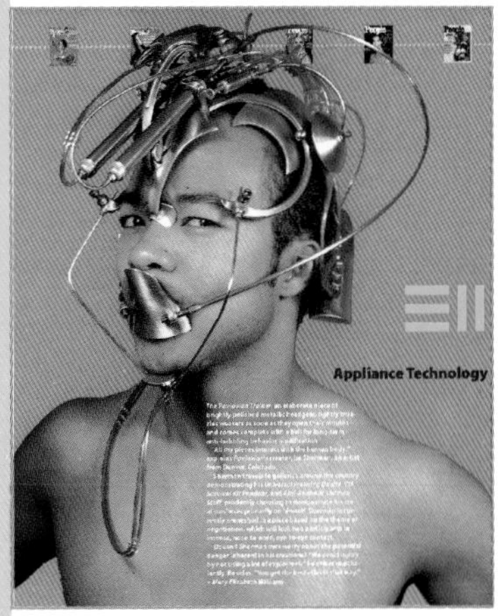

The Pavlovian Trainer, **an elaborate piece of brightly polished metallic headgear, tightly muz-**

P E O P L E

By EMILY MITCHELL

Summer Studies

While on a 1953 summer program at Harvard, **JACQUES CHIRAC**, then 20, was a waiter at a local restaurant. There, as biographers record, he fell for a "Southern belle." Her identity was unknown to the public until now, when the magazine *Paris Match* followed a magnolia trail to Columbia, South Carolina, and discovered **FLORENCE HERLIHY**. She fondly remembers how they tooled about in a white Cadillac. He called the 18-year-old beauty *"Ma chérie"*; she called him "Honey Chile." She introduced the future President to "American life, hamburgers and music"; he taught her how to kiss. Chirac wanted to marry, but their parents intervened and the sweethearts parted. Divorced after a 37-year marriage to a Navy officer, the gracious grandmother of two has just sent Chirac a note with a recipe for *semoule de maïs*. That's grits, honey chile.

Up-to-Date in Beijing

People tell **WAYHWA**, 32, they liked her better as an anchorwoman. Dismissed for appearing on the U.S. news program *Nightline* during 1989's Tiananmen protests, she streaked her hair and joined a rock group. Last year she changed her name from Wang Weihua. Now she has a solo album, *Modernization*, and says, "I do want to push people, make them think." Uh-oh, there she goes again.

А. Карпов Г. Камский

Yes, but Where's the Real King of Chess?

Two men—ANATOLY KARPOV, 45, and the bespectacled GATA KAMSKY, 22—are duking it out in the ongoing World Chess Federation title face-off. Two other powerful men loom behind every move. Kamsky's father and coach Rustam, who masterminds his son's brilliant career, is on hand for the matches in Elista, capital of the remote Russian republic of Kalmykia. Also hovering but not present is Gary Kasparov, the world's No. 1 player. He defeated Karpov in 1985 and then set up the breakaway Professional Chess Association. Whoever wins, Kasparov will still hold the throne. But Elista's divvied-up $2 million purse should be sweet consolation.

S E E N & H E A R D

For those who were outbid at the auction of Jackie O.'s knickknacks, there's always one of **Elton John's** flashier discards. An AIDS charity benefited from the sale in Atlanta of 4,000 shiny shoes, glitzy glasses and designer concert costumes donated by the pop star. Say, what kind of closets does this man have?

In his upcoming book, *Jack and Jackie: Portrait of an American Marriage*, Christopher Andersen reveals that **Marilyn Monroe** was frisky indeed the evening she sang *Happy Birthday* to J.F.K. At a party for him later that night, Monroe headed for a window to do a striptease for government sharpshooters stationed on a roof nearby. That's patriotism.

72 TIME, JUNE 17, 1996

NOTEBOOK

MILESTONES

TUTU ABIOLA IN 1995 LORENGAR IN 1972 GARFIELD IN 1980

RESIGNED. MESUT YILMAZ, 49, Turkey's Prime Minister, after just three months at the head of a center-right coalition government; in anticipation of a censure motion because the Constitutional Court ruled illegal the vote of confidence that brought him to power, in Ankara. The collapse of Yilmaz's coalition gives the Islamic Refah (Welfare) Party—which won the most seats (158) in Turkey's 550-member parliament last December—an opportunity to form a government. Yilmaz will remain as caretaker Prime Minister until another leader can assemble a coalition.

RETIRED. DESMOND TUTU, 64, South Africa's spiritual guide, whose early and eloquent crusading against apartheid won him the Nobel Prize in 1984; from his post as Archbishop and leader of Southern Africa's Anglican Church; in Cape Town. From the pulpit of St. George's Cathedral, Tutu preached the sins of apartheid—a singular voice during the 1980s, when most other black leaders were jailed. One of the first to call upon other nations to impose economic sanctions against his country's white-minority regime, Tutu warned leaders of newly democratic South Africa a decade later against the "gravy train" of privilege.

MURDERED. KUDIRAT ABIOLA, 44, critic of Nigeria's military junta who campaigned tenaciously for the release of her jailed husband Moshood Abiola, a wealthy businessman widely believed to have won the West African nation's annulled 1993 presidential election; by unknown gunmen who ambushed her car; in Lagos. Mrs. Abiola was scheduled to stand trial on charges relating to her repeated calls for her husband's release. He is serving his 24th month in prison for treason and may not have been notified of his senior wife's assassination.

DIED. PILAR LORENGAR, 68, Spanish diva whose shimmering soprano gave radiant life to opera's greatest heroines, such as the Countess in Mozart's *The Marriage of Figaro*; of breast cancer; in Berlin. The glory of Lorengar's higher register coupled with her warm stage presence drew fans on both sides of the Atlantic. She was a regular of the Deutsche Oper in Berlin, where she had lived since 1958, and a frequent guest star at New York City's Metropolitan Opera House. Though purists considered her vibrato a trifle uncontrolled and her emotional repertoire somewhat limited, her soaring renditions of Mozart's *Dove Sono* and Federico Mompou's *Cantar del Alma* effectively silenced her detractors.

DIED. LEON GARFIELD, 74, British children's storyteller who peopled his extravagant yarns with plucky orphans, lusty gods and shamelessly outsize villains; in London. A biochemist until age 48, Garfield turned scribe by concocting out of seemingly familiar elements—18th century England, Greek mythology—literary compounds such as *Smith* (1967), a Dickensian tale of a pickpocket who steals a document that becomes his death warrant. Garfield's writing was permeated by a clear humanity, justifying his claim that "one does not write *for* children. One writes so that children can understand."

28 YEARS AGO IN TIME

The R.F.K. Assassination

"[Robert] Kennedy fell ... The gun, waving wildly, kept pumping bullets, and found five other human targets. Eight men in all, including Rafer Johnson, an Olympic champion, and Roosevelt Grier, a 300-lb. Los Angeles Rams football lineman, attempted to overpower the slight but lithe assailant. Johnson finally knocked the pistol out of the stubborn hand [and together with Grier held the suspect] spread-eagled on the counter. Several R.F.K. supporters tried to kill the man with their hands. Johnson and Grier fended them off. Someone had the presence of mind to shout: 'Let's not have another Oswald!' Johnson pocketed the gun ... [S]cores of people pressed in." —June 14, 1968

Cover: First J.F.K., then R.F.K. too

—By Janice M. Horowitz, Nadya Labi and Megan Rutherford

TIME, JUNE 17, 1996 17

BRIEFINGS FROM THE EDITORS

Better use of current failures helps turn red ink to black.

ture as the impetus to overhaul the way in which all ventures were authorized and monitored.

2. *Disappointments get the attention of senior management.* Sometimes projects don't receive the necessary resources until they start sending out distress signals, notes McGrath. Early poor performance in the bank's credit-card venture led to a concentrated effort by experienced employees who had not been involved previously. "The unparalleled quality of focus turned the situation around," she says.

3. *Disappointments can create a perverse motivational effect.* Proponents of an idea will often rally to prove its worth. McGrath cites as an example the reaction to major financial setbacks in the bank's consumer effort. The team in charge became determined to prove the correctness of their vision, and their division is now the most profitable in the bank.

4. *Disappointments can create powerful symbols.* A company's persistence with a venture that is going badly demonstrates its ability to withstand punishment, a symbol that can deter competitors from entering the field. Such disappointments can also serve as strong internal symbols of top management's commitment to stick by its people, McGrath believes.

While any company would prefer black ink to red when a new venture's results come in, managers might ensure more future successes by making better use of current failures. As McGrath says, "You've already paid for the disappointment; you might as well use it."

Motivation

Don't Forget the Middle Manager

"Unsophisticated" is the term Michael Gibbs finds himself using when asked to describe the incentive strategies of large U.S. companies. Gibbs, a visiting assistant professor at the University of Chicago Graduate School of Business, was surprised to find in his recent study that typical incentive structures seem to ignore the motivation of approximately half of middle management, the half that has been passed over for promotion.

Gibbs notes, "This phenomenon becomes of even greater concern as businesses downsize and restructure and are thus less able to use promotion as a source of motivation."

Gibbs looked at two key types of motivation available to large companies: promotion-based motivation and within-job motivation, such as raises, bonuses, and the threat of dismissal. He found promotions to be a primary motivational tool: they were awarded to those with higher performance ratings, and they were critical to salary growth over the long run. Indeed, most managers had roughly zero real salary growth once they stopped moving up the corporate ladder.

Gibbs expected that management would use more within-job incentive pay for such employees, since that group might otherwise be poorly motivated. To the contrary, he found that as a person's tenure in the same job lengthened and thus the chances of promotion diminished, raises and bonuses were smaller and less variable, pay was less sensitive to performance ratings, and the likelihood of leaving the company was no greater than that of a colleague who was moving rapidly down the hall to a corner office. "Pay became less variable and more bureaucratic at the same time that incentives from possible promotion decreased," he explains.

How Promotions Affect Motivation

Before being passed up for promotion, over 30% of managers received the highest performance rating.

Highest (>30%) Lowest (<20%)

After being passed over for five years, less than 20% received the highest rating.

Highest (<20%) Lowest (>30%)

12 HARVARD BUSINESS REVIEW November-December 1993

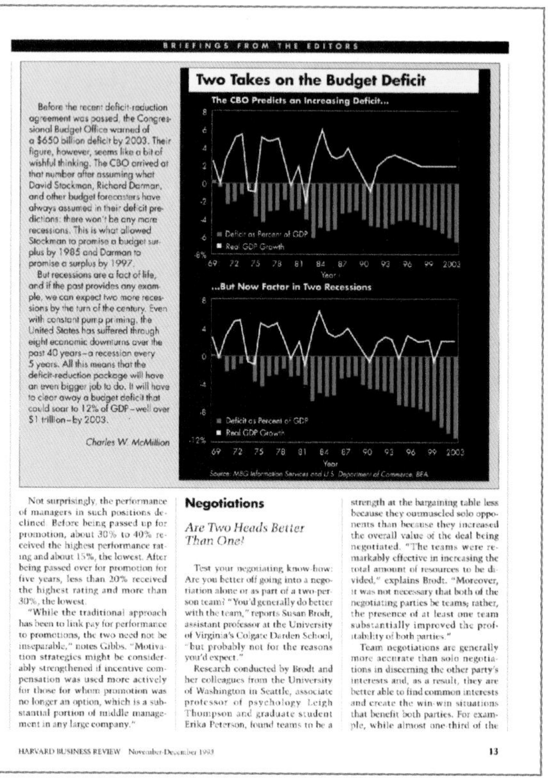

BRIEFINGS FROM THE EDITORS

Before the recent deficit-reduction agreement was passed, the Congressional Budget Office warned of a $650 billion deficit by 2003. Their figure, however, seems like a bit of wishful thinking. The CBO arrived at that number after assuming what David Stockman, Richard Darman, and other budget forecasters have always assumed in their deficit predictions: there won't be any more recessions. This is what allowed Stockman to promise a budget surplus by 1985 and Darman to promise a surplus by 1997.

But recessions are a fact of life, and if the past provides any example, we can expect two more recessions by the turn of the century. Even with constant pump priming, the United States has suffered through eight economic downturns over the past 40 years—a recession every 5 years. All this means that the deficit-reduction package will have an even bigger job to do. It will have to clear away a budget deficit that could soar to 12% of GDP—well over $1 trillion—by 2003.

Charles W. McMillion

Two Takes on the Budget Deficit

The CBO Predicts an Increasing Deficit...

...But Now Factor in Two Recessions

Deficit as Percent of GDP
Real GDP Growth

Year

Source: MBG Information Services and U.S. Department of Commerce, BEA.

Not surprisingly, the performance of managers in such positions declined. Before being passed up for promotion, about 30% to 40% received the highest performance rating and about 15%, the lowest. After being passed over for promotion for five years, less than 20% received the highest rating and more than 30%, the lowest.

"While the traditional approach has been to link pay for performance to promotions, the two need not be inseparable," notes Gibbs. "Motivation strategies might be considerably strengthened if incentive compensation was used more actively for those for whom promotion was no longer an option, which is a substantial portion of middle management in any large company."

Negotiations

Are Two Heads Better Than One?

Test your negotiating know-how: Are you better off going into a negotiation alone or as part of a two-person team? "You'd generally do better with the team," reports Susan Brodt, assistant professor at the University of Virginia's Colgate Darden School, "but probably not for the reasons you'd expect."

Research conducted by Brodt and her colleagues from the University of Washington in Seattle, associate professor of psychology Leigh Thompson and graduate student Erika Peterson, found teams to be a strength at the bargaining table less because they outmuscled solo opponents than because they increased the overall value of the deal being negotiated. "The teams were remarkably effective in increasing the total amount of resources to be divided," explains Brodt. "Moreover, it was not necessary that both of the negotiating parties be teams; rather, the presence of at least one team substantially improved the profitability of both parties."

Team negotiations are generally more accurate than solo negotiations in discerning the other party's interests and, as a result, they are better able to find common interests and create the win-win situations that benefit both parties. For example, while almost one-third of the

HARVARD BUSINESS REVIEW November-December 1993 13

Is Microsoft Finally Headed for a Fall?
If Operating Systems Were Airlines
Desktop Diving
The Continuing Investigation of Phil Zimmermann
Pop Culture Overload
the Spam
dictment Thrown Out!
then leverage it into all others, including retail.
This is... computer warehouse
MAC 630
7200 SERIES
A REAL CW MULTIMEDIA BARGAIN!
NEW POWERBOOKS @ CW NOW!!
CHECK OUT THIS GREAT MAC OS COMPATIBLE!

TIME 25
TIME'S 25 MOST INFLUENTIAL AMERICANS
COMPILING A LIST OF THE MOST INFLUENTIAL PEOPLE IN AMERICA, BESIDES BEING A PROVOC-

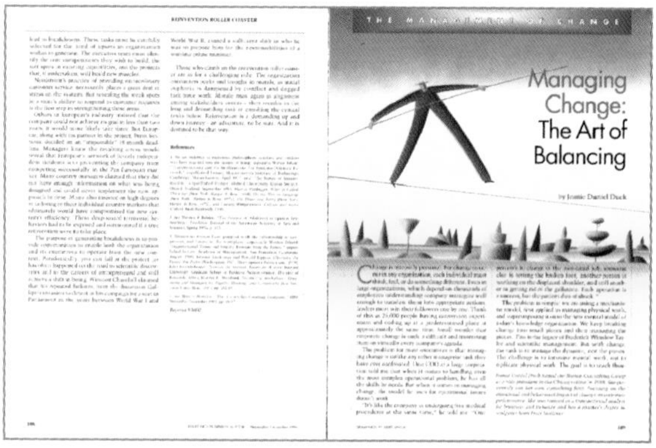
THE MANAGEMENT OF CHANGE
Managing Change: The Art of Balancing

A JOURNEY OF 10,000 MILES BEGINS WITH THE SHOES
TIME 25
NIKE

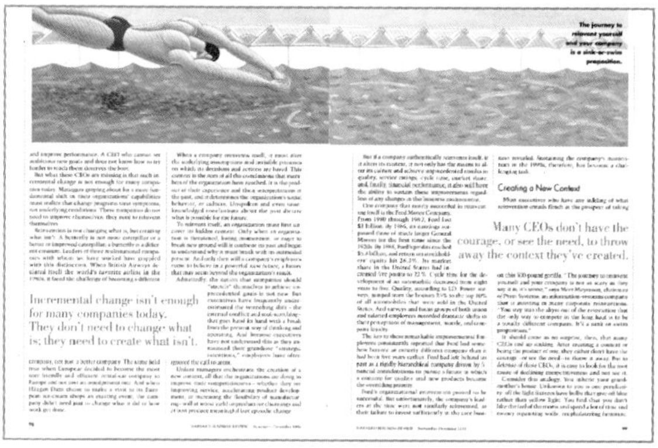
The journey to reinvent yourself and your company is a sink-or-swim proposition.
Incremental change isn't enough for many companies today. They don't need to change what is; they need to create what isn't.
Many CEOs don't have the courage, or see the need, to throw away the context they've created.
Creating a New Context

ONE MAN

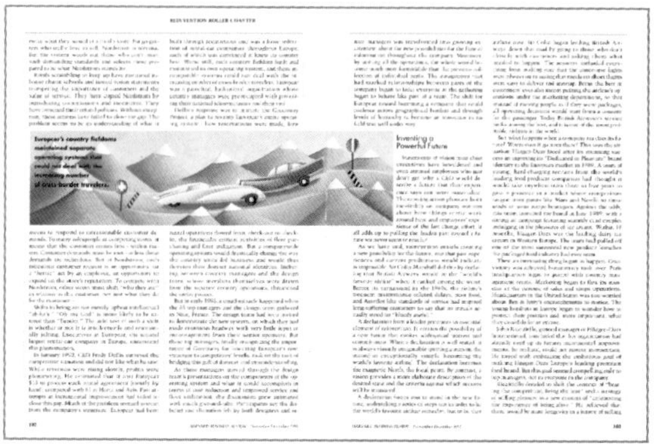
Inventing a Powerful Future

THE MILLION MAN MARCH ASSEMBLED AT FARRAKHAN'S FIERY BECKONING

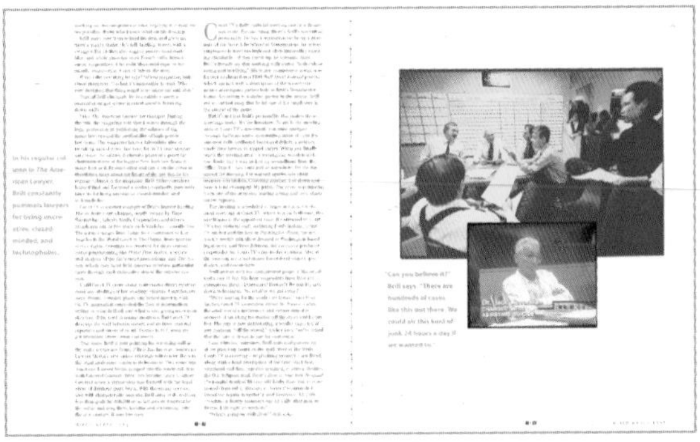

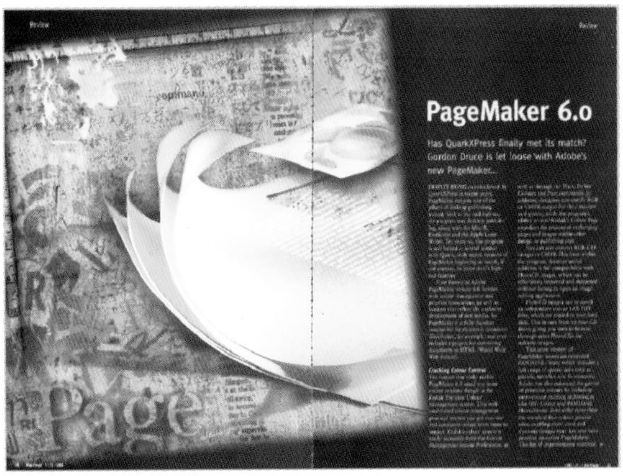

Given that these apparently dissimilar magazines work under very similar restraints of comprehensibility, what is amazing about the spreads on this page is not the similarity of the results but the great variety each set of designers has achieved in working towards almost identical objectives. This observation is reinforced by the articles on the next spread.

Time's grids are tight on white space. As the only weekly, its designer naturally gives it more urgency, a more newspaper-like feel. But the grid's apparent simplicity is deceptive; there is more than enough space and flexibility to give many entertainment magazines a run for their money – as the backdrop enlargement from one of its pages makes only too brilliantly clear, ***Time*** is a sister-magazine of ***Life***, the home of exemplary photography.

But it is the communications industry magazines which, in their feature articles, look almost conservative. ***Wired*** in particular plans swathes of white space into the grid to lend grave importance to their feature articles.

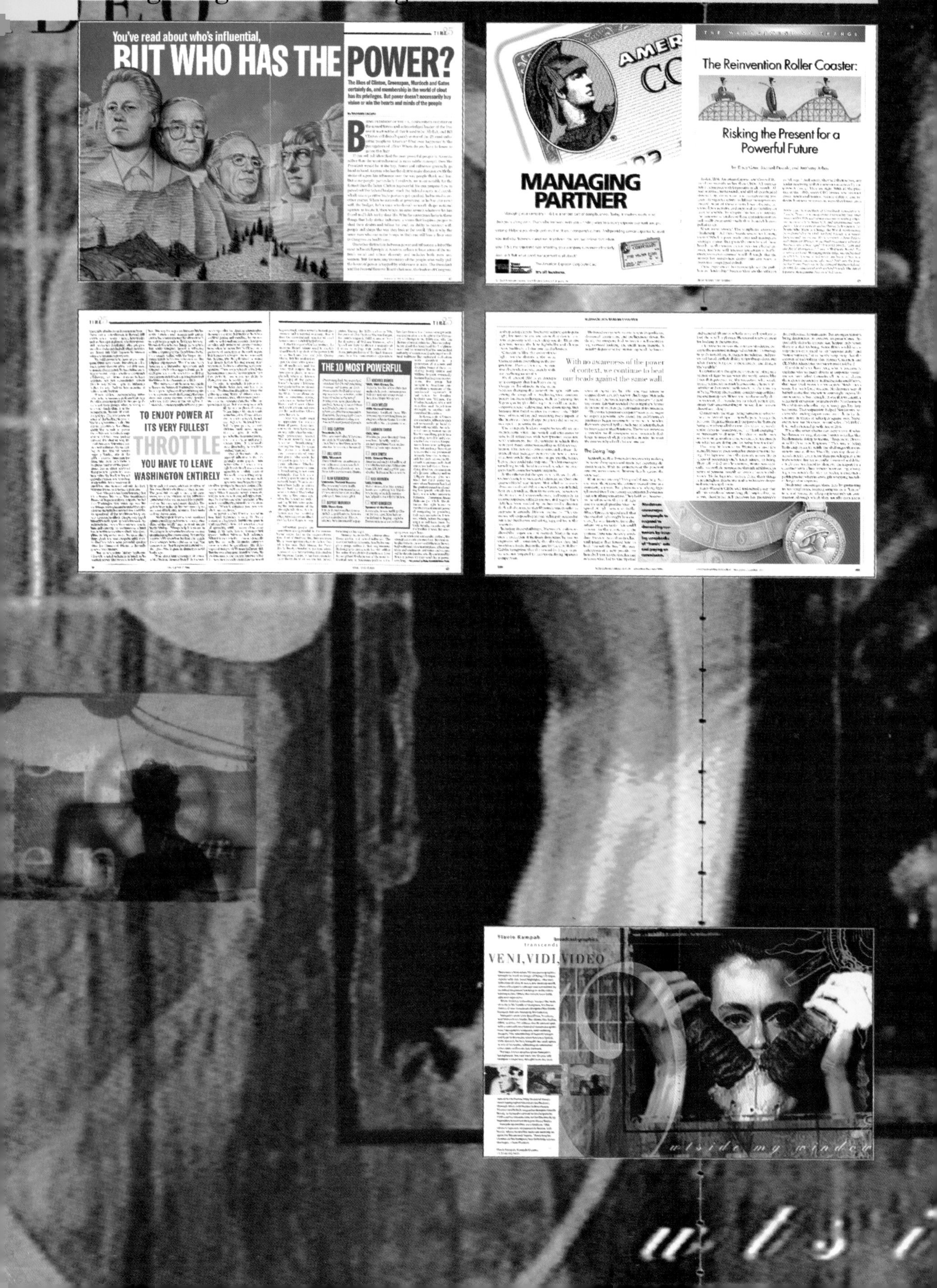

You've read about who's influential,
BUT WHO HAS THE POWER?
The likes of Clinton, Greenspan, Murdoch and Gates certainly do, and membership in the world of clout has its privileges. But power doesn't necessarily buy vision or win the hearts and minds of the people
MANAGING PARTNER
THE MANAGEMENT OF CHANGE
The Reinvention Roller Coaster:
Risking the Present for a Powerful Future
TO ENJOY POWER AT ITS VERY FULLEST
THROTTLE
YOU HAVE TO LEAVE WASHINGTON ENTIRELY
THE 10 MOST POWERFUL
With no awareness of the power of context, we continue to beat our heads against the same wall.
The Giving Trap
VENI, VIDI, VIDEO
outside my window

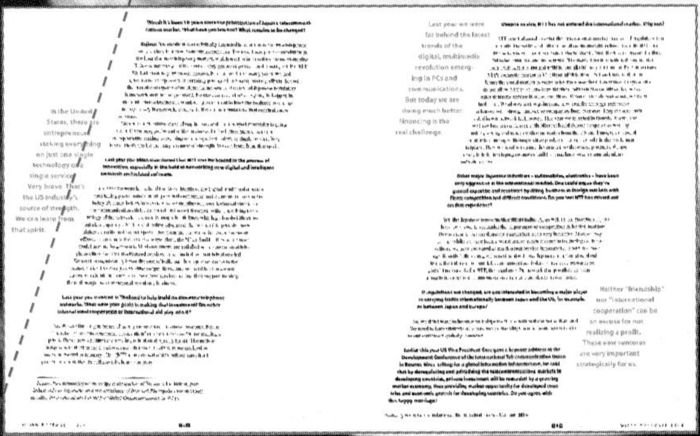

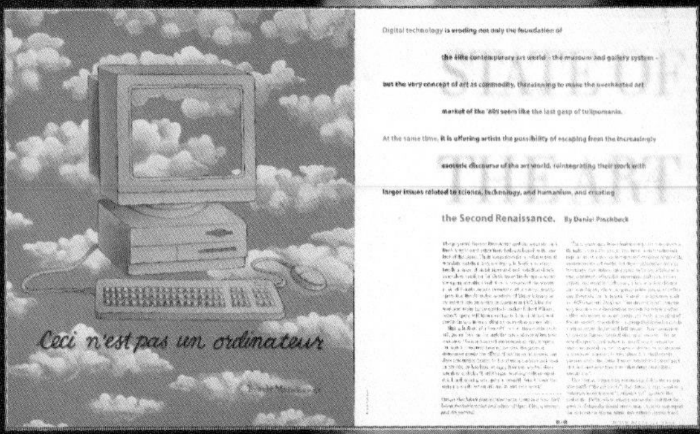

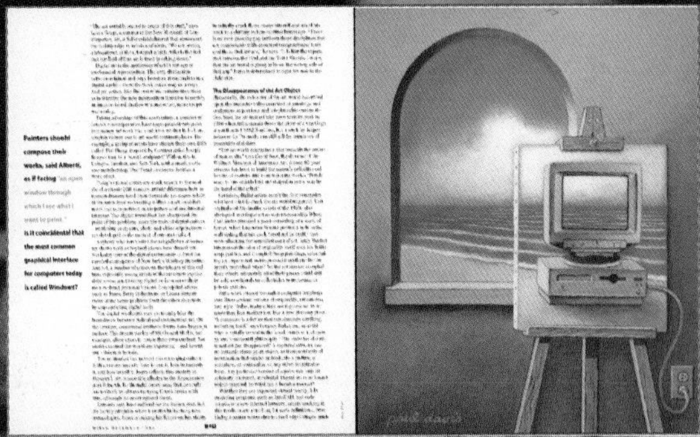

The *Time* designers have linked a much-wordier follow-on article to the main item by using a similar-sized illustration across the spread.

In the *HBR* article, the bar across the top refers back directly to the cover page of the magazine, and its color links to the illustration overleaf which itself links the pages of the continuation spread. It is often a problem in professional-type magazines that relevant photographs – never mind relevant photographs of reproducible quality – are exceedingly hard to come by, but the designers have managed in this magazine to turn that disadvantage into a feature by the consistent use of commissioned illustrations.

The ***Wired*** designers have in one article angled the illustration and then carried the angles of the pillars into the background through to the setting of text and pull-quotes. It works brilliantly. The unillustrated, text-heavy second spread is visually linked by its grid not only to the first page but indelibly to the otherwise unexciting opening illustration. In the second article the computer is a link, but of equal importance is carrying alternate lines of the strapline (the subsidiary headline) into the sidebar space, which is used for pull-quotes on the continuation spread. The grid itself is thus used as a link.

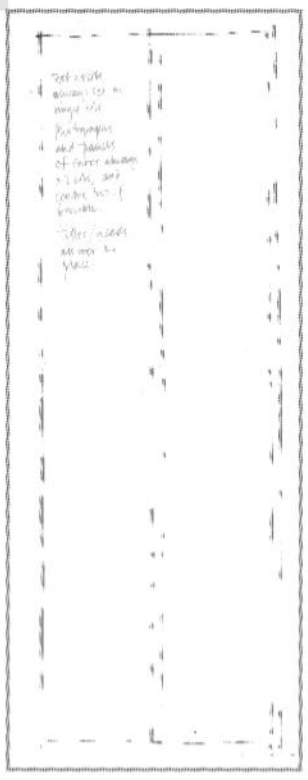

Philip Quested has turned the quick sketch made in the client's office into an art form. He deliberately eschews the computer as too clinical, preferring the individuality of handmade art and layout. Often enough his first sketch, with photocopied arts pasted on, is sent straight to film.

Students, who travel on a budget, would be put off by glossy travel brochures. It is thus unsurprising that the print buyer for several student travel organizations knows the Quested studio number off by heart.

Even his grids, of which three are reproduced here, are first sketched freehand on to tracing paper. 'But,' notes Quested, 'one must still have a grid to organize the masses of necessary information contained in travel promotion literature. Without the grid, one would simply have a mess. Users must absolutely be able to find relevant information predictably and reliably.'

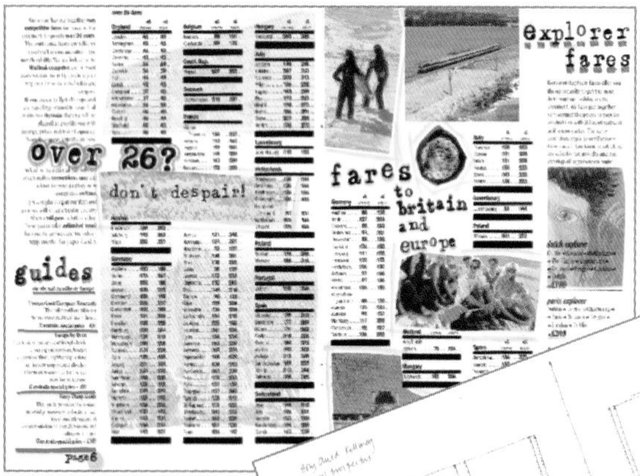

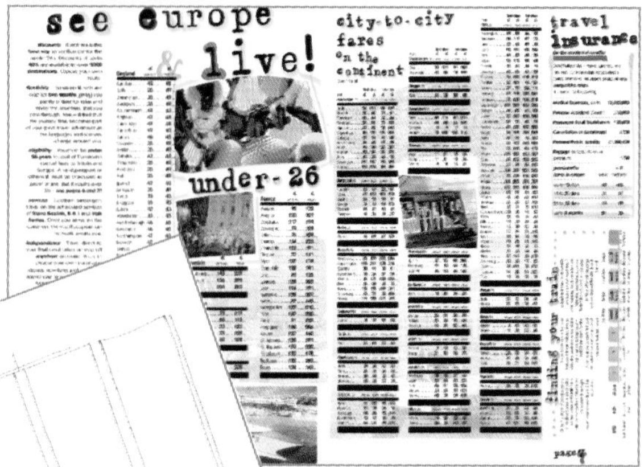

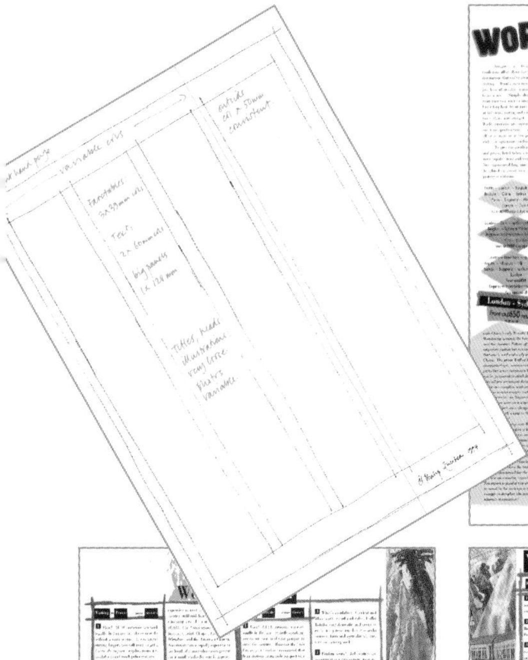

lately? If not, why not?
Long haul packages
Sample winter fares to Faraway Places
London - Sydney
London - Mexico
3

TWO Card TRick
The International Student Identity Card
European Youth Card
Been around the
Destinations with a difference and distance
London - Casablanca
2

Dublin - Brussels
Dublin - Paris
7

Working
Sample winter fares to Europe
Dublin - Brussels, Amsterdam or Paris
6

usit
A break away
Insurance
Christmas cheer
Usit offices
GLOBETROTTER
8

Working
abroad
USA
5

WORKing aBROad
Dublin - New York
Sample winter fares to North America
4

usit
IndePENdENT TRAVeL gUide
Ski '94
Contents
London calling & beyond
Sample winter fares to Britain
GLOBETROTTER

OPS 60-9206
Francesco Landini and the Italian Ars Nova
+ Works by Piero Ghirardelli da Firenze, Jacopo da Bologna and Lorenzo da Firenze
Alla francesca
Vocal and instrumental ensemble

OPS 30-68
Codex Las Huelgas
Motets, proses, tropes, conduits, sequences, organum
Discantus
Female-voice vocal ensemble

OPS 30-79
Russian Orthodox M
Early Russian Plainc
The Russian Patriarch
Choir
Anatoly Grindenko

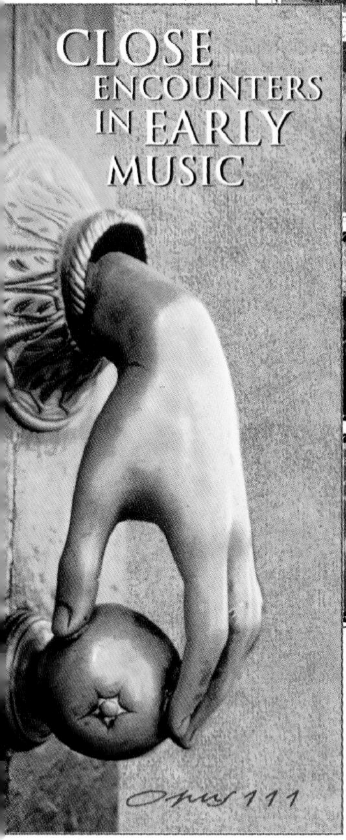

OPS 30-101
Johannes Ciconia
Motets, virelais, ballate, madrigals
Alla francesca + Alta
Vocal and instrumental ensembles

OPS 30-102
Campus Stellae
St Martial de Limoges
Santiago de Compostela
Discantus
Female-voice vocal ensemble

OPS 30-97
Panikhida
17th century
Orthodox Requiem
The Russian Patriarch
Choir
Anatoly Grindenko

OPS 30-131
Llibre Vermell
de Montserrat
Cantigas de Santa Maria
Alla francesca
Vocal and instrumental ensemble

OPS 30-134
Ave Eva
Songs of womanhood from the 12th century
Brigitte Lesne

OPS 30-120
Russian Medieval Ch
The Divine Liturgy
of St John Chrysost
The Russian Patriarch
Choir
Anatoly Grindenko

OPS 30-146
Gautier de Coincy
Les Miracles de Nostre-Dame
Alla francesca
Vocal and instrumental ensemble

OPS 30-143
Eya mater
Chant grégorien & polyphonies des XIᵉ et XIIᵉ siècles
Discantus
Female-voice vocal ensemble

OPS 30-145
Orthodox Easter Litu
The Easter Canon
of St John Damasce
The Russian Patriarch
Choir
Anatoly Grindenko

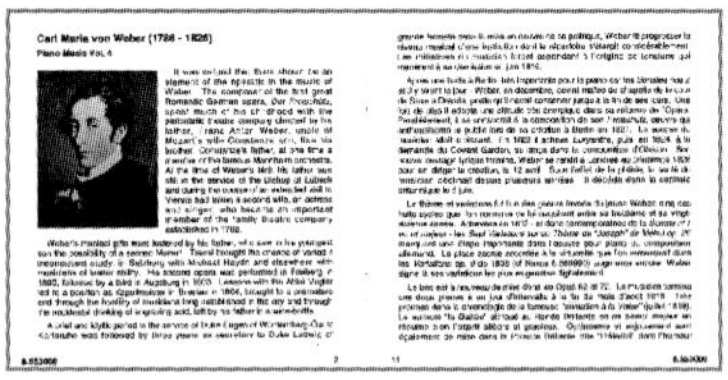

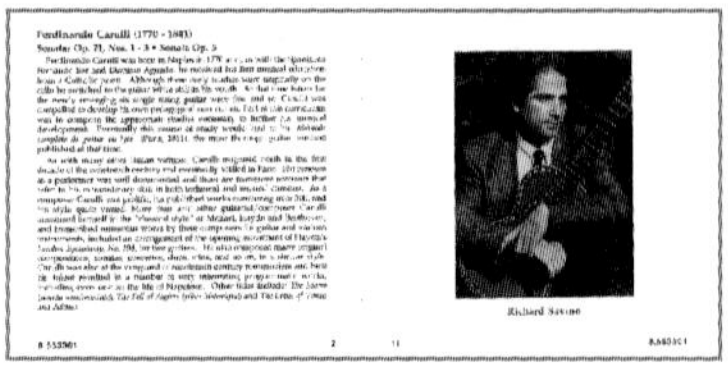

The Naxos covers, right, seem almost wilfully to disregard the possible excitements, but their iterated simplicity hammers their corporate image home from shelf after shelf. It is difficult not to conclude that Naxos' continuing loyalty to their flexible, ultra-simple grid has contributed largely to building an obscure cut-price label into a great recording house. That their designers apparently have no personality is apt: it is the crystal goblet in action.

A uniformly square product: selling music

Huge reputations have been made in designing for the music business, and a steady stream of distinguished or otherwise good design originates in the promotion of recorded music. In addition its management is long accustomed to giving the young and untried a chance: it is axiomatic to them that their business depends on discovering new talent.

Here we ask not which grids will win prizes, but which work, and continue working by selling records, establishing artists and, above all, labels.

Music promotion offers a rich kaleidoscope of different media. They include leaflets, opposite top; disc covers, opposite bottom, which are an exercise in packaging; extended text setting for 'liner notes', shown with the Naxos covers; prestigious booklets, second column left; even postcards, left, used as reminders to dealers, reviewers and as economical up-market give-aways to favored customers; catalogs, overleaf; and folders for publicity material, also overleaf.

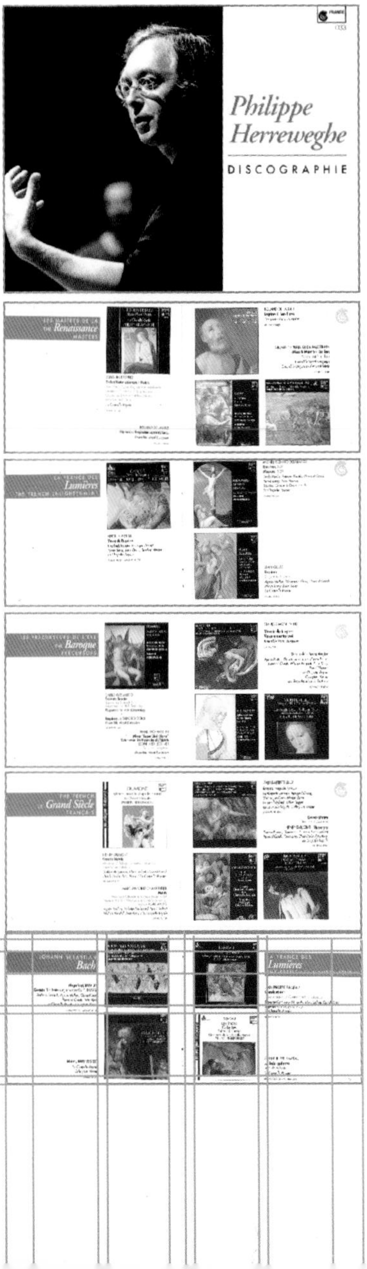

Grids are generally so simple that they may be grasped at a glance. That is to be expected when the square format of the product is considered. It is a challenge for the innovative designer. Asymmetrical layouts are one solution, bottom left.

The booklet cover could be improved by flipping the photograph to look into the opening side. But many people, and especially performers, resent having their photographs flipped and many designers avoid complaints by not doing it.

It is not difficult to see why the music business attracts so many fine designers. Not only are the challenges of all those little square products an exciting inducement, the opportunities for working with high-class materials are endless.

On the folder, below left, overlook for the moment the richness of the art and presentation which the subject material supports. Look behind the clever font combinations. Then we see a standard three-column grid, with each column divided in half, and two pieces of text shifted left the width of the column divider, all to make a certain flow possible in the layout. Its front and back covers are on a four-column grid with centerlines.

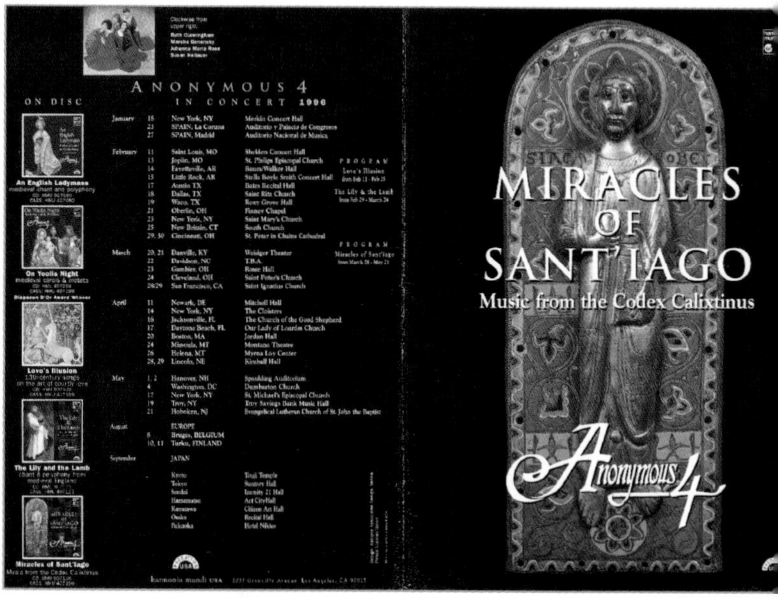

International Distribution
Collins Classics
COLLINS CLASSICS
96
Exploration and Excellence

Collins Classics
February 1996 releases
Witness

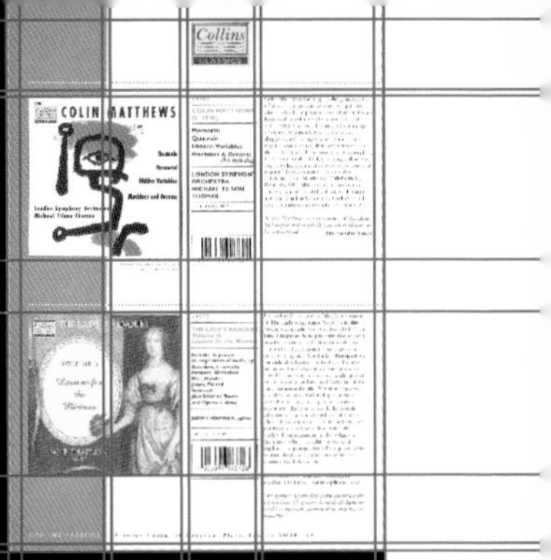
Collins Classics
COLIN MATTHEWS

Collins Classics
FRANK MARTIN
SCHARWENKA

Collins Classics
April 1996 releases
HARRISON BIRTWISTLE
GAWAIN

BARTÓK
TO BE RELEASED IN 1996
1
2

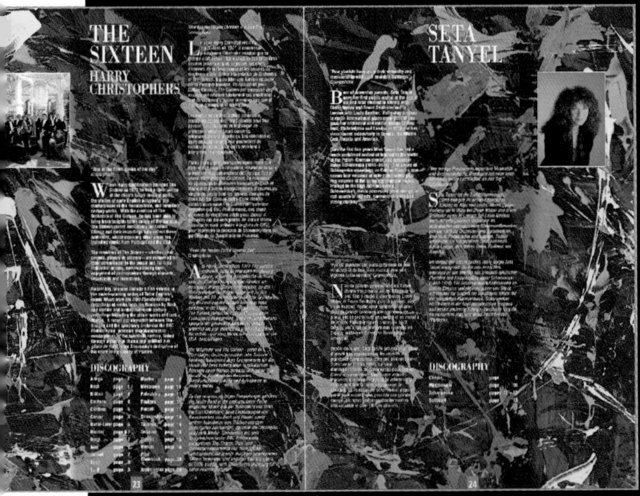
THE SIXTEEN
HARRY CHRISTOPHERS
SETA TANYEL
DISCOGRAPHY
23
24

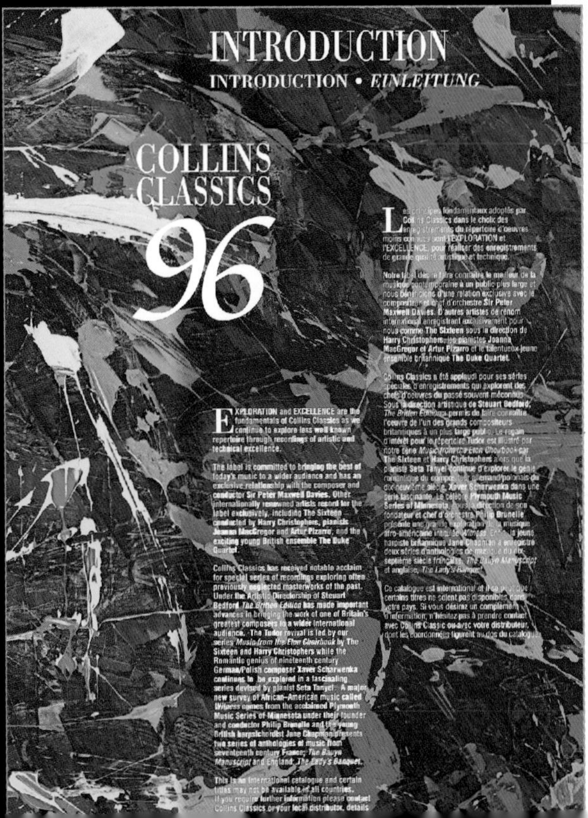
INTRODUCTION
INTRODUCTION • EINLEITUNG
COLLINS CLASSICS
96
EXPLORATION and EXCELLENCE are the fundamentals of Collins Classics as we continue to explore less well known repertoire through recordings of artistic and technical excellence.
The label is committed to bringing the best of today's music to a wider audience and has an exclusive relationship with the composer and conductor Sir Peter Maxwell Davies. Other internationally renowned artists record for the label exclusively, including The Sixteen conducted by Harry Christophers, pianists Joanna MacGregor and Artur Pizarro, and the exciting young British ensemble The Duke Quartet.
Collins Classics has received notable acclaim for special series of recordings exploring often previously neglected masterworks of the past. Under the Artistic Directorship of Steuart Bedford The Britten Edition has made important advances in bringing the work of one of Britain's greatest composers to a wider international audience. The Tudor revival is led by our series Music from the Eton Choirbook by The Sixteen and Harry Christophers while the Romantic genius of nineteenth century German/Polish composer Xaver Scharwenka continues to be explored in a fascinating series devised by pianist Seta Tanyel. A major new survey of African-American music called Witness comes from the acclaimed Plymouth Music Series of Minnesota under their founder and conductor Philip Brunelle and the young British harpsichordist Jane Chapman presents two series of anthologies of music from seventeenth century France; The Bauyn Manuscript and England; The Lady's Banquet.
This is an international catalogue and certain titles may not be available in all countries. If you require further information please contact Collins Classics or your local distributor, details

Towards the Ockeghem 500th Anniversary
Kids' Books You Can Enjoy
What qualifications are needed for becoming a children's book author/illustrator?
In addition to possessing exemplary drawing, writing, and storytelling skills, having been a child is a reasonable prerequisite.
Fitcher's Bird
The Tallis Scholars in concert

Cinderella
Roarr Calder's Circus
The Stinky Cheese Man

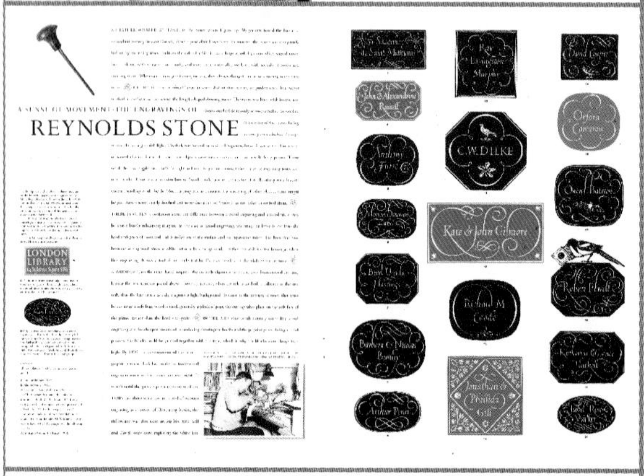
REYNOLDS STONE
C.W. DILKE
Kate & John Gilmore
LONDON LIBRARY

EX LIBRIS
ETON SCHOOL LIBRARY
THE LEAGRAVE PRESS LTD

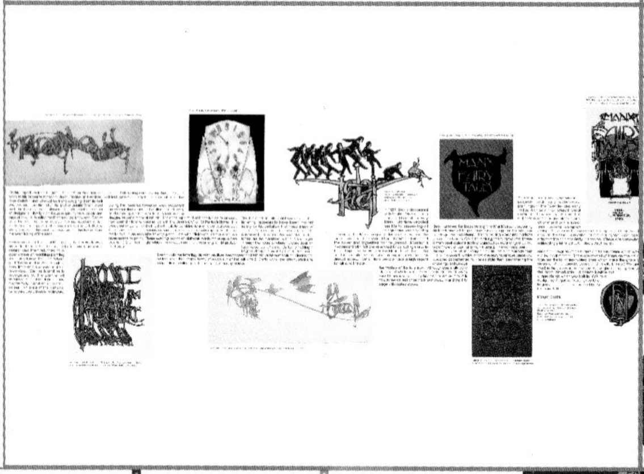
MANN FAIRY TALES

LETTERING &
ILLEGIBILITY
ON ENGLISH
CANAL BOATS
IPOMŒA
MIDDLEWICH
DRAGONFLY
LAPWORTH

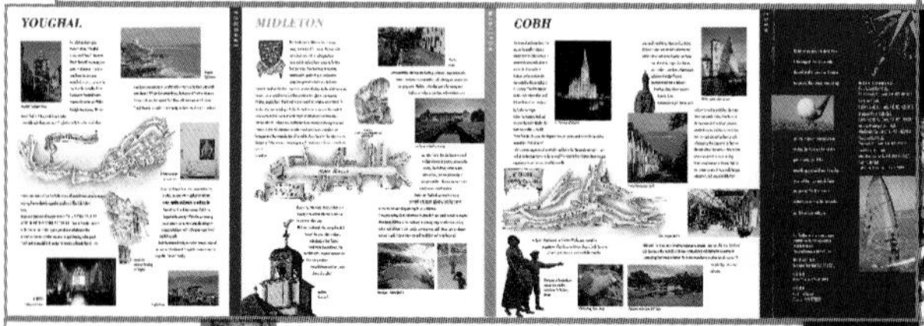
YOUGHAL
MIDLETON
COBH

Then let Ray Dream Designer help you achieve a real life adventure in 3D.
Ray Dream Designer
When you want to make your ideas stand out from the crowd, add real graphic impact with AddDepth.
AddDepth

MacLine
Jaggies.
JAG
A really SMOOTH utility
The Dream Pack
Buy all 3 products for only £129.95
Are you ready to dream?

The complete grid expert?

No one ever knows everything about grids. Designers with a future cannot even be heard to say they know enough about the grid.

Study of the grid renders its own reward. But every time the designer grasps it, it moves on. Graphic design is like that.

To prove that the grid is an enigma wrapped in a riddle, we reward all the hard work many readers have put into this book with a puzzle. Which of these pages and spreads, judging on their grids, belong together, and how were they made?

Three tips: Answers are not provided because any thoughtful designer's answer is probably a good one. Not all the effects were created in layout programs; Adobe Illustrator and Macromedia Freehand are normally used to attach text to a curve and manipulate its shape. Some of the illustrations, including one which really looks like it belongs to some very similar, are orphans, unrelated to any other page.

Good luck!

Grids – the future

As the world becomes increasingly automated, with communications between individuals, multinational corporations and governments becoming ever more complex and complicated, so the need for the unequivocal transmission of information, by whatever means, will become ever more indispensable.

The rapid development of communication technology during the 21st century, together with its inherent promise of chaos, will ensure that the need to create order by the basic means of a grid system, whether on printed page, screen or any other future medium, will apply to an even greater degree than at present.

The advent of the Internet and its development during the opening years of the next millennium, will bring in its wake a host of unforeseen problems of communication, many of which will carry implications of potentially apocalyptic proportions. Far from replacing the need for a grounding in the science of basic communications, the Worldwide Web, and its as yet undreamed of successors, will create a whole new range of problems. The solution to these will, despite the blessings of ever advancing technology, require the same common sense approach as that adopted five centuries ago by the first printers – The grid.

The grids on the bundled disk

For those who prefer to read on-screen, an expanded version of this text is also on the disk in:
README.MAC for users of Apple's Macintosh
README.TXT for MSDOS or Windows systems

Using the bundled disk

The disk is formatted for the lowest common denominator of DOS. Mac owners should have a DOS disk-opening utility installed to use the disk; PC Exchange comes free with Apple's system.

All the grids are scaleable EPS format
The files all contain fully scaleable Encapsulated PostScript (EPS or EPSF) graphics. They are saved for Macs with the word 'MAC' in the title and for DOS and Windows machines with the word 'IBM' in the title. All files have the suffix EPS.

Designing with the grids on the disk
Use them by dragging the chosen grid into a page layout program like Adobe Pagemaker or QuarkXPress.

Detailed instructions are given in the book for copying the formatting on the grids, drawing quick frames over them, adding guides, and scaling them to whatever format suits the job at hand.

Customizing the grids on the disk
The grids were created in Adobe Illustrator, and can be opened and altered in Illustrator or any other compatible vector drawing program and modified to suit your own needs.

These are the grids on the disk

A43CMAC
A43CIBM
A4 three-column

A44CMAC
A44CIBM
A4 four-column

USL3CMAC
USL3CIBM
US letter three-column

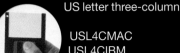

USL4CMAC
USL4CIBM
US letter four-column

A423FMAC
A423FIBM
A3 two- and three-fold leaflets

L23FMAC
L23FIBM
US letter two- and three-fold leaflets

A3PTRMAC
A3PTRIBM
A3 poster

TAPTRMAC
TAPTRIBM
Tabloid poster

PACKMAC
PACKIBM
Packaging design

BKMAC
BKIBM
Book design

FILMMAC
FILMIBM
Acetate overlay and printable grid.

For those who prefer doing layout the traditional way, all the grids on the disk are also described in the book, with measurements and names of display and text faces used.

For those who prefer doing layout the traditional way, all the grids on the disk are also described in the book, with measurements and names of display and text faces used

Index

acetate overlays 84
  computerized layout 87
  grid 109
  specific purposes 86
angling text and illustrations 100–1
baselines 62
blocks
  different depths 74
  sizes 65
book grid 109–11
bundled disk grids 102–21, 157
  acetate overlay 109
  books 109, 110–11
  film 121
  introduction 105
  leaflets 114–15
  multi-fold leaflets 106
  multimedia 121
  multiple grids 107
  newsletters 112–13
  packaging 109, 118–19
  posters 1 08, 116–17
  printed grid 109
  TV 121
  using 104
catalogs 130–5
color specification 98
columns 34–5, 50, 51
  allocation 34
  dividers 91
  mixed 70–1
  stylebook 91
  width and typesize 58–9
complete drawn grid 65
computer setting, style-sheets 94–5
contents 138
cropping 76–7, 85
curved grids 120
decorations 97
design bands 75
design brief 49
display text 63
dividers, stylebook 91
external factors 48–50
feature articles 144–5
film design 121
folios 82
golden section 32
graphic elements 97
grids
  at work 122–55
  basic 40–2
  blocks 65
  bundled disk 102–21
  catalogs 130–5
  columns 34–5
  communication 11
  composition 10
  construction 46–79
  curved 120
  design bands 75
  elements of 12–37
  external factors 48–50
  future of 156
  historical perspective 4
  linking mechanisms 146–7
  margins 32–3
  mixed columns 70–1
  multiple 107
  overlays 80–101
  purpose of 6–11
  quick grid design 38–45
  refinement 43
  regular items 126
  repeatability 9
  running items 67
  service items 67, 126, 140–3
  specific purpose 44
  standard 68–9
  stylebook 80–101
  templates 80–101
  viewing 66
  white space 36–7, 132–3
illustration
  angling 100–1
  baseline shift 62
  color specification 98
  cropping 76–7, 85
  decorations 97
  depth 64
  miscellaneous graphics 97
  perception 78
  scale 78
  scaling 79, 85
  style-sheets 96
  text runaround 73
information 128–9
leading 60–1
leaflets 114–15
line-space 57
linking mechanisms 146–7
margins 32–3, 50
  color 32
  defining elements 32
  golden section 32
  page 32
  spread 32
  stylebook 91
mixed column grids 70–1
multi-fold leaflets 106

multimedia design 121
multiple grids 107
music promotion 150–3
newsletters 112–13
overlays 80–101
acetate 84
computerized layout 87
special purposes 86
packaging 109, 118–19
page titles 45
pages, stylebook 91
paper 14–16
American sizes 15
DIN sizes 14
finish 16
Imperial 15
ISO sizes 14
stylebook 91
typeface choice 16
perception, illustration 78
posters 108, 116–17
print area, stylebook 91
printed grid 82–3, 109
professional journals 136–47
Quested, Philip 148–9
quick grids 38–45
regular features 126–7
reprographic style-sheets 99
rules 97
running items 67
scale, illustration 78
scaling 79, 85
screamer headlines 63
serenity, design feature 124–5
service information 132–3
service items 67, 126, 140–3
short takes 140–3
sophisticated guides 52–3
standard grids 68–9
straplines 82
stylebook 80–101
style-sheets 90
computer setting 94–5
illustration 96
page information 91
paper information 91
reprographic 99
text 92–3
teasers 139
templates 80–101
text
angling 100–1
baseline shift 62
extraordinary displays 63
inset 72
runaround 73
style-sheets 92–3
thumbnails 51
trim marks 82
TV design 121
type area 50
type selection 54–6
typesize and column width 58–9
typography 17–31
Anglo-American measuring system 20–1
ciceros 20
computer measuring system 21
Didot measuring system 20
drop caps 23
expert fonts 25–6
font collection 28–9
leading 60–1
measuring systems 20
naming type parts 17
paper finish 16
sans serif faces 19
serif faces 18
styling 24
swash caps 23
text inset 72
text runaround 73
type classification 18–19
type combinations 30–1
type manipulation 24
type sizes 22
typeface choice 16
typesize and column width 58–9
weight 27
width 27
white space 36–7, 132–3
distribution 36

Acknowledgments

Original illustrations are by the author unless otherwise indicated. Additional original illustrations and other art used for decorative purposes in this book is used only by authority of the copyright holders, whose names and addresses are below.

The published material used for instructional purposes is gratefully acknowledged. If you contributed design, typography or art to the examples or printed materials used as examples in this book, drop a note to RotoVision, Sheridan House, 112/116A Western Road, Hove, East Sussex BN3 1DD, England and we will do our best to give you an individual credit in the next edition.

- Stock photography throughout this book is exclusively from the several fine CD-ROM series by PhotoDisc Inc, 2013 Fourth Ave, Seattle, WA 98121, USA and The Old Workshop, Retreat Road, Richmond, Surrey TW9 2NN, UK. Phone, in the USA/Canada 800 528 3472, in the UK 0800 697 622, international to USA +1 206 441 9355, international to UK +44 181 332 2020; more contact information on their Web site http://www.photodisc.com. Special thanks to Susan Dotterweich in Europe and Dan Saimo in the States.
- Page 20 Flags and map from Magnum's *All of instant art*; Magnum Software, Sampford Peverell, Tiverton EX16 6YZ, UK.
- All other original illustrations are made by the author exclusively in Adobe software except:
  • Page 23 Swash caps from the Ekol-V series by André Jute, Bandon, Co Cork, Ireland, on paintings by Vicky Saunders Guillane, Rosscarbery, Co Cork, Ireland.
  • Page 23 Decorative numbers by Michael O'Dwyer, 24 Willington Grove, Templeogue, Dublin 6W, Ireland.
  • Page 87 Pagecurl graphic by André Jute on visiting card graphics by Michael O'Dwyer; addresses above.
  • Pages 148–149 Hand drawn grids by Philip Quested, 13 Sallymount Ave, Ranelagh, Dublin 6, Ireland.
  • The 'Russian' dummy text used is in fact Latin, chosen and translated for us by Philip Weaver pweaver@cris.com and also at: http://www.concentric.net/~pweaver
  • The 'Esperanto' in the section *Grids at Work* was created by Jabberwocky.
  • Pages 110–111 The text in the book sample is by Damien Enright. Ekol-V swash capitals as credited above on page 31.
  • The 600 odd fonts used in this book are all, with the exception of the custom-designed decorative fonts on page 23 and pages 110–111, available in the Adobe and Monotype catalogs.

Jean Koefoed

1923–1996

This book is dedicated to the memory of Jean, who for more than the last half century was the guardian of the very best in graphic design. He inspired authors and designers to the highest levels and the subject of this book, being the basis of all good design, was very dear to his heart.
We mourn this humble man, whose name never appeared in the books that he conceived and loved so much, but we are fortunate to have worked with him on this, his last work.

The Publisher — December 1996